THE MARINE SOCIETY

AND SEA CADI

D0765806

Is yours an
SS Great Britain
family?

by Adrian Ball

**Foreword by HRH The Duke of York CVO ADC
Patron of the SS Great Britain Project**

m KENNETH MASON

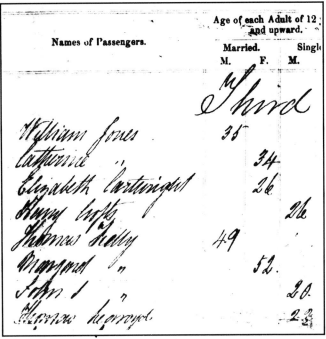

Names of Passengers.	Age of each Adult of 12 and upward.		
	Married.		Single
	M.	F.	M.
	Third		
William Jones	35		
Catherine "		34	
Elizabeth Cartwright		26	
Henry Wills			26
Thomas Kelly	49		
Margaret "		52	
John "			20
Thomas Heproyd			23

Acknowledgements

The passenger lists published in this book are reproduced by kind permission of the Keeper of Records at the Public Records Office in Melbourne. The SS Great Britain Project wishes to record its warm appreciation to that department for preserving the records so efficiently over the years and for supplying the lists for publication.

Carole Drewett of Wrington, Avon, the Project's volunteer genealogist, carried out the considerable task of transcribing all details from the Melbourne lists. The fragment above from a typical hand-written record shows just how consuming and skilled her work was.

Vera Madan prepared the master list for the printer from Mrs Drewett's hand-written copy and coded the 14,000 names for easy reference. The Project and the author express their deep gratitude to both ladies for their inestimable contributions to this published work.

Of the archive material to which reference is made in these pages, we thank the State Library of Victoria for the diary notes of emigrant John McLennan and the University of Melbourne for permission to use the drawings aboard the *Great Britain* by Herman Zumstein, a Melbourne silk merchant who sailed in the ship.

The Marylebone Cricket Club provided the author with invaluable information on the first two England tours of Australia and also gave permission for the use of the photographs appearing herein.

The diary of Daniel Higson is held by the Preston City Library and was submitted to the SS Great Britain Project by Arthur G. Credland, Keeper of the Town Docks Museum in Hull, who has made a study of Mr Higson's later life in England.

The warm thanks of the Project and the author also go to the following private individuals, often direct descendants of passengers, who donated shipboard diaries or personal letters. The name of the 19th century passenger is given in brackets in each case:
Mrs Nora Skevington of Derby (George Greaves).
Mr James H. Whitehead (Richard Pope).
Neil Campbell of El Toro, California, U.S.A. (John Campbell).
Mr J. Lowe of Lyndhurst, Hampshire (Stephen Perry).
Miss E. M. Taylor of Ringwood, Victoria, Australia
(Elizabeth Joseph).
Mrs Rose Jenkins of Blackheath, London (Rosamond D'Ouseley).
Mr J. Alastair Peck (Margaret Brown).
Mrs Margery Grace (Dr E. M. Grace).

Except where otherwise credited, the illustrations come from the archives of the SS Great Britain Project. We are indebted to Dr Ewan Corlett OBE, the Project's Hon. Naval Architect, for his line drawings of the ship as she appeared during her service on the Australia run.

Finally, the author wishes to thank Dr Basil Greenhill CB CMG, the Chairman of the SS Great Britain Project, and his fellow members of the Council of that body for the encouragement and support they gave him during the preparation of this book. The ready co-operation and help at all times of Captain C. J. Young RN, the Project Director, and Brian Wheddon, the Commercial Director, are also acknowledged with gratitude.

• **(Front cover): An artist's impression of the scene as the *Great Britain* left for Melbourne for the first time from Prince's Dock, Liverpool**

Published by Kenneth Mason
The old harbourmasters, Emsworth, Hampshire PO10 7DD

© Adrian Ball and the SS Great Britain Project 1988.

All rights reserved. No part of this publication may be reproduced, stored in a retrieval system, or transmitted in any form or by any means, electronic, mechanical, photocopying, recording or otherwise, without the prior permission of the copyright owners.

British Library Cataloguing

Ball, Adrian
    Is yours an SS Great Britain family?
    1. Passenger transport. Shipping. Steam liners.
    (Ship) Great Britain. Passengers, 1852-1875
    I. Title
    387.2'432

    ISBN 0-85937-342-8

Typesetting and artwork production by Articulate Studio, Hampshire
Printed by Redwood Burn Limited, Wiltshire

BUCKINGHAM PALACE

The SS Great Britain was brought home from The Falkland Islands in 1970. Since then, she has been and is still undergoing restoration in the Great Western Dock in Bristol.

The Great Britain served in many theatres of commercial operation - the Atlantic Run for which she was designed, but then more shrewdly, on the run to Australia between 1852 and 1875 taking many thousands of people to Australia. She also saw service of a military nature, taking troops to the Crimea and India.

With the detailed research so far carried out in Bristol by the SS Great Britain Project, we know the identities of more than 60,000 Victorian men, women, and children who sailed in the ship.

This book is intended to be a permanent source of information and be updated as new and fresh material emerges. Few vessels can ever have had such documentation built into their archive. We hope the pages that follow will stimulate you to visit or learn more about this ship, even if our information does not add any new twigs to your own family tree.

Andrew

Introduction

Thousands of Americans are proud to proclaim (accurately or otherwise) that their forebears 'came over in the *Mayflower*'. A far greater number of Australians – perhaps a quarter of a million or 300,000 – can probably claim that their folks sailed in the *SS Great Britain*. Such a total would represent about two per cent of the population of Australia today.

Our cousins down under have a further edge on our friends across the Atlantic. While the *Mayflower*, for all her historical and sentimental significance, was no more than a typical modest vessel of her times, the *Great Britain* was (and is) one of the most important ships ever built.

Mayflower carried 149 passengers and crew to New England in a single voyage in 1620. The Brunel liner made 32 round voyages between Britain and Australia between 1852 and 1875/76, carrying some 15,000 passengers on the outward journeys and perhaps 10,000 people home to Liverpool.

No other ship was more closely associated with the remarkable development which took place in Australia in the third quarter of the nineteenth century. And no vessel was held in ever higher regard, as her reputation for reliability and regularity increased with each year that passed.

The *Great Britain* was not designed for the long and challenging Australia run; Isambard Kingdom Brunel conceived her as being a fast and profitable contender on the much shorter trans-Atlantic route. But a shrewd commercial decision, influenced by the post-Gold Rush demand for berths to Australia, led to the fortunes of the vessel being linked inextricably with those of the booming Australian colonies.

Thanks to the diligence of the Public Records Office in Melbourne, nearly all the outward passenger lists have survived the years. Records of the homeward journeys, however, appear sadly to have been destroyed or lost.

The names and some personal details of passengers on 29 of the 32 voyages to Australia are known and have been transcribed from faded, hand written originals in a labour of love by well-wishers of the SS Great Britain Project. We are still engaged in trying to trace the names of the remaining 1,000 or so people who travelled on the three 'missing' voyages.

This book contains information on 14,000 men, women, children and infants who sailed to Melbourne or other Australian ports in the 23 turbulent years between the Augusts of 1852 and 1875. As such, it must be priceless source material for genealogists on both sides of the world and a fascinating document for the average Australian interested in the history of his or her own country and family.

The value of this alphabetical record for compilers of family trees is surely that whole families are here chronicled together with ages and occupations at a point in time. The records drawn up for the colonial authorities in Melbourne listed, too, births and deaths aboard and even the lamentable cases of persons being pronounced insane between Liverpool and Melbourne.

Although the intention is to make this book a permanent source of information, it is appropriate that its first publication is taking place in the bicentennial year of 1988 when even the busiest and most forward looking Australians must be tempted to take occasional backward glances.

These pages should also be a timely reminder of the fact that, for all the importance of the First Fleet and the survival of the Australian settlement in the early part of the nineteenth century, the country was largely shaped by the sturdy settlers who paid their way and are typified by the thousands of ordinary people whose names we record.

Since her return to Bristol from the Falklands in 1970, the *Great Britain* has been undergoing restoration in the city's Great Western Dock. Numerous Australians have found their way to the dock over the years as part of pilgrimages to the 'Old Country' but we very much hope that this book will persuade many more to visit the Brunel masterpiece in the future. After all, almost half a million Australians visit Britain each year and that number rivals the population of the City of Bristol itself.

According to our staff in Bristol, Australian visitors are the most enthusiastic of the people from overseas who walk the decks of the liner. What they see is the 1845 version because she is being restored, understandably, to her original six-masted appearance. As time progresses, we plan to provide graphic representations at the dock of the three guises in which she appeared during her long Australian service – with two funnels and four masts; two funnels and three masts; and finally one funnel with three masts.

We hope this book will circulate widely in Australia and persuade many more people there to search their family archives for mentions and mementoes of the ship. A useful amount of material, notably letters and diaries written aboard, has already been donated or lent to the SS Great Britain Project by Australians; but we believe that much more must exist. A modest museum already exists at the ship in Bristol; in time we trust it will be extended into a display of major Anglo-Australian and Anglo-American significance.

Hitherto there has been an inevitable tendency for greater emphasis to be placed on the *Great Britain*'s epochal early years in the Atlantic than on her calmer times in the Antipodes, or on the sterling service she rendered the nation in the Crimean War and the Indian Mutiny. We have researched the names and regimental details of 44,000 officers and men she took to the Crimea. Thus, as HRH The Duke of York points out in his foreword, we know the identities of more than 60,000 Victorian men, women and children who sailed in the ship, as passengers or crew.

The Grand Concept

A marine historian of the 1920s, writing about the SS *Great Britain*, described her as 'the most famous ship which ever floated, excepting Noah's Ark'. Many Brunel devotees would accept this as a fair description; others would want to know more about the specifications of Noah's Ark before giving the palm to any other vessel!

Without doubt the *Great Britain* is one of the most significant ships ever built. In her was combined for the first time all the elements of the modern vessel: iron construction; a steam-driven screw propeller; and a great bulk designed to achieve economical and efficient running. This early Victorian marine masterpiece has a proud and permanent place in marine history. By a mixture of good luck, foresight and daring she is still with us, undergoing complete restoration in the dock where she was laid down almost 150 years ago. Craftsmen and artists are serving her today with the same skill and diligence as did their predecessors in the middle years of the nineteenth century.

Although a surviving monument of Britain's industrial and marine pre-eminence in the last century, she is part of American history because of her epochal Atlantic crossings and the threat she represented to the fast and efficient US sailing packets of the day. But her greatest achievements were recorded between Liverpool and Melbourne rather than New York.

The *Great Britain* achieved her legendary reputation on the Australia run because of her utter reliability over a vast distance. When she was first conceived, in 1835, she was envisaged as being ideal for much shorter journeys to and from a New York growing each year in prosperity and importance. In modern parlance, she began as a Concorde, but settled down to being an efficient and profitable airbus.

The ship's story, however, really begins in the 18th century, in 1769, a year which saw the birth of Napoleon Bonaparte in Corsica – and of Marc Isambard Brunel in Normandy. The young Brunel was first destined for the Church but later joined the French Navy and became a junior officer. By 1793, with Napoleon's star beginning to rise, Marc Brunel was under suspicion as a Royalist sympathiser and fled the country to the United States. The Americans soon recognised Marc Brunel's technical skills and he was appointed Chief Engineer of New York City. By the end of the century, however, the brilliant young Frenchman felt there was greater opportunity in Britain for his innovative skills.

Marc Brunel had invented a machine for the assembly line production of naval blocks and he calculated, shrewdly, that it would be in great demand in a country engaged in a world-wide maritime struggle with revolutionary France. His machinery went into production at the Maudslay works and in 1799 Marc Brunel came to Britain to supervise the block-making operation.

In Britain he renewed the acquaintance of an Englishwoman, Sophia Kingdom, whom he had met in France when both were fleeing from the terror which came in the wake of the revolution. They were married and settled near Portsmouth Dockyard. Their son, Isambard Kingdom Brunel, was born there in April 1806. Tutored by his remarkable father until the age of nine Isambard was then sent to school in Hove, Sussex, where he distinguished himself as a bright and resourceful pupil. At 14, with Britain at peace again with France, he was enrolled at the College of Caen in Normandy, then at a famed mathematical establishment, the Lyceé Henri Quatre in Paris. Finally, he was apprenticed to a French manufacturer of chronometers and scientific instruments.

While the young Brunel was studying, his father was struggling with large debts at home for which he was arrested in 1821 and spent almost three months in gaol. Upon the intercession of the Duke of Wellington, he was given a state grant of £5,000 which enabled him to clear his debts. In the following year Isambard, now in his 17th year, returned from France to work in his father's London office. He soon became involved in the extraordinary variety of engineering projects which Brunel senior tackled to keep his head financially above water. Through his father he met many of the great scientists, engineers and public men of the day whose views and advice helped mould his character and gave him an assurance beyond his years.

The biggest father-and-son adventure was the design and construction of the Thames Tunnel at Rotherhithe, the first in the world beneath a navigable river. This took 18 years to build, between 1825 and 1843, and the younger Brunel bore the brunt of

● **Isambard Kingdom Brunel, taken in 1856 or 1857 against a background of the checking chains to be used in the launch of his *Great Eastern***

• The *Great Britain* is floated out of her dock on 19 July 1843 after being launched by Prince Albert

the work, public controversy over disasters and delays, and real physical dangers. He almost drowned in 1828 when the river burst into the workings.

In March of 1843, with both Brunels national figures, the tunnel at last opened to the public. Queen Victoria herself walked through it having knighted Marc Brunel as a tribute to all the ageing engineer had done for his adopted country. Fifty thousand people followed the monarch in strolling beneath the Thames in the first 27 hours after the official opening.

During all the years of struggle beneath the river, both Brunels were engaged on many other engineering projects in Britain and abroad. Young I.K. Brunel began a 20-year association with Bristol through his celebrated design for the Clifton Suspension Bridge and various projects done in the docks. He also became closely involved in the developing railway systems of the 1830s as consulting engineer to the Great Western Railway which was linking London and Bristol.

It was at a meeting of directors of that company in a Blackfriars, London, hotel in 1835 that the 29-year-old I.K. Brunel made a quip which was to lead him ultimately to the design of the *Great Britain*. Talk turned to the 120 miles of railway line projected between the capital and Bristol. Isambard Brunel suggested, either seriously or jokingly, that the line could be extended to New York if they built a steamboat – to be called the *Great Western* – which could ply between Bristol and New York. His suggestion was taken seriously and a Great Western Railway committee was formed at once to consider the economics.

In January of 1836 the committee produced an encouraging report on the venture with Brunel stressing in an accompanying statement the need for the vessel to be as large as possible to carry sufficient fuel and a payload which was economically viable. The GWR directors were urged to construct a vessel of at least 1,200 tons which could make the journey to New York in less than 20 days and return in 13. (Comparable figures for the sailing ships of the day were 36 and 24 days respectively.)

Those were the early days of paddle steamers and it was assumed that the *Great Western* would be so propelled. (The first Atlantic crossing with paddles working all the way had been made by a Nova Scotian-built vessel, the *Royal William*, in 1832.) The Great Western Steamship Company was formed and work on the ship entrusted to three men – Thomas Guppy, a businessman and engineer, Captain Christopher Claxton, a retired Royal Navy officer, and William Patterson, a Bristol shipbuilder.

Work on the *Great Western* began in Patterson's shipyard in July of 1836. Oak-built, she was larger than any other steamship in the world and the Maudslay engines designed for her were of similar unprecedented size. She was launched on July 1837 and then sailed to London to take her engines on board.

This, the first of I.K. Brunel's trio of steamships, made her maiden voyage from Bristol on 8 April 1838 and arrived 15 days later with a quarter of her bunkers still full. She was pipped into New York by the small British paddle steamer *Sirius* which beat her by one day for the title of the first passenger steamer across the Atlantic.

The real triumph, however, belonged to the *Great Western* because the *Sirius*, of only 700 tons, was too small to be a genuine Atlantic competitor. As the Great Western Steamship Company was able to boast at the time, the Brunel paddler was 'the first ship regularly laid down, equipped and sent to sea for the purpose of establishing a steam line between America and England'.

Great Western settled down quickly to a routine of successful service making in all a total of 74 Atlantic crossings. Britain, under challenge for so many years from the fast American sailing packets, was once again supreme in the Atlantic. So it was no surprise when the Great Western Steamship directors announced in September 1838 (as their first ship was making her fourth voyage) that they were to build a sister vessel to be known as the *City of New York*.

In time, this was to become the *Great Britain* we know today but, at first, the intention was to make her another wooden paddleboat and a large quantity of African oak was purchased. During 1838 and the following year, under Brunel's guidance, five designs were prepared, each providing for a larger and more powerful vessel than its predecessor. The first two schemes were for wooden ships but then, in January 1839, a revolutionary design for an iron vessel appeared on the drawing board. By July of that year the tonnage of the proposed ship had increased to 3,443 from the original 1,340, and the ship's name had been changed to the *Mammoth*. The first plates for the iron keel were laid down in July 1839 in a dock bought and equipped specially for her.

While Brunel and his colleagues debated the economics of ever larger vessels, a major development was taking place in marine engineering: the development of screw propulsion. Two patents were taken out in 1836, one by a British farmer named Francis Pettit Smith, the other by Captain John Ericsson, once of the Swedish Army. Both men arranged trials of their inventions on the Thames in small experimental craft during 1837.

Subsequently, the Ericsson plans attracted the attention of the United States Navy and one of his experimental craft crossed the Atlantic for further development there by the naval authorities. In Britain, a vessel named the *Archimedes* was built to demonstrate the potential of the Pettit Smith designs. In 1839 it began trials under government supervision and in May 1840 arrived in Bristol during a demonstration tour. Guppy sailed in the *Archimedes*, was impressed by screw propulsion, and interested Brunel in the system. The vessel was hired by the Great Western Steamship Company for several months after which Brunel came to the conclusion that all plans for a new paddleboat should be scrapped and screw propulsion adopted. His report proposing this was finally approved by the directors of the company in December 1840.

The decision to make the switch meant the cancellation of contracts for paddleboat engines. Francis Humphrys, who had designed the engines was asked to start again making provision for screw propulsion. It was too great a blow for the man; he 'fell ill with a brain fever' and died. Brunel and his team then tackled the enormous job of designing and building the necessary steam engine themselves, in Bristol. The design of the fabulous engine – of which a full scale replica is shortly to be installed in the ship – owed much to a celebrated power plant, called the 'Triangle' which Sir Marc Brunel had invented in 1822. In its final version it was a 1,000 horsepower, 18 revolutions-a-minute engine, the first 'vee' engine which drove upwards to a crankshaft above the cylinders.

In the spring of 1841 the revised construction programme got under way and the vessel was renamed the *Great Britain*. Her launch took place on 19 July 1843 – the anniversary of the launch of the *Great Western* – and four years from the day on which her own first plates had been laid.

Prince Albert, the Prince Consort, the great-great-great grandfather of the present day Patron of the SS Great Britain Project, travelled to Bristol on the Great Western Railway for the floating-out ceremony. One of his many distinguished fellow guests was the 74-year-old Sir Marc Brunel, a proud and excited parent. Queen Victoria's consort was supposed to launch the vessel himself but he surrendered the honour to Mrs John Miles, the wife of a Great Western director. Her aim was, however, faulty and she missed the ship. Prince Albert saved the day by grabbing another Champagne bottle and smashing it against the side of the *Great Britain* as she was floating slowly out of the dock.

The banquet, in a specially built white and crimson pavilion, was one of the most magnificent occasions Bristol had seen. Six hundred guests crowded the pavilion and tens of thousands of Bristolians packed every vantage point around the docks. It was ironically the most splendid marine occasion in the city until the same day of the month in July 1970 when the ship finally came home from the Falklands . . .

The Atlantic Years

The early Victorians talked of the *Great Britain* with the same pride as their successors were to show in Concorde: there had never been anything like her. The liner's final displacement was an unprecedented 3,675 tons, her overall length exceeded 322 feet, and her breadth was 50 feet 6 inches. There were innovations throughout: a six-bladed propeller, the first balanced rudder in any sizeable ship, six masts to carry the auxiliary sail, and wire rigging instead of hemp.

With the budget already exceeded by a wide margin, the Great Western Steamship Company directors hoped the vessel's maiden voyage to New York could take place in May 1844. In the event, the first crossing was delayed until July of the following year. The sheer size of the ship was the main reason.

Fitting out in Bristol was prolonged from July 1843 until the end of the following year. She was almost too large for the city's inner harbour system, developed in the early years of the century. Pressure had to be exerted by the Board of Trade to force the Bristol Dock Board to widen the locks. This was sanctioned in the autumn of 1844 and the *Great Britain* was able to squeeze out of the dock system and into the River Avon on 12 December.

After all the anxieties of 1844 Brunel and his colleagues were exulted by the magnificent way the vessel performed during her trials. A speed of 11 knots was achieved during her first spell at sea and Guppy reported to his board on the 'triumphal result' of the switch from paddle wheels to screw propulsion. In official trials in January 1845 she achieved 12½ knots in short bursts.

On 26 January 1845 *Great Britain* arrived at Blackwall, on London's River Thames, for final furbishment of the interior. Her size and bizarre appearance aroused the excited interest of crowds all along the river. For Brunel the arrival in London after a voyage around the south coast in choppy weather was more important than the public adulation: the first passage of a modern steamship had been a total success.

Queen Victoria put the stamp of Royal approval on the venture on 23 April 1845 when, with Prince Albert, she came aboard after a lavish procession up river from Greenwich Palace. The Queen expressed herself as being 'quite amazed' at the length of the liner, one-third longer than any battleship in her service. Throughout the month of May, Londoners visited the ship in their thousands until on 12 June she left for Liverpool to begin her working life.

At that point, she had cost her owners £117,295, against the £76,000 originally budgeted. That did not include £53,000 for the construction of the Great Western Dock which remained a separate asset. Of the ship total, 73 per cent represented the hull and machinery and 15 per cent fittings, rigging and stores, while the balance covered financial charges and other items. The directors then calculated that management and running costs, plus depreciation, would claim just over £60,000 a year. Income from seven round trips to New York each year could reach a theoretical £100,000 from passengers and £35,000 from cargo charges. So all the investment and the anxiety could prove to have been worthwhile – if the ship was well patronised.

Public clamour to sight-see aboard the iron leviathan delayed her departure for New York until 26 July 1845. And there were still trippers aboard for the first few miles of her passage down the Mersey. Not many people, however, had been prepared to put complete faith in the new form of propulsion. There were only 45 passengers out of a possible 252, but paid-for cargo comprised a commercially useful 360 tons.

Those passengers who braved the elements were rewarded with a magnificent maiden voyage. The *Great Britain* arrived in New York in just under 15 days, having covered 3,304 nautical miles at an average speed of 9.4 knots. If anything, the welcome from the New Yorkers surpassed even the displays of public warmth in London and Liverpool. Some 21,000 members of the public toured her within the next fortnight.

The return crossing, as anticipated, was faster with Liverpool being reached by a shorter route in 13½ days. Two more round trips were made in 1845 until the vessel was laid up for a winter overhaul. The main features of that early 1846 refit were the scrapping of a mast (the one behind the funnel), replacement of the original six-bladed propeller by a four-bladed unit, improvements in the boilers, a return to the use of hemp for the rigging, and the strengthening of the fourth mast to carry more sail.

The year 1846 seemed likely to be commercially successful for the ship. She made round trips between Liverpool and New York in May/June and in July/August. On the latter voyage, both the outward and homeward legs were completed in just over 13 days. What was more important, she carried 110 passengers to New York, indicating that the public at last was beginning to show confidence in screw propulsion.

Was the commercial tide about to turn? The owners certainly believed so when the *Great Britain* sailed from Liverpool for New York on 22 September 1846 with an unprecedented passenger list of 180. In our chronology, this was the seventh voyage – and it came perilously close to being the last. The ship was under the command of Captain James Hosken, a highly experienced officer and former Royal Navy man. Although he had shown some navigational failings in early passages of the *Great Britain*, he enjoyed the full confidence of the Great Western directors. But on the evening of the day she left Liverpool the ship ran aground at Dundrum Bay, Northern Ireland. Hosken had missed the lighthouse on the Isle of Man and, instead of carrying on along the Irish coast, had sailed straight into the bay.

The passengers were evacuated the next morning in carts normally used to gather seaweed and the iron ship was driven further up the shore to protect her from future gale damage. The directors generously accepted the Captain's claim that he had been misled by inadequate Admiralty charts but the general view in maritime circles was that Hosken had made a terrible and inexplicable blunder.

The ship was destined to remain stranded in Dundrum Bay for 11 months, protected by improvised breakwaters during the winter and then ingeniously refloated after she had been lightened by the removal of stores, furniture and fittings. With temporary repairs made to her hull, she was towed back to Liverpool on 28 August 1847, under the direction of Captain Claxton. The first survey in Prince's Dock, Liverpool, was encouraging. The hull and frames were found to be safe and sound and, according to a contemporary report, 'not bent, shaken or strained, nor indicating in the slightest degree anything that would lead to the supposition that her back had been injured while embedded in the sands of Dundrum Bay'.

But, while the ship was still in a robust state, the affairs of the Great Western Steamship Company were not. *Great Britain* had been grossly under-insured at £17,000 – one seventh of her cost. Now an expert survey stated that £16,000 would be required to repair the hull and rigging and £6,000 to put the machinery back into service.

The directors had sold the *Great Western* in April 1847 and had no further source of income. There was no hope of restoring the *Great Britain* to service so the inspired idea of 'extending the Great Western Railway to New York' came to an end. Winding up proceedings began and the assets of the company were auctioned. In September of the following year the *Great Britain* was put up for auction – but only half the reserve price of £40,000 was bid for a ship which had cost almost £120,000 only three years earlier.

Between 1847 and 1850, the iron ship remained in Liverpool's Coburg Dock, awaiting a buyer. It seemed that Brunel's masterpiece – still the greatest vessel afloat – was doomed to a premature death in a breaker's yard. Then she was reprieved by events on the other side of the world. The Australian colonies were starting to boom and gold had been discovered in Victoria. The most successful chapter in the *Great Britain*'s extraordinary history was about to open . . .

● **Many Victorian households boasted prints of this painting of the ship in heavy seas by the noted artist J. Walter**

Australia Bound

As the second half of the nineteenth century dawned, no section of the British commercial population was better placed than the shipping men and merchants to judge the potential of the Australian colonies. And among that fraternity, few were more knowledgeable than the Gibbs and Bright families of Bristol and Liverpool. They owned Gibbs, Bright & Company which operated the Eagle Line of sailing packets which traded between Britain and Australia.

This enterprise bought the *Great Britain* for only £18,000 in December, 1850, ending the ship's long period of idleness in Liverpool. The new owners knew the vessel well: Robert Bright had been one of the Great Western Railway directors who discussed the original Atlantic steamship venture with Brunel and Guppy in 1835. George Gibbs had been on the London board of the railway company. Both appreciated the qualities of the ship and realised the bargain they were getting. Their payment enabled the winding up of the steamship company to be completed in February 1852.

The business partnership of the Gibbs and Bright families had started in Bristol in 1818 but the enterprise was now firmly Liverpool-based. In 1853 an associated company known as Bright Bros & Company opened its doors for business in Melbourne, acting as agents for the Eagle and Blackwall sailing ships. The *Great Britain* was therefore acquired just as the trading activities of the company were about to enter the most vigorous stage of their development.

Gold was discovered in Victoria in 1850 and more substantial alluvial deposits in the following year. With the Californian gold rush still fresh in everyone's memory, there was a rush for berths on ships plying between Britain and Australia. Apart from the prospect of sudden wealth in the diggings, there were jobs a-begging in Melbourne where a large part of the local population had downed tools to pick up nuggets in the bush.

The Gibbs, Bright directors had made a shrewd assessment of Australia's potential and the discovery of gold endorsed their decision to place their main faith on the colonies down under. The first ship to reach Liverpool with Victorian gold was one of their own fleet – the Eagle Line packet *Albatross* which arrived with £50,000 worth of gold in August of 1852. (The first gold to be landed in the UK was from the Aberdeen White Star liner *Phoenician* which docked in February of that year.)

The *Great Britain* was to prove to be the right ship, at the right time, for Gibbs, Bright but even that company's far-sighted directors did not realise just how successful she was going to be. Clearly, her size would enable her to carry many passengers and a good cargo and, being steam-powered, she should be able to complete the passage in around 60 days against the 80 to 120 days taken by sailing vessels.

William Patterson, the Bristolian shipbuilder involved with *Great Britain* from the outset, was commissioned to oversee the reconstruction of the ship for the Australia run. New engines were essential and more space had to be found for cargo. At the same time, there was a requirement for extra passenger accommodation and this was achieved by building a new complex of cabins on the once uncluttered deck.

The 1852 engines, built by John Penn & Company, of London, were totally different in design from the originals, incorporating two oscillating cylinders driven upwards to a crankshaft; but their total horsepower approximated to that of the 1845 plant. Considerable modifications had to be made to the structure to accommodate the machinery and to allow for more cargo space and coal bunkers. Two funnels, placed side by side, and a new three-bladed propeller, were other features of the reconstruction.

Externally, the vessel changed dramatically. The number of masts was reduced from five to four (although the total sail area was increased to 27,000 square feet against the original 16,000). A deckhouse, about 300 feet long and running almost the entire length of the ship, was built for passenger use. A hurricane deck was provided above for promenading during long days in the tropics. The after part of the deckhouse was occupied by a magnificent dining saloon of which, happily, an artist's impression has survived. All these changes increased the carrying capacity of the world's largest liner to an unprecedented 730 passengers, of whom 50 could travel first class.

The work was completed by the spring but Gibbs, Bright felt there should be a shake-down round trip to New York before the first long voyage to Melbourne. She left on 1 May 1852 and made New York in 13 days seven hours under the command of Captain Barnard Robert Matthews. *Great Britain* came home in fine style with the new engines doing all required of them and by August she was ready for Antipodean service.

Great Britain's Voyage 9 began from Liverpool on 21 August with a phenomenal passenger list for the day of 630 people and a heavy mail. The passengers paid a total of £23,000, an average of £36 a head. Gibbs, Bright forecast that the ship would reach Melbourne in 56 days but she ran into headwinds in the South Atlantic and had to return 1,100 miles to St Helena to take on more coal, at an exhorbitant cost. Matthews was not a popular captain and a meeting of passengers protested about conditions aboard and the irregularity of meals. Critical letters were sent home to the press from St Helena, some casting doubt on the seamanship of the captain.

In the event, that first journey took 83 days, the *Great Britain* arriving off Melbourne on 12 November. After a great reception there and a five day stay she sailed on to Sydney with 300 passengers, to another round of civic receptions and public sight-seeing. On 20 December 1852 she sailed again from Sydney to Melbourne where, three days after Christmas, a magnificent ball was held on board attended by some 400 colonial notables.

When she sailed back to Liverpool on 4 January 1853 she carried 161 passengers and 100,000 ounces of gold. Again it was a slow voyage, and the owners were forced to re-think their basic strategy, making more use of sail when conditions were right. So during the summer of 1853 the ninth version of the *Great Britain* materialised, with two funnels and just three masts. She was now a conventional three-masted ship, able to enjoy the best of both

• Australia-bound: the great iron ship, pictured in her earliest Antipodean guise, drops the pilot off Liverpool

worlds under sail and steam. In that guise she sailed again to Australia on 11 August 1853.

The advertised fares for that passage ranged from 70 and 65 guineas for first class accommodation to 42 and 25 guineas in the second class. (A guinea was 21 shillings.) We do not have the rates for third class and steerage although a few years later they were being quoted at 18 or 20 guineas, and 14 or 16 guineas respectively. Scheduled time for the passage was 65 days and the owners bravely agreed to pay a penalty of two pounds per ton on freight for each day exceeded.

Great Britain sailed to Melbourne precisely on schedule, in 65 days, with 319 passengers and 600 tons of cargo. She came home in even better time – 62 days – and the foundation of her reputation for reliability had been laid. The cargo she landed at Liverpool included almost seven tons of gold, wool – and 23 bales of cotton, the first to be exported from Australia. The conversion to a square-rigged sailing ship with auxiliary screw propulsion had proved to be a complete success.

Captain Matthews retired and John Gray, the First Mate was promoted to Captain in April 1854. A bluff Shetlander with a skill for command as well as for getting on well with passengers, he was to be associated with the ship for almost her entire Australian career. Twice, during 1854, the ship was involved in starting 'Russian invasion' scares. Upon returning to Liverpool on 24 February, Matthews fired an exuberant salute from the ship's small cannons. No doubt he was delighted to be home in record time, but the country was then on the eve of the Crimean War and rumours quickly spread on Merseyside that the Russians were landing.

When the *Great Britain* next arrived in Melbourne on 18 August 1854 she had smallpox cases on board and the medical authorities put the ship in quarantine for three weeks. When finally released,

she sailed towards Sandridge (now Port Melbourne) and a jubilant Captain Gray fired cannon and sky rockets to celebrate his evening arrival. Once more, the local citizens decided the Russians had arrived. The military called its men to the colours, a small cavalry force galloped towards the port, and civilians armed with guns or sticks advanced to deal with the invaders. A local journalist reported the next day, 'Byron's description of the excitement in Brussels on the eve of Waterloo can alone give any idea of the state of Melbourne last night . . .'

• Captain John Gray RNR, the bluff and popular Shetlander who commanded the *Great Britain* for 18 years, then disappeared at sea

But officialdom was not pleased and a report went to the Colonial Office. The Melbourne Argus said sternly, 'The firing of rockets and guns was but a demonstration of joy and self-congratulation indulged in by the commander of the liberated ship to gratify his passengers. This was a piece of exhilaration which might have been dispensed with'. The newspaper's angry editorial went on to comment, 'Should it ever happen that an enemy should enter our port the people, if armed, would fight like tigers. They were by no means pleased, however, at the Captain of the *Great Britain* for creating this alarm and we think he acted very indiscreetly in doing what he did'. The only beneficiaries, apparently, were the newspaper boys who went around selling papers with the cry, 'Full particulars of the Battle of Melbourne'.

While the ship was on the outward leg of Voyage 11, in July 1854, Gibbs, Bright transferred ownership to their own subsidiary, the Liverpool & Australian Steam Navigation Company. She was re-registered thus in February of the following year following her return from Melbourne. But that was to be her last Australian trip for two years as the government now required her for trooping service during the Crimean War with Russia. Between March of 1855 and her return to Liverpool in June 1856 she carried a total of 44,000 fighting men and horses on a variety of journeys around the Mediterranean, four of them culminating in Constantinople. All of this war service is regarded as Voyage 12 in the SS Great Britain Project's chronology of the ship's career.

Upon release from government service, the owners had the time (and no doubt, the profits from trooping) to contemplate the most thorough refit yet of the *Great Britain*. Captain Gray played a prominent part in the planning of what we now know as the '1857 refit' which achieved the vessel's most successful guise, in which she had her longest and most profitable work period. Her sailing rig this time was changed completely. Three new massive masts were fitted, each made from four tree trunks bound together with iron bands. These masts were destined to survive for the remainder of her working life and were only taken down for the ship's return to Bristol in 1970. The ship's sail area was enlarged further to 33,000 square feet and the deckhouse was extended to the stern, increasing the first class accommodation to 85 (with 500 other passengers). Henceforth, she was destined to follow sailing ship routes, utilising the most favourable winds at all times. This normally meant sailing out around the Cape of Good Hope and home around Cape Horn.

Engine improvements were made, too, and a single oval funnel replaced the rather incongruous twin funnels installed five years earlier. A two-bladed propeller was fitted which could be lifted out of the water when the vessel was under sail to ensure the smoothest possible transition from steam. Many passengers were later to comment favourably on this device.

This major refit took eight months to complete and the *Great Britain* was not able to leave for Melbourne again until 16 February 1857. Her appearance then has been described by Dr Evan Corlett, the distinguished naval architect whose enthusiasm for the ship sparked the campaign to save her in 1968, 'Little of the ship's original lightness and grace remained. Nevertheless, she was undeniably impressive – heavy, powerful and reminiscent of the steam frigates of her day. Indeed, anybody might be excused for mistaking her for a warship'.

That early 1857 Voyage 13 was a speedy one, Melbourne being reached in 62 days. She came home, however, in 93 days and then went into government service again, this time taking British troops to India to help quell the Indian Mutiny. It was not until April 1858 that she was freed for civilian duties again and Voyage 15 was a round trip to New York, between July and September 1858.

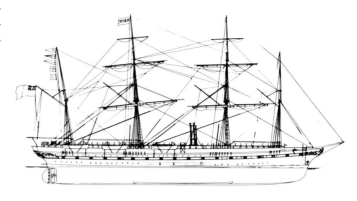

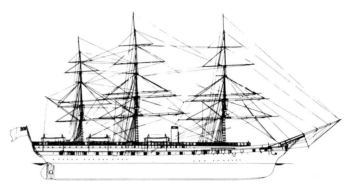

● Line drawings which illustrate the four-masted appearance of the early Australia years and (below) their final configuration

Voyage 16 was another round trip to Melbourne, followed by the last passage to New York in July and August of 1859. Then came 16 unbroken years on the Australia run, during which the ship set new standards for punctuality and reliability. Isambard Kingdom Brunel lived to see the ship re-established on the Melbourne run after the Indian Mutiny but died of Bright's Disease in September 1859, a few days after a boiler explosion while his third, and largest, ship the *Great Eastern* was undergoing trials in the English Channel. He was aged 53.

Some of the most interesting and significant information on the voyages in those years come from the diaries, letters and ship's newspapers produced by passengers. Thus, we know that during Voyage 18 (March to May 1860) *Great Britain* was under sail alone for 52.8 per cent of the time, combined steam and sail for 31.7 per cent, and solely steam for 15.5 per cent. The main cargo items were 592 bales of wool and 7,472 ounces of gold. That voyage carried 504 passengers and the following menagerie of animals and fowl to ensure that first class meals could be served to the saloon passengers throughout the voyage, 133 live sheep, 38 live pigs, two live bullocks, one milch cow, 420 live fowl, 300 live ducks, 400 live geese and 30 live turkeys. Two tons of fresh beef were also carried.

We have an excellent ship's newspaper account of Voyage 21, a 64-day journey to Melbourne between October and December of 1861. On this occasion there were 551 passengers and 140 crew and even more livestock was required: 140 sheep, 36 pigs, 528 fowl, 444 ducks, 96 geese and 48 turkeys. The problems of coping with such a collection of livestock must have been enormous and are difficult to imagine today.

The newspaper's main concern, however, was for the celebrities on board – the All England Eleven, the first England cricket team to play against Australian sides. They were confident of whipping the colonials although fellow passengers worried whether their incessant quoit playing aboard would be sufficient preparation for the matches against the enthusiastic Australians. Some of us today still look askance at commercial sponsorship of cricket but

• The members of the England cricket team which toured Australia in 1861/2 after practising at quoits on deck. From left to right the players and sponsors are George Wells, Mr Spiers, George Bennett, William Mortlock, Roger Iddison, William Caffyn, H. H. Stephenson (Captain, seated), Mr Mallam, Thomas Sewell, George Griffiths, William Mudie, Edward Stephenson (seated), Mr Pond, Charles Lawrence and Thomas Hearne

that very first tour was a 100 per cent sponsored venture. Victorian cricket lovers had failed to raise the funds to finance an England tour so Spiers & Pond, a wine and spirit firm, decided to promote it themselves. Their agent, a Mr Mallam, came to England in 1861 and signed up a team of mainly Surrey men with the promise of a fee of £150 each plus all travelling expenses. H H Stephenson was the captain.

The England side contracted to play 22-man teams, although their first match was against an 18-strong Victoria side. Some 15,000 people – an enormous crowd for those times – watched the first day's play in Melbourne. Altogether, Stephenson's men played 12 matches and two exhibition games. They won six, lost two and drew four times. The first big defeat was at the hands of

• Dr E. M. Grace (centre below) sporting the floppy white cap which he said caused a 'sensation' among passengers

22 men from Victoria and New South Wales when, it is alleged, the visitors lost because of the off-field wining and dining to which they were being subjected!

The 1861/62 tour was followed by another visit by England cricketers – this time more representative of the whole country – in 1863/64. Once again the team, captained by George Parr, sailed in the *Great Britain* (Voyage 24). They played 14 games in Australia and five in New Zealand, all against 22-man sides, and were undefeated throughout. This time the tour was worth £250 to each man, a useful sum in those days for a professional sportsman.

We have a delightful memoir of the second tour in the form of a fragment of the diary kept by Dr E M Grace (not W G), one of the England players. He showed little of the mock modesty we expect from nineteenth century gentlemen. He wrote in his diary on 24 October 1863, 'I appeared for the first time in my white cap with the rose in front and my canvas shoes with the red tapes which caused quite a sensation!' In Australia, Dr Grace challenged six local players to a match after an exhibition game at Maryborough. The locals could not dismiss the doctor who was 106 not out at the end of the day.

A theatrical drama was played out aboard the ship in 1865 when Mr G V Brooke, a theatrical manager, booked a passage home to Liverpool in the company of a young actress, Lavinia Jones. He was alleged to have absconded with some £30,000 and police searched the ship before its departure from Melbourne. The couple were hidden aboard by one of the ship's officers and travelled to Liverpool openly, giving theatrical performances for their fellow passengers. The charges against Brooke were later dropped and he and Miss Jones embarked for Melbourne in another ship, the *London*, in 1866 but they were drowned when the ship went down in the Bay of Biscay.

The ship's strangest and saddest drama occurred during Voyage 39. *Great Britain*, captained by John Gray, left Liverpool on 27 July 1872 and made her fastest journey ever, reaching Melbourne in just 54 days. On the return trip, she was 34 days out of Melbourne when Captain Gray disappeared from the ship. His servant went to his cabin to call him, but found it empty. The cabin was at the stern and one of the large square transom windows was wide open. It was surmised that he had somehow fallen through it, but he might have taken his own life during a spell of ill-health. There were even rumours that he might have been murdered for money he kept in his cabin.

But John Campbell, the Chief Steward (later to become the ship's Purser) noted in his diary entry for 26 November 1872, 'Listless and heartless we all are and those of us who sailed so long with the late Captain Gray aback. This sad end is so unexpected. Sick we knew him to be, and downhearted, as he always was in sickness but we never thought of this. He has to all appearances got out of bed in the middle watch, gone through the saloon to the lower saloon and unscrewed the port. There is a lamp hangs by it all night and he had taken time to lift the lid and put out the light before he dropped through. Our stewards saw the port down; little they thought what put it down till his servant went with his tea as usual in the morning. Dark to us all why he has done it. No letters can be found though his servant saw him writing'.

In a diary entry the next day, Campbell lamented the fact that the stewards had not watched Captain Gray more closely. After recalling the captain's penchant for medicines to cure his internal disorders, the Chief Steward declared, 'Thou art gone; live the many good qualities thou had, the good thou hast done. Thy faults fade in the distance. From the humblest part of the profession he rose to be made of as much as any Master in the Merchant Service. His name a home word in the Colonies of Australia and to the soldiers of the Crimea and the East Indies. And this is the end they will hear of the genial Captain Gray'. Captain Gray, born in Unst, the most northerly of the Shetland Isles, was 53 at the time of his death and left a widow and family.

Peter Robertson, the First Officer, took command of the ship but upon return to Liverpool the job of Captain was given to George Chapman, the former First Mate. Chapman captained the vessel on three uneventful trips, Voyages 40, 41 and 42, but Robertson succeeded him for what were to be the ship's last two round trips. The last Australian journey began on 26 August 1875 and the *Great Britain* came home to Liverpool on 30 January 1876. That was the end of her life as a steamer; she was to be laid up again, this time for six years in Birkenhead.

• The *Great Britain* riding at anchor in Liverpool, apparently fully laden, prior to one of her later runs to Melbourne

Life on Board

There was a happy consequence, for later generations, of the two months at sea spent by *Great Britain* passengers. The long journey, in usually tranquil conditions, made them hungry, thirsty and sometimes troublesome; but it also prompted many of them to write. From ship's newspapers (hand written at sea and then printed properly upon arrival in Melbourne or Liverpool) from diaries, logs and lengthy letters home we have fascinating pen pictures of life afloat in the iron ship.

The passengers in the early voyages in the 1850s were often heading for the diggings in Victoria. As with California a few years earlier, the lure of gold threw together people from every social background. Young men from sheltered middle class homes abandoned professional appointments or training and rubbed shoulders aboard with the impoverished and criminals of all nationalities. Young women seeking well paid appointments in a Melbourne crying out for labour, or just in search of husbands, found themselves in a ship with more than its fair quotas of gamblers and drunkards.

A letter survives from a young man Stephen Perry (Voyage 9) who wrote to his parents on 7 October 1852. He described fellow passengers thus, 'We are a rough looking lot; there is a dash of every nation here and I begin to know some of them by this time . . . Nearly all the passengers are going to the diggings and I only hope there is gold enough for all. We have had many applications to join our party but we do not intend to take on any more'.

The Gold Rush folk had a taste for gambling, drinking and violence. Stephen's letter went on to give this pen portrait of some personalities aboard, 'We have a gentleman by the name of Scott who has a pretty wife and I believe he thinks she will leave him and take another lord even before we arrive at our destination. There has been what the ladies call miffs and he won't leave her a moment.

'Then we have some young men who go below at midnight drunk and come out in the passages with a little bowie knife exercise. Then others that get chained up for being drunk and disorderly, and some fond of calling meetings and making speeches as to the badness of the food. In fact, we have all sorts. You only have to pay your money and take your choice'.

They were still drinking hard aboard in December 1867 (Voyage 31) when a 20-year-old Scots ploughman, John McLennan, committed these notes at different times to his shipboard diary, 'The ship was rolling very much last night. Some of the Irish were afraid to go to bed with their clothes off. The sailors were telling them she was going to founder so they treated the sailors with grog to see them safe in the lifeboat . . .

'Two young Irishmen were put to gaol for being riotous and annoying the rest of the passengers . . . There was a row in the third cabin between two women. One was married and she was for thrashing the other for winking at her husband . . . There is one young fellow I have noticed that drunk and gambled all his money and clothes so he is turned out a shoe black, a penny a head. In fact, there is plenty as bad as him. There was a while

there was nothing but raffles – on watches, rings, pipes, cigars, unicorns, clothes. Everything they raffled to get money they would drink so you may guess what sort of people we have got on board . . .'

Voyage 31 was particularly well chronicled. George Greaves from Derby, a 21-year-old labourer, left a detailed and chatty account of the passage. He recorded the same heavy drinking and fights aboard as John McLennan but also noted what must have been agreeable and amusing shipboard concerts. There was one minstrel show with the 'smell of burnt cork and no mistake. We had fiddle, concertina, drum, triangle and bones . . .'

Another labourer on that voyage, an Irishman named Richard Pope, 30, recalled later how he and other immigrants were robbed by a confidence trickster even before they had left Liverpool. Writing about events on 13 December 1867 he said, 'A minister visited the ship who gave us a farewell address and distributed tracts to all on board. He also collected a great deal of money to pay for printing an account of our leaving England, the same to be sent to our friends at home for which purpose he took the addresses of all who gave him money. But the old rogue never fulfilled his promise as we heard no more about him or his tracts'.

The accounts of Pope, and of his contemporaries, treat life (and death) aboard in the matter of fact, almost callous style, which was customary in an age more accustomed to shortened lives than we are today. On 8 January 1868 he noted, 'A child died of measles in the steerage and was thrown overboard this evening'. The following day he recorded, 'A child born in the second cabin, making the second birth on board'. Then on the 10th came an entry familiar in various accounts of shipboard life, 'One of the second cabin passengers put in irons for committing a nuisance'. Later that month his 26 January entry said tersely, 'A child born in the steerage last night and committed to the deep this evening. A sailor locked up for using insulting language to the first officer'. The next day's entry concluded, 'Another child born in the steerage'.

It was not only the men who caused problems for the officers, crew members and their fellow passengers. Sea journeys traditionally stir up all kinds of strange feelings in the feminine gender and that was certainly the case aboard the *Great Britain*. John Campbell, then Chief Steward, often complained of troublesome females. In one log entry he declared, 'I do wish that women would never come to sea. They are the top and bottom of every trouble, but when one sees one acting the part of the working Christian woman she sparkles like a diamond among rubbish and renews the faith of man in woman . . . God needs to help those who go to sea in emigrant ships on long voyages . . .' The following day his log noted tersely, 'Crazy females giving as much trouble as possible . . . Our good old ship does well in this dirty weather but if any sudden emergency should come these troublesome selfish folk would cry out. How few of us, God's creatures, try to live for others and as little as possible for self'.

Diary comments suggest that Victorian ladies were not always treated with the deference and respect which we imagine to have

• Life on board during an 1863 voyage, as captured by Herman Zumstein, a passenger who worked in Melbourne as a silk merchant

been obligatory at the time. One shrewdly observed shipboard account was kept by the 25-year-old Elizabeth Joseph of Bryn-mawr, Wales, who travelled on Voyage 35. She was destined to marry in New Zealand two years later, to give birth to eight children, and to die aged 95 as recently as 1940.

She wrote in one entry, 'Captain Gray and the Doctor come down every morning to see if we are all out of bed and ready to go on deck; if not, they wait till we are ready and drive us all up. Captain came down one morning and found some of the ladies in bed – they had been sick all night. "Now then," said he, "get up. If you don't upon my word I will take you out and dress you," stamping his foot at the same time. I can assure you they got up as soon as he left the room and on deck in a few minutes.'

Miss Joseph enjoyed the trip. 'The sea agrees with me first rate. I get up at six o'clock every morning and take a walk on deck and stay there until breakfast. The bell rings about half past eight and I go down as quick as I can. We have coffee for breakfast every morning. We have dinner at half past 12, pork and preserved potatoes. The pork is very good but I don't care for the potatoes. I wish I had brought some with me. They don't sell any here but, after all, I make a very good dinner. Other times we get beef, and rice and plum puddings. We get fresh bread three times a week in little loaves – Sunday, Tuesday and Friday. I can get anything here at the store. The bread gets short every week. I am only sorry that I did not bring flour with me. It is very dear here, four pence a pound, sugar one shilling and Tea four shillings. I have bought Tea, Flour and Sugar. It is a great comfort to get it at any price, on such a voyage.'

Elizabeth Joseph, to whom we are indebted for many shipboard observations, was surprised how 'dressy' life often was on board. She had thought that 'anything would do' but in fact life afloat en route to Australia often resembled a fashion show. She noted one day, 'They are very gay here – especially the saloon ladies. They had on their silks and white muslins when we crossed the Line. I thought anything would do on board ship but I was greatly mistaken. I am sorry I did not keep some of my dresses out of my box. I found my walking dress very handy on board to run up and down the stairs and there are a great many of them here.'

In one diary entry in April 1870 Miss Joseph reported three deaths – two men, and a woman of 72 – and a birth. She noted, 'One of the dead gentlemen filled himself with drink. He brought a large quantity with him, besides what he bought at the bar. He

left a wife and family in Liverpool to mourn after him. He was a lawyer's son. The other was one of the saloon waiters – the cramp took him in his stomach. This was his first voyage. He was about 20. The lady and her little son are getting on nicely. I have been seeing them many times. I was going to make her something to eat but she said she had everything she needed – better than she could have at home. She has a very nice room.'

Rosamond D'Ouseley, aged 24, was a lively middle class girl with a great (if often snobbish and critical) interest in people around her during Voyage 34. She was travelling to spend some time with relatives in Melbourne before sailing on to Sydney. Her initial comment on her fellow passengers at Liverpool was, 'The ship presented a rather wild appearance to my astonished gaze. A motley assembly of saloon, second, third and steerage passengers being all jumbled up together – some of the latter being exceedingly dirty and ill favoured in countenance . . .'

Describing the traditional final banquet on board before landing at Melbourne, Miss D'Ouseley wrote, 'We had a swell dinner in comparison to those we have been accustomed, given by the Captain as usual at the end of a voyage – roast boiled mutton, pastries and puddings in abundance, raisins and nuts and two decanters of Sherry and Port at each table. The latter was indifferent, the former very hot but it was thankfully received by us starving beggars who have been fed five times a week on salt meat and twice on fresh and that not *ad libitum* . . . As usual one or two got intoxicated before the day was over.'

A common sight on the *Great Britain* was the young man from a well-to-do home being shipped to Australia by his family because he had disgraced himself in some way or another, or was an incorrigible drunkard. These were to become the familiar class of 're-mittance men' – so called because their income derived from remittances sent by their families which could only be cashed in some distant Australian city.

Margaret Brown, 24, was one of the early travellers in the iron ship, arriving in Melbourne in August 1854 after Voyage 11. She was on her way to marry James Hoey, a Scot, but did not know she had a heart defect which was to end her life at the age of 28 after having mothered two children. A carefully brought up lass from Old Cumnock, Ayrshire, Miss Brown was horrified at the dissipated young men she saw aboard. 'There are some nice-like people and some very much the opposite; some very well-doing

15

Discipline on board

Victorian Britain was a disciplined society and most passengers did not question the strong rules imposed by the owners of such vessels as the Great Britain. *For those who caused particular trouble on board – such as fighting or being drunk – the ship's officers were able to impose the ultimate sanction of imprisoning the offender. Numerous accounts survive of passengers so losing their liberty for varying periods. One of the strictest rules was a total ban on the taking aboard of any alcoholic liquours – 'an ample stock being provided on board at moderate prices'. But we know from memoirs that the rule was often flouted. There was one celebrated case of a digger who had made a fortune in the goldfields and resolved to drink all the way home to Liverpool, drawing upon his own stocks and those of the ship. He died before reaching his native land.*

One of the regulations for the convenience of women aboard concerned seating arrangements at table for the saloon passengers. Because of the long bench-type seating, it was useful to be near the end of the seat. Saloon passengers were advised, in writing, 'The passengers are respectfully required to allow the ladies to occupy the seats most convenient for their retiring from the dinner table; and the places taken by the whole of the passengers at the first dinner after the ship leaves port are to be considered theirs during the voyage; this rule is not, of course, to prevent parties from changing seats with each other.'

The discipline extended to all classes and research has disclosed the following 17 'rules and regulations' to govern the conduct of the fore saloon passengers:

1 *When desirable, the sashes to remain open all night; if circumstances prevent this, to be opened at 5 in the morning in summer and 7 in winter.*

2 *The saloon and ladies' boudoir to be swept every morning before breakfast, beginning at 5 o'clock.*

3 *The stewards and boys to attend at meals neatly dressed.*

4 *Bedding to be turned down as soon as passengers quit their rooms.*

5 *The State Rooms to be swept every morning after breakfast. Slops emptied and basins cleaned at the same time. Beds to be made once only during each day (except in cases of illness), and within one hour after the breakfast things are removed.*

6 *Bed linen to be changed on the eighth day.*

7 *One towel to be hung up for each passenger, and to be changed every second day.*

8 *Breakfast to be on the table at 8 o'clock, and at 9 o'clock the cloth to be removed; after which nothing will be served till dinner.*

9 *The before-dinner gong to strike at half-past 12 o'clock, and dinner to be on the table at 1; the cloth to be removed the instant it is over.*

10 *Tea to be on the table at 6 o'clock.*

11 *Passengers' servants to take their meals at the fore saloon table.*

12 *Lights to be put out in the saloon at 11 o'clock, and in the state rooms at 12.*

13 *No meal to be served on the upper deck, nor in the state rooms, unless in cases of real illness.*

14 *No silver or glass to be used out of the saloon or state rooms.*

15 *The stewardess will be in attendance on the ladies exclusively, and make their beds at the time before stated.*

16 *Smoking not allowed under deck, and not abaft the funnels on deck.*

17 *Gambling is strictly prohibited, and card playing on Sundays will not be permitted, on which days Divine Service will be performed, weather permitting.*

and some very dissipated, particularly among the young men. Some of these young men might have been very different who had bright prospects before them at home and very likely the flowers of the family to which they belonged, but had got so dissipated that their friends would not insist on them staying at home. The youth who possesses the finest face on board this ship belongs to that class. He is a young Englishman, a medical student and as gentlemanly a lad as I ever spoke to, poor fellow. I often feel very sad when I look at him . . .'

Daniel Higson, aged 20 from Preston, Lancashire, was forced by his family to travel to Australia to advance his career. Sailing on Voyage 34, he left poignant diaries of his unhappiness at being separated from his parents and his girl friend Esther. 'I am determined to get back as soon as I can. The only comfort I can find is in that thought. When I get home I will not leave it again if I can help it. Oh, if they only knew how miserable I am they would not oppose my coming home . . . What a monstrous life this is – perspiring all night without clothes on the bed; all day reading, mauling about on deck wishing to be home and almost starving . . . A child died and was buried at sea, thrown from a port on the starboard side, I believe. Read the "Young Man's Guide". It is a good book but I cannot do as it says. I always wish to be at home on Saturdays and Sundays more than other days. I looked at Father's and Esther's portraits and I wished that I had one of my Mother. I cried when I thought that if I was at home I should be with Esther in Ashton Road or some other such place.'

Other accounts are happier chronicles of days in the sun, reading, chatting, playing cards and sewing. The celebrated Victorian novelist Anthony Trollope completed a novel between Liverpool and Melbourne when he and his wife sailed on Voyage 37 in 1871 to visit a son in Australia. With them travelled the family cook as Trollope had been given lurid accounts of the terrors of bush cuisine. The writer started on his novel *Lady Anna* on the first day at sea, and wrote a precise 66 pages by hand each day. He had the manuscript ready for the publisher by Melbourne.

A memoir of a passenger who sailed on the same journey as Trollope gives a glimpse of the 'simple diversions on board: reading and sketching for the studious, singing and dancing for the more exuberant . . . Among the steerage passengers the music of two professionals enable dancing to be gone into with spirit, and a few of the more intelligent public give recitations and readings in good taste, with a few songs to enliven their entertainment. In our case a concert or two, and a mask ball, successfully managed, give a little life to our otherwise monotonous voyage.'

Although the passengers were chiefly young and youngish people, death aboard was a commonplace event. Some were in advanced stages of consumption when they came aboard; others were suffering from years of under nourishment or the effects of excessive alcohol. Childish ailments were often fatal. The death of two young sisters aboard in August 1853 was described tersely in a letter to his wife by John Lewis, a steward. He wrote on the 23rd, 'I am sorry to say we have had a death on board. It occurred this afternoon. It was a sweet little girl about seven years old from bronchitis in the throat. I saw it breathe its last in its mother's arms. It will be some time before the scene will be erased from my memory . . .'

The next day Lewis penned a further note, 'I mentioned the death of a sweet child and have now to say that its sister, a younger one Elizabeth is just gone into the world of spirits. It was unwell when its sister died but not dangerous. The poor mother is almost broken hearted. I think if she does not get better soon, she will be the next.' The sisters were buried in the sand at St Vincent, one of the Cape Verde Islands. According to Lewis, their father was in Australia, 'holding a situation under the English Government of great responsibility'.

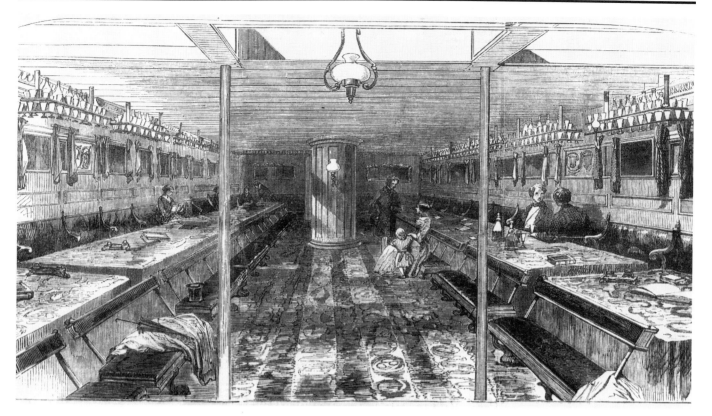

● The capacious dining saloon provided in the long deck house built to accommodate more passengers on the run to Melbourne

Food for all classes

Catering for anything up to 780 passengers and crew during two months at sea was a tremendous problem, normally solved to general satisfaction. The ship's stores were supplemented by fresh food killed aboard and a cow provided milk daily for the first class passengers. But the vast number of animals and fowl required their own considerable supplies – on one typical voyage in 1861 there were four tons of hay, two tons of mangold wurzel and 120 bushels of grain among the animal feedstuffs.

You got precisely what you paid for in Victorian times. The class of accommodation you could afford dictated not only the quality of your food but also its quantity and whether you were served at table or attended to your own messing arrangements, having been provided with cooked or uncooked provisions by a steward. Those able to pay for the best saloon accommodation were assured in the literature of a 'first rate table' and surviving records indicate this promise was well kept. A dinner menu surviving from 1861 shows that the first class passengers had Vermicelli Soup, followed by a choice from 22 main courses, five vegetable dishes, nine pastries and six dessert items. At the same time, the second cabin passengers had Mutton Soup, a choice from three dishes and two vegetables, with three pastries to follow. In the third class and steerage, it was simply Preserved Meat and Plum Pudding.

'Everything was provided' for those in the first class cabins. Those in the second were supplied with crockery and glass but had to provide their own bedding, linen and soap. In third class and steerage the passengers had to come with their own bedding, linen and soap together with eating utensils, a drinking can, coffee or tea cup, and a keg to hold three gallons of water. Food supplies were issued according to a fixed, weekly scale but it was also possible to purchase extras such as ham, bacon, pickles or sauces to supplement the rations.

The first class passengers must have spent a good part of each day at table, with a set breakfast, luncheon, tea and dinner. In the steerage it was very different; miss your allocation of food and you went hungry. An Irishman emigrating in 1875 wrote in one diary entry, 'Our breakfast was none of the best today – nearly impossible to break the biscuit

and if it had not been for the butter I had it would have been wasted. I made a blunder today in not attending at the butcher's shop for my pork so we had only pea soup and preserved potatoes for dinner.' On the following day he noted, 'I got a few pounds of bacon at 1s 6d a pound and a three pound loaf for 1s 6d; it is a fearful price but the biscuit is too hard.'

The weekly scales of provisions in the 1860s for passengers other than first class make fascinating reading. Second class passengers were allocated three pounds of biscuits whereas those in the third and steerage were given three and a half pounds each. There was one and a half pounds of beef and the same quantity of pork for the second class but the ration was reduced to one and a quarter pounds in the third and (in the case of pork) to only one pound in the steerage. The second class folk were given two and a half ounces of tea and coffee each week; in the third this became two ounces while in the steerage it was only an ounce of tea and one and three quarter ounces of coffee.

Treacle was a curiosity – none went to the second class passengers but those travelling third received half a pound and in the steerage the allocation dropped to a third of a pound. Some categories of food, notably cheese, pickles, jam, milk and tripe, did not figure at all in the foodstuffs given to the third class and steerage inmates. Sugar was rationed with an awesome precision: 16 ounces in second, 15 in third and 12 in steerage, each week. Some rations were the same for all classes, notably oatmeal (one pound); raisins (eight ounces); suet (six ounces); lime juice (six ounces) and water (21 quarts).

The Irish immigrant whose comments are quoted above used butter liberally to soften his biscuit. We do not know the class in which he travelled. If it had been second he would have received 12 ounces a week; in the third it would have been six ounces and in steerage only four ounces. But the steerage folk came into their own in the allocation of peas; somehow these were deemed to be an essential for the lower orders. One pint of peas each week sufficed for the second and third class passengers; in the steerage you could tuck into a pint and a half of them . . .

The Last Journey

In her Australian heyday, the *Great Britain* had an almost awesome reputation for speed. Through a combination of her fast passages (and voyages by the swifter sailing ships of the day), it was possible for letters to be sent to Melbourne and replies delivered to officialdom or commerce in London in a total period of 18 or 19 weeks – rapid communication for the day. But the iron ship's later journeys were slow and leisurely, and her last voyage of all lasted 84 years and 149 days, surely the slowest sea passage in history!

After her return from Melbourne in early 1876, the ship was laid up at Birkenhead for more than five years while her owners pondered whether there was still profit to be gained from her operation. The maritime scene was changing speedily and insurers were wary of providing cover for an ageing vessel carrying passengers. Finally, in July 1881, she was put up for auction by Messrs C. W. Kellock & Company of Liverpool. Gibbs, Bright felt her passenger days were at an end but that she might appeal to a firm handling animals or general cargo.

The advertisements for the sale make poignant reading today. Kellock's auction details declared: 'For the cattle trade across the Atlantic, she is admirably adapted, her high 'tween decks and side ports affording grand ventilation; she can carry livestock on three decks. For a sailing ship, her beautiful lines peculiarly adapt her and, with the machinery taken out, she is calculated to carry upwards of 4,000 tons dead weight'. The auctioneers suggested that 'with a certain outlay she could be made a most desirable merchant ship'.

But the blurb did not excite the hard headed shipping men of Liverpool. Bidding began at £2,000 and moved slowly to £5,000; then £6,000 was offered but the bidding stopped there. It was well below the reserve figure and, for the second time in her career, the *Great Britain* was withdrawn from sale.

The ship was saved from the scrapheap by internal changes within Gibbs, Bright. Late in 1881 the London trading firm of Antony Gibbs & Sons (controlled by another branch of the Gibbs family) absorbed Gibbs, Bright and re-named it Antony Gibbs, Sons & Company. The *Great Britain* came with the deal and the new owners soon decided they had a use for her, but as a large sailing vessel engaged in the North and South American trades.

Antony Gibbs had many connections on the Pacific coasts of both continents and the directors felt they could transport large consignments in both directions at an economic cost if the engines were removed. Accordingly, in 1882, she became a sailing ship with all machinery and passenger accommodation gone. The three great masts remained but the main was moved forward to achieve a correct balance following the removal of the funnel. Three new cargo hatches were inserted and the hull was sheathed in pine from eight feet above the keel to the 25 feet level. This area, in turn, was covered in zinc, as an anti-fouling measure or to protect it from being damaged by lighters.

Re-registered A1 at Lloyds in November 1882 as a cargo vessel, the *Great Britain* sailed for San Francisco on 2 December, skippered by Henry Stap who was to be her last captain. She loaded almost 3,300 tons of coal at Liverpool but at Montevideo, as a result of

protests by the crew, 200 tons were offloaded. This delayed the trip and 183 days had elapsed by the time the ship reached San Francisco. But some of the old aura still clung to her and the American press gave her an admiring welcome. One newspaper commented that she 'shows conclusively they put good work and good materials in vessels in early times'.

Great Britain sailed home in August 1883 with a large cargo of wheat, taking 154 days for the journey and thus completing Voyage 45. In 1884 she made another round trip between Liverpool and San Francisco, taking 160 days on the outward journey and 145 coming home. The pattern had been the same as the previous journey – coal to the West Coast and American wheat back to the U.K. That was her last complete passage on her own bottom: Voyage 47 was to see the end of her career as a sea-going vessel.

That journey began from Penarth, Cardiff, on 6 February 1886. It was an uneventful passage until the ever hazardous rounding of Cape Horn. On 18 April the crew begged Captain Stap to take the ship back to Port Stanley but he refused. For three and a half weeks, *Great Britain* struggled to round the Horn against hurricane force winds. Two of the top gallant masts were smashed in the storm conditions and the cargo began to shift. On 13 May the crew again appealed to the Captain and this time he relented and took the veteran back to Port Stanley on 24 May 1886.

As in the aftermath of the Dundrum Bay disaster almost 40 years earlier, the *Great Britain* was acknowledged to be in a robust condition by surveyors in Port Stanley. But the cost of repairing the decking and the masts was put at £5,500. Antony Gibbs felt this expense was not justified and the ship was sold for just £2,000 to the Falkland Islands Company which happened at the time to be seeking a floating storehouse for locally produced wool.

For just over half a century the vessel rode anchor in Port Stanley, at first holding wool and later being reduced to being a store ship for coal. In the First World War, the coal she held was taken on board by the British warships which were to triumph in the Battle of the Falklands. By 1933, however, she was not even required as a hulk and there were fears she might sink and block the harbour at Port Stanley.

In 1936, to avoid her destruction, the Governor of the Falklands, Sir Herbert Henniker-Heaton, launched an appeal for the return of the ship to Britain and her restoration. Between £10,000 and £15,000 would have been needed then but there was little public interest. In the following year the Royal Navy was told to take her out into the Atlantic and sink her for target practice. Naval officers in the Falklands declined to destroy the ship in this way and, instead, *Great Britain* was towed into the remote Sparrow Cove, three miles from Port Stanley. There, holes were made in her side and she settled down in the mud, apparently to die quietly in one of the most remote corners of the earth.

Thirty years passed with little interest in the historic hulk. Then in 1967 Karl Kortum, Director of the San Francisco Maritime Museum, and William Swigert, another enthusiast for old ships, went to the Falklands to study the vessel and take photographs. Their hope was to take the ship to San Francisco, or interest the

British in saving her. In November of that year Ewan Corlett, a naval architect and Brunel enthusiast, opened a public campaign in Britain with a letter to *The Times* urging the recovery and preservation of the 'forefather of all modern ships'.

The public interest aroused by Dr Corlett led to the formation of the SS Great Britain Project in May 1968. The American well-wishers agreed to stand back if a British rescue effort could be mounted. In November of that year Dr Corlett was able to travel to Port Stanley in HMS Endurance to make a proper technical survey of the ship. As with all previous surveys, he found *Great Britain* in remarkably good heart.

He reported to Project colleagues that she was in 'surprisingly sound overall structural condition'. He felt the vessel was capable of salvage and 'very well worth the effort'. So fund-raising began and in 1969 the Bahamas-based millionaire Jack Hayward promised to underwrite the cost of bringing her home to Bristol. A Hull tug company was appointed to tow the *Great Britain* home and prospects looked bright. Then, in November, the towing firm decided not to participate on the grounds that the iron plates were too far gone to be made seaworthy.

We will never know whether the iron ship could have been patched up and towed home on her own bottom. Instead, the Project approved a scheme by an Anglo-German concern, Risdon Beazley Ulrich Harms, to bring the ship home on top of Mulus III, a large floating pontoon. A further survey in January 1970 resulted in a report that there was an '80 per cent chance' that such an operation would be successful.

In March of that year Mulus III, towed by the tug Varius II, arrived in the Falklands and the pontoon was moored alongside the iron ship in Sparrow Cove. The plan was to make temporary plugs in the ship's holes, pump her out, then get her floating again. That was accomplished, the pontoon was sunk beneath her, then raised. On 13 April she was safely secured on top of the Mulus, ready for the tow to Bristol.

Ownership of the vessel was now transferred to the SS Great Britain Project and the 7,000-mile tow began. By 2 May she was in Montevideo for further inspection prior to the long Atlantic crossing. The final leg of Voyage 47 began four days later and by 24 June she was in Avonmouth, having achieved, at best, five knots an hour on the last epic passage. After minor patching up in Avonmouth, she was towed up the Avon to Bristol's floating harbour on 5 July – her first visit to her original port since 11 December 1844. A vast crowd gave the ship the warmest welcome in Bristol's history.

After a brief spell in the harbour, she was returned to her original dock on 19 July 1970, the anniversary of the laying of her first plates in 1839 and of her launch by Prince Albert four years later. Again, a Queen's consort was on hand that day, in the person of Prince Philip. He watched with fascination as the ship was positioned directly above the original keel blocks on which she would rest again once the water had been pumped out of the dock.

The great adventure of restoration began with the dismantling of the wooden cladding and the removal of hundreds of tons of mud, scale and rotting marine life. Cleaning of the iron plates was then put in hand. All this preliminary activity took two years. When this phase was over, the portholes could be seen again, revealing something of the ship's appearance in the 1840s.

Encouraged by the public interest – which has not flagged since – the Project embarked upon the awesome task of restoring *Great Britain* to her six-masted 1845 splendour. At first we reckoned a decade would suffice with the income available from admissions, other sales, and donations. Now it seems it will take double that time – but, fortunately, our visitors seem to derive as much pleasure from the continuing work as they might in the final perfection. At time of writing, 2,600,000 visits to the ship have been recorded. We hope that, henceforth, their ranks will be increased by a growing number of Australians now that the identities of most of her passengers can be disclosed . . .

● **The deck of the *Great Britain* as it appeared in the late 1880s when the vessel began her long exile in the Falkland Islands**

SS Great Britain's Australian voyages

The *Great Britain* made 47 voyages between leaving Bristol for trials in January 1845 until she was brought back to the same port in July 1970. Of these round trips, 32 were between Liverpool, or London, and Australian ports.

The first two voyages were from Bristol to London for fitting-out on the Thames, then from London to Liverpool. Voyage 3 was her maiden run from Liverpool to New York which began on 26 July 1845. She remained on the Atlantic route until Voyage 8 in May/June of 1852.

The *Great Britain's* legendary service on the Australia run started with Voyage 9 from Liverpool in August 1852. The last journey to Australia was Voyage 44 which began on 26 August 1875 in London. She arrived back in Liverpool in January of 1876, destined to be laid up for more than six years.

Readers seeking to trace their forbears in the passenger lists which begin overleaf should refer to the log at right for the voyage dates. Twenty nine outward passenger lists appear to have survived the years. We do not have details of those who sailed to Australia on voyages 18, 19 and 44.

Except where indicated, all the outward journeys were from Liverpool to Melbourne. The tables in the next column give the date of departure, the time taken for the voyage and (where known) the crew complement and the numbers of passengers aboard.

The entries on the pages which follow begin with the surname of the passenger, followed by the forenames or initials. Then come (if known) the person's age and occupation if disclosed at the time of ticket purchase.

All passengers were English except those marked S (Scottish), I (Irish) or OP (signifying to the chauvinistic Victorian English that they came from 'Other Parts'). The entry concludes with a dash and then the voyage number.

Thus, Armstrong George 20 labourer I-22' refers to a George Armstrong, aged 20 an Irishman who travelled to Melbourne on Voyage 22 which left Liverpool on 15 June 1862 and arrived in Melbourne 60 days later. Occasionally, passengers travelled on to other Australian ports in vessels other than the *Great Britain*. In these cases, to help identification, the final destination is indicated by a symbol at the end of the line such as Sy (Sydney) and Br (Brisbane). For the full list of abbreviations, see the footnote in the next column.

Family relationships may be presumed from the groupings of adults and children travelling on the same voyage. All such groups who journeyed together are kept in sequence in the lists which follow. Although the ship's papers do not necessarily identify a husband, wife and children – where say a John and Jane Smith booked berths in the ship on the same voyage with a number of children and infants of the same name it is a fair presumption that they were a family.

Because of the necessity for genealogists of keeping families together, only the surnames are in alphabetical order. People with the same surname are listed in numerical voyage order so that *Smith, Adam* does not necessarily come before *Smith, William*. In looking for a possible ancestor, readers must check through all passengers with the same surname.

Finally, it must be observed that these names have been taken from hand-written lists on faded documents so minor discrepancies in the spelling of names must be expected occasionally. Also, over a period of a century or more, some families change the spelling of their names slightly, by accident or design.

Outward (Liverpool-Melbourne)

No	Date	Days	Crew	Pass
9	21.8.52	81*	143	630
10	11.8.53	65	141	319
11	13.6.54	66	138	349
12	7.3.55 to 14.6.56 (Trooping in the Crimean War).			
13	16.2.57	62	133	469
14	24.9.57 to 10.4.58 (Trooping in the Indian Mutiny).			
15	28.7.58 to 7.9.58 (Round trip, Liverpool-New York).			
16	21.11.58	86	165	332
17	1.7.59 to 10.8.59 (Round trip, Liverpool-New York).			
18	11.12.59	56	120	–
19	20.7.60	62	130	404
20	17.2.61	75	137	406
21	20.10.61	64	141	535
22	15.6.62	60	165	544
23	25.1.63	69	142	536
24	15.10.63	63	146	589
25	26.5.64	60	140	451
26	17.12.64	62	139	478
27	25.7.65	56	142	504
28	18.2.66	58	157	436
29	27.10.66	59	161	331
30	19.5.67	59	147	328
31	15.12.67	57	–	512
32	9.7.68	58	156	616
33	3.2.69	59	152	561
34	12.8.69	62	169	490
35	19.3.70	57	170	618
36	6.10.70	59	144	509
37	24.5.71	64	153	391
38	17.12.71	66	149	396
39	27.7.72	54	132	337
40	30.3.73	57	163	386
41	27.10.73	56**	161	591
42	4.6.74	56	160	369
43	11.1.75	67	157	387
44	26.8.75	54***	144	355
45	2.11.82 to 1.2.84 (Round trip, Liverpool-San Francisco).			
46	11.5.84 to 8.7.85 (Round trip, Liverpool-San Francisco).			
47	6.2.86 (Penarth to San Francisco but voyage ended at Falkland Islands on 24.5.86 where she was later converted to a hulk. Voyage 47 was resumed in April 1970 when, after refloating, she was taken back to Bristol, arriving on 19.7.70).			

Great Britain sailed on to Sydney
**Great Britain* sailed on to Brisbane.
***This last voyage began in London, not Liverpool.

Abbreviations for destinations other than Melbourne:
ca Cape of Good Hope; ho Hobart; sy Sydney; ad Adelaide;
la Launceston; ge Geelong; ly Lyttleton; we Wellington;
br Brisbane; ot Otago; du Dunedin; ho Hollister; au Auckland.

● **(Top opposite): The iron ship comes home on top of the vast Mulus pontoon and (below) the return in triumph to Bristol**

The passenger lists 1852–1875

Aaron Henry J 55 agent–41
Aaron D 25 traveller–41
Aaron Philip 20 OP–42
Abadd James 8 OP–30
Abbot Miss Hannah 19 I–24
Abbott Samuel 26–28
Abbott Fanny 24–28
Abbott Florence 4–28
Abbott Edith infant–28
Abbott Thomas 42–36
Abbott Fanny 7–36
Abbott Thomas 5–36
Abbott Mary E 18–36
Abbott Susannah 14–36
Abel W –9
Abel A J –35
Abel Elias J –37
Abercrombie Isabella 27 S–11
Abern Miss Bridget 25 I–24
Abrahall J –9
Abraham R 24 blacksmith–11
Abraham George 24 labourer–23
Abraham Ann 28 spinster–23
Abraham I P 30 labourer I–26
Abrahams Bolina 26 spinster–37
Acheson William 26 labourer S–22
Ackroyd Francis 41 labourer–23
Ackroyd Mary 32–23
Ackroyd Elizabeth 18–23
Ackroyd Harriet 14–23
Ackroyd Frances J 1–23
Ackroyd Jonathan 29 labourer–24
Ackroyd Mary 24–24
Ackroyd Mrs Adelaide 34–36
Ackroyd Mary J 6–36
Acres Mrs Sarah 45 I–37
Acrees William 28–41
Adam Archibald–9
Adam James–9
Adam Thomas adult–10
Adam John–22
Adam Mrs–22
Adam Archibald 33 S–31
Adam Margaret 13 S–42
Adams Joseph–9
Adams William 45–11
Adams George 40 miner–21
Adams Emily 20 spinster–21
Adams Mrs Sarah 26–21
Adams John 17 labourer–22
Adams Julia 39 matron–25
Adams Alfred 11–25
Adams Edward 8–25
Adams Samuel 19 labourer I–26
Adams William 38 labourer I–30
Adams J D –34
Adams W A –34
Adams James 31–36

Adams Anne 31–36
Adams F Ernest 5–36
Adams Cecil 3–36
Adams Edith M 2–36
Adams Maria F infant–36
Adams Elizabeth 32 spinster–37
Adamson Alexander 21 S–13
Adamson John 64 grocer–38
Adderley James 33–11
Adderley Jane 37–11
Addis Heber 29–28
Addison James C 18 labourer–30
Adrain Jacob 48 labourer I–31
Adrain Jacob N 19 I–31
Agan Thomas 25 farmer S–13
Agnew Thomas 30 I–21
Agnew Andrew 25 I–29
Ahders August OP–41
Aherne Eugene 24 I–40
Aiken James 35 painter S–10
Ainscough Richard 21–36
Ainscough Thomas 34 labourer–36
Ainscough Ann 30–36
Ainscough Aaron 2–36
Ainscough John infant–36
Ainsworth Roger 44 labourer–26
Ainsworth Martha 42–26
Ainsworth James E 2–26
Ainsworth Benjamin 16–26
Airey Jonathan 20 labourer–24
Airey Jonathan 19 labourer–24
Airey H B –29
Aisbett Joseph 22 labourer–21
Aitchison Peter 30 farmer–11
Aitchison Alexander 25–11
Aitken Miss Ann 39 S–22
Aitken D –33
Aitkin James 30 merchant S–13
Aitkin Catherine 23 S–13
Aitkin Mary A 20 spinster I–22
Aitkin Miss Margaret E 26 S–22
Aitkin Mary 41 spinster S–22
Aitkin William 26 labourer S–23
Aitman Joseph H 28 labourer–26
Aked John 24–42
Akid John 46 labourer–26
Akroyd Priestly 1–24
Alderdyce James 13 S–11
Alderson James 48 labourer–22
Alderson Henrietta 50–22
Alderson Emma 18–22
Alderson Mosse 8–22
Alderson Albert 11–22
Alderson James 23 labourer–26
Aldgry Mary J 35 I–35
Alexander James–9
Alexander Thomas–9
Alexander J N –9

Alexander William 25 labour S–26
Alexander Emma 26 S–26
Alexander James 30 labourer I–27
Alexander Mary 28 spinster–29
Alexander Robert 24 S–36
Alexander William 20 artisan I–38
Alexander William 57 farmer I–38
Alexander Letitia 55 I–38
Alker William–9
Alkinson Jonathan 34 labourer–27
Allan David 15 labourer S–20
Allan William 25 labourer–26
Allan Frederick 31 labourer–26
Allan Jessie spinster 38–35
Allan Robert 40 I–36
Allan Fanny 40 I–36
Allan Jane 11 I–36
Allan John 8 I–36
Allan Fanny 9 I–36
Allan Charles 21 I–36
Allan Robert 39 merchant S–37
Allan Margaret 39 S–37
Allan William George 10 S–37
Allan Robert 7 S–37
Allan Archibald D 3 S–37
Allans Thomas–9
Allardyce Alexander 30 lab. –23
Allardyce Margaret 21–23
Allardyce Jane 25 spinster–23
Allardice William 23 labourer–24
Allardice James 18 labourer–24
Allbrook John 27 labourer–22
Allbrook Charles 25–22
Allcock Thomas 22 labourer–20
Alleman John 51 labourer–21
Allen George–9
Allen Ambrose 30 pawnbroker–11
Allen John 45 cabinetmaker–13
Allen Joseph 14 miner–13
Allen George 50 brickmaker–16
Allen Mrs Jane 35–23
Allen Miss Kate 24–23
Allen Capt Wm–23
Allen Mrs Eliza widow 60–24
Allen Frederick 26–24
Allen Frederick 16 labourer–28
Allen John 29 labourer S–30
Allen Rev Henry–31
Allen James 30 grocer–32
Allen Phillipa 30–32
Allen Thomas 21–34
Allen Harry 20–36
Allen Helena 40 servant–38
Allen Moses 50 blacksmith–39
Allen Alexander 57–41
Allen Martha 18 spinster–41
Allen John 21–42
Allen William 21–42

Allfrey Ernest H 28-30
Allinson John-9
Allison John 27 labourer-23
Allison James 20 labourer I-24
Allison John 23 OP-28
Allison Frederick 27 joiner-39
Allison Charlotte 27-39
Allison Frederick W 4-39
Allison Archibald 3-39
Allison Walter C 1-39
Allport Herbert 37 labourer I-31
Alpin Christopher 23-36
Alpin Catherine 20-36
Alpress Ezra 20 labourer-23
Alren Edward 21 labourer-21
Ambler Mrs Catherine 48-23
Ambler Catherine 20-23
Ambler Robert 18-23
Ambler Mrs Catherine 50-34
Amstell John William P -21
Andelson Christian 38 lab.-25
Anderson C -9
Anderson James-9
Anderson M adult-10
Anderson P 28 OP-10
Anderson John 25 carpenter I-13
Anderson Robert 21 wareh'seman-13
Anderson Robert 18 labourer I-23
Anderson Andrew 38 S-24
Anderson George 28-24
Anderson James 28 labourer-25
Anderson Rosa 30-25
Anderson William 31 labourer-26
Anderson A W 14 labourer-27
Anderson H H 39-27
Anderson James 32 S-29
Anderson Thomas-29
Anderson Elant 40 labourer S-31ge
Anderson Jane 34 S-31ge
Anderson Henry 11 S-31ge
Anderson Eliza 10 S-31ge
Anderson Maria 8 S-31ge
Anderson Elant 6 S-31ge
Anderson John 4 S-31ge
Anderson Ellen infant S-31ge
Anderson Miss I-31
Anderson Margaret-31
Anderson Francis 32 labourer-32
Anderson Henry 35 S-32
Anderson Alexander 20-33
Anderson Miss S-33
Anderson Thomas 26 S-33
Anderson J W 25 I-34
Anderson Mrs Mary 50 S-35
Anderson Farquar 50 S-35
Anderson William 35 labourer-35
Anderson Elizabeth 29-35
Anderson Alice 4-35
Anderson John 2-35
Anderson Richard 28-35
Anderson Sarah 20-35
Anderson Richard 1-35

Anderson John S-36
Anderson William 31 I-36
Anderson Jane 27 I-36
Anderson Agnes 4 I-36
Anderson Mary 3 I-36
Anderson Marian 1.1/2 I-36
Anderson M A spinster S-37
Anderson Samuel 25 I-37
Anderson Mary 50 widow-39
Anderson Thomas 53 S-39
Anderson Catherine 49 S-39
Anderson Hugh 13 S-39
Anderson Patrick 11 S-39
Anderson Catherine 15 S-39
Anderson Mary 17 S-39
Anderson T 46 workman-40
Anderson Mrs 42 wife-40
Anderson Mary 11-40
Anderson John 30 carpenter S-41
Anderson John 20 S-42
Anderton Benjamin 40 butcher-37
Anderton Bridget 34-37
Anderton William 7-37
Anderton Frederick 4-37
Andrea Joseph 23 OP-35
Andred Christine 16 OP-40
Andrew J-9
Andrew Hendra 21 miner-11
Andrew Henry-11
Andrew Joshua 33 labourer-26
Andrew Mary 23-26
Andrew Richard 37 labourer S-31
Andrew Mary 35 S-31
Andrew Richard 9 S-31
Andrew Stephen H 4 S-31
Andrew Michael J infant S-31
Andrew John-41
Andrews George 34 labourer-20
Andrews William 13-20
Andrews B H 26-34
Angelo Michael 15 OP-32
Angivin Andrew 26 labourer-21
Anglin Patrick 21 I-28
Angus George millwright S-16
Angus Silvanus 25 coachbuilder-11
Anthony Thomas 30 labourer-21
Anthony Mrs 26-21
Anthony Louis 1-21
Anthony David 24-21
Anthony Capt-22ad
Anthony Jno-23
Anthony William I-26
Antonio Gabrilo 24 OP-33
Applehay August 26 labourer-25
Appleyard John 52 miner-41
Appleyard Faith 49-41
Appy Julietta 52-37
Arbuckle Joseph 24 labourer I-24
Archer Adam 23 stonemason-27
Archer Isabella 33 servant-37
Arenas Martin-36
Arenas Mrs-36

Arenas Marriella 6-36
Arenas John-36
Arenas Phillip-36
Argyle Edward 49 S-29
Argyle Mrs M 30 S-29
Argyle Reginald 6 S-29
Argyle Charles 4 S-29
Aria H -29
Armanasco Giacomo 29 OP-42
Armand Margaret 34 servant-41ly
Armitage J J 21-26
Armitage Mrs 55-26
Armitage Mr 28-27
Armitage Mrs 28-27
Armitage Frederick 3-27
Armitage Harry 2-27
Armour Robert L 22 S-23sy
Armstrong Joseph 28 miner-11
Armstrong Walter 32 ironworker-13
Armstrong Phoebe 30-13
Armstrong Margaret 11-13
Armstrong Joseph 8-13
Armstrong John 6-13
Armstrong George 3-13
Armstrong Mrs Ann 27-21
Armstrong George 20 labourer I-22
Armstrong G W 38 labourer-22
Armstrong William 26 labourer-22
Armstrong George labourer-23
Armstrong Thomas 48 labourer-23
Armstrong Jane 44-23
Armstrong Mary 18-23
Armstrong James T 11-23
Armstrong Agnes 10-23
Armstrong Jane 8-23
Armstrong William 6-23
Armstrong Samuel 3-23
Armstrong Susan 1-23
Armstrong Robert 14-23
Armstrong William 23 labourer-23
Armstrong James 35-23
Armstrong Andrew 20-28
Armstrong Michael 49 lab. I-31
Armstrong Aaron 31-36
Armstrong Mary 28-36
Armstrong William 3-36
Armstrong John 28 S-36
Armstrong Isaac 22 S-36
Armstrong William 27-36
Armstrong Susan 23-36
Armstrong William 29 farmer I-40
Armstrong Mrs F L -42we
Arnold Robert 18 labourer-27
Arnold John-28
Arnold Miss Jane Ellen 21 I-30
Arnsall Thomas 37 labourer-24
Arnsall Elizabeth 33-24
Arnsall Elizabeth 11-24
Arnsall Ann 8-24
Arnsall Elizabeth 6-24
Arnsall Thomas 3-24
Arnsall Mary J infant-24

Aronson J W 19 labourer–22
Arroyads East.D 8 I–29
Arthur Henry 28 moulder–41
Arundel Henry–36
Asbeck A 27 OP–10
Ash Ruth 34–33
Ash Sophia 13–33
Ash Alma 12–33
Ash William 9–33
Ash Arthur 4–33
Ashe Julia spinster–25
Ashmore Charles 40–24
Ashmore Catherine 40–24
Ashton Miss Maria 54–23
Ashton John 42–33
Ashton Mary 30–33
Ashton Mary 16–33
Ashton Josiah 21 labourer–34
Ashton James 44–40
Ashworth John–9
Ashworth Mark–23
Ashworth John 48 merchant–37
Ashworth William 12–37
Ashworth John 21 engineer–40
Askew Maggie 30 spinster–29
Asnip John 37–41
Asnip Susan 22–41
Asnip Sarah 2–41
Aspinall Mrs Mary–23
Aspinall Hugh R –23
Aspinall Butler–23
Aspinall Miss E –29
Aspinall William 26–29
Aspinall Joseph 47 labourer–30
Asten Michael 24–34
Aston John 25 labourer–23
Astrella Tommizo 41 lab. OP–37
Astrello Francisex 10 OP–32
Atchison W –9
Atherton James 41–35
Atherton Francis 33–36
Atherton Anne E 21–36
Atherton James 43 miner 38
Atkinson Samuel 50 farmer–13
Atkinson James–23
Atkinson Thomas 36–24
Atkinson Margaret 22–24
Atkinson Robert 20–24
Atkinson Richard 33 labourer S–31
Atkinson William 26–33
Atkinson Thomas–34
Atkinson Henry 48–36
Atkinson James 22 farmer–37
Atkinson Fanny 47–38
Atkinson Stephen 55–39
Attenborough Robert 25 labour–20
Attrill Thomas–9
Aubrey Margaret 20–24
Auderoft John 21–43
Audley Sarah 28 spinster I–30
Auger Neskett 38–40
Auger Sophia 11–40

Auger Ottelie 9–40
Auld Sarah 53 spinster–27
Auld Sarah 24 spinster–27
Auradii Andrea 34 OP–35
Austin B –21
Austen J H –9
Austin J 24–33
Austin Charles 35–34
Austin W H –39
Autagnoli Giovanni OP–38
Aveline James 25 farmer I–37
Aver Luke 33 miner–11
Avery Barry 18 labourer–27
Aynsley Robert J 23–42
Aynsley James–42
Ayres Miss–23
Ayton James 47 labourer–26
Azzapardi Margaret matron–25
Azzapardi Claudina 14–25
Azzapardi Valetta 11–25
Azzapardi Galliloo 8–25

B

Babington G M –9
Babington J N –9
Bable Thomas 21 labourer–22
Bach Robert–9
Backman J S 48 labourer–30
Badcock William 25 labourer–25sy
Badcock Susan 24–25sy
Badcock Emily infant–25sy
Baddull William 58 farmer–41
Badger Thomas 29 labourer–22
Badger Ellen 25–22
Baditati A 20 OP–26
Bage Edward adult–10
Bage Anna adult–10
Bage Edward 2–10
Bage Robert 1–10
Baggaley T –9
Baggott William 55–34
Baggott Francis 18–34
Bagley John 40 labourer–24
Bagley Eliza L 34–24
Bagley William 13–24
Bagley Mary 11–24
Bagley Ann 10–24
Bagley James 8–24
Bagley Annadalia 6–24
Bagley Samuel 4–24
Bagley Eliza infant–24
Bagnall Mrs 36 I–10sy
Bagshaw Joseph–9
Bagshaw Mrs–9
Bailes Joseph 26 joiner–21
Bailey Samuel–23
Bailey John 42 labourer S–31
Bailey W John labourer I–32
Bailey Violet 6.1/2–41
Baillie Thomas 40 labourer–24
Baillie Elizabeth 36–24
Baillie Mary D 10–24

Baillie George 7–24
Baillie Elizabeth 5–24
Baillie Robert A 3–24
Baillie William 2–24
Baillie Mrs E J 27–26
Baillie Miss M G 7–26
Baillie George 23 engineer S–32
Baillie Mary 22 S–32
Baillie William 32 coalminer I–38
Baille Ann 30 I–38
Baille Elizabeth Ann 8 I–38
Baillie Joseph 4 I–38
Baillie John 3 I–38
Baillie J H J –40
Bain Henry 34–29
Baird Miss S–29
Baisbeck Mary A –37
Baister Robert W 27 labourer–23
Baker E –9
Baker George C –11
Baker John–21
Baker Mrs E–21
Baker Elizabeth–21
Baker Margaret–21
Baker Mary Jane–21
Baker Thomas–21
Baker James–21
Baker John–21
Baker William M 29 labourer–22
Baker James 31 S–38
Baker Jane 24 S–38
Baker Thomas–43
Bakmann Frank OP–41
Balcraig William 34 compositor–11
Balderstone John 21 farmer–40
Balding Joshua J 38 labourer–23ge
Balding Mary 46–23ge
Balding Mary E 11–23ge
Balding William 9–23ge
Baldwin Miss Bertha 23 S–24
Baldwin David 20 labourer–25
Baldwin Elizabeth 15 spinster–27
Bale George Elliott 25 I–11
Bale George E 26 merchant–13
Bale Jane 26–13
Bale R H 29 butcher–21
Ball Henry–11
Ball Hannah–11
Ball John 25 I–35
Ball James 18–41
Ballantine William 33 labourer–24
Ballingoll Miss I–21
Bane William 25–41
Banister Joseph 45 labourer–31
Banks T –9
Banks Ellen 23–10
Banks Jessie 26–42
Banley Thomas 25–42
Bannon Patrick 19 I–33
Bantley Anthony 30–34
Bantley Bridget 27–34
Bantley Elizabeth 10–34

Bantley Margaret 6-34
Bantley Mary A 4-34
Bantley Esther 1-34
Banwell John 20 labourer-27
Barber William 18 labourer I-22
Barber James 24-22
Barber Mrs Anna 22-24
Barber Charles S 25-37
Barclay J 31 labourer-27
Barclay Sarah 34 labourer-27
Bardsley Rev W J -35
Barendale Richard 42 labourer-35
Bargon Cammillo OP-35
Bargstedt Carl 28 OP-42
Barinston George 27 cornfactor-11
Barkas William 30 labourer-24
Barkas Isabella 28-24
Barker Anne 42-11
Barker Evan 24 miner-16
Barker D -21
Barker George 40 labourer-24
Barker Lady-27
Barker George 26 labourer-30
Barker William 17 traveller-34
Barker Charles 15 traveller-34
Barker Edward B -43
Barker Margaret-43
Barley William 30 labourer S-31
Barley Isabella 48-31
Barley George 27-31
Barley Mary 25-31
Barlogie Guiseppe 19 OP-23
Barlow Mrs J 26-22
Barlow William 6-22
Barlow Emma 4-22
Barlow Jane 22 spinster I-37
Barnard Thomas C 24 draper-11
Barnard David-38
Barnard Mrs-38
Barnard William-43
Barnel Samuel 40 farmer-38
Barnel Jacob 27-38
Barnes R -9
Barnes Joseph 20 miner-16
Barnes Miss Margaret 30-21
Barnes John D 36 labourer-23
Barnes John George 26-27
Barnes Sarah 21-27
Barnes William 37 labourer I-31
Barnes Mary A 43 I-31
Barnes T 36 S-32
Barnes John 39 miner-40
Barnett John 27 miner-13
Barnett George J 30 labourer-26
Barnett Mary A 30 spinster-26
Barnett Walter infant-26
Barnett William 18 labourer I-26
Barnett John R 32-29
Barnett Charles-39
Barnett Charles 29-42
Barnett Elizabeth 29-42
Barnett Ada 2-42

Barnett Mable W infant-42
Baron Ralph 24-38
Baron Mary A 23-38
Barr Robert 21 labourer-24
Barr Agnes 37 spinster-29
Barr Andrew 21 labourer I-37
Barraclough George 30-41
Barratt John-28
Barratt Mrs M-28
Barratt William 7-28
Barratt Annie 5-28
Barratt John 33-33
Barratt Rosannah 32-33
Barratt George G 11-33
Barratt Arthur J 5-33
Barratt Esther 2-33
Barratt Walter 1-33
Barratt John 24 I-33
Barret Thomas I-35
Barrett Joseph-9
Barrett John-23
Barrett Jno 26 labourer I-31
Barrett Thomas 22 miner-31
Barrett Ellen 21-31
Barrett Susannah 1-31
Barrett George G 25 I-38
Barrett Isabella 23 I-38
Barrett Arthur L 2 I-38
Barrett George G 1 I-38
Barrop Christopher 20 miner-13
Barrow Margret 15 servant I-42
Barry John Michael 24 archt. I-11
Barry S Augustine 17 archt. I-11
Barry Patrick 36 labourer I-22
Barry Miss Mary 20 I-23
Barry Thomas 30 labourer I-24
Barry John 39-27
Barry Richard 21 labourer I-31
Barry John 22 labourer S-32
Barry John 22 I-32
Barry Rev David-33
Barry Susan spinster I-41sy
Barry Nicholas 29-41
Barry Thomas 21-41
Barry Dennis 33 I-42
Barry John 22 I-42
Bartalli Antonio 28 OP-43
Barth Jacobine 25 spinster OP-29
Barthold John C 42 OP-38
Barthold Caroline 40 OP-38
Barthold Paul W 4 OP-38
Bartlett John 48 farmer-38
Bartole Feudo 26 OP-33
Barton S -9
Barton W R 29 carver-39
Bartram James 39 labourer-27
Bartram M Mary 45 spinster-27
Bartram H William 13 labourer-27
Bartrom Miss 21-22
Barwick Elizabeth 40-29
Basi Isago 11 labourer OP-26
Baskervill James 35-28

Bassett Henry J 30 clerk-13
Bassett John 70 miner-21
Bassett M 65-21
Bassett Daniel 28 labourer-22
Bastian Thomas 65 S-35
Bastiman Mary 27 spinster-20
Bate Hannah 19 spinster-25
Bateman Thomas 60-34
Bateman James 23-34
Bates Samuel 25-28
Battaglio Pietro OP-38
Battalia Fran A 23 OP-41
Batterby H -9
Batterby James-41
Batterby Sarah-41
Batterby Caroline E 1.1/2-41
Batterby James R (infant)-41
Battinson John 21 woodcarver-13
Battye R -9
Baugy Elizabeth de 30-42
Baunow Miss Mary 18 I-21
Bawn Sigismund 18 OP-28
Baxter Charles 21 labourer I-27
Baxtor Janet spinster-25
Bayldon Mary 22 spinster-22
Bayley John 25 labourer I-26
Bayne John 19 labourer-34
Beaham James 25 miner-37
Beale Alfred 21 labourer-24
Bealy David B 35-28
Bean Margaret-9
Bean Alexander 27-34
Bean Agnes 26-34
Bean William 5-34
Bean Alexander 4-34
Bean Agnes 2-34
Bean Margaret 1-34
Beard Thomas 21-39
Beardsworth Jeffraison 36 farm-13
Beardsworth Martha 30-13
Bearteam Jane 28 spinster-20
Beath Joseph 29 S-10
Beaton Euph 22 spinster S-28
Beattie William 30 labourer S-23
Beattie John 24 labourer-26
Beattie Robert 23 labourer I-31
Beatty James M 30 I-13
Beatty George M 45 I-13
Beaumont Charles 25 labourer-22
Beaumont Rev G P 40-29
Beaumont Joseph 37-42
Beaumont Joseph 11-42
Beaver Albert 16 labourer Op-28
Bebarfield Barnett 17 lab. I-24
Beck 17-13
Becker Charles 17-33sy
Beckett James 25 labourer-25
Bedat William I 22 labourer I-26
Bedson Mrs John 50-41
Bee John-9
Beech George 41 labourer-23
Beechins Rev M I-28

Beeston J C –11
Begg David–21
Begg Francis J labourer–30
Begg Agnes spinster–34
Beggs Margaret 28 spinster S–29
Begley Patrick 18 I–43
Behesy J –9
Behrendo Albert 17 labourer OP–21
Beicroft Mathew 20–29
Belden James 23 labourer–35
Belden William 21–35
Belford Thomas 27–37
Belford Rebecca 22–37
Belisini Andresa 24 OP–35
Bell H –9
Bell Henry–9
Bell John–9
Bell Thomas junior–9
Bell Robert 25 joiner–11
Bell George 28 miner–13
Bell George 32 miner–13
Bell James 32 labourer–20
Bell Isabella 25–20
Bell Joseph R child–20
Bell James 29 miner S–21
Bell Sarah 45 spinster–21
Bell Robert 28 labourer S–22
Bell Samuel 23 labourer I–22
Bell George J 29 labourer–24
Bell Jane 29–24
Bell Hannah 8–24
Bell Robert 6–24
Bell Annie 4–24
Bell Miss Jane 22–24
Bell Hugh 23 labourer I–24
Bell Joseph 29 labourer–24
Bell Margaret 29–24
Bell Bridget 4 (died at sea)–24
Bell Anne 2–24
Bell Ruth 20–24
Bell William 36 labourer–24
Bell Mr–30
Bell Mary 27 spinster–31
Bell Joseph 39 labourer–34
Bell Bessey 37–34
Bell Mary H 11–34
Bell Richard 31–34
Bell James 38–36
Bell William 40 coachmaker–38
Bell Ann 36–38
Bell Mary E 15–38
Bell Jane 12–38
Bell William 9–38
Bell Henry 5–38
Bell George 2–38
Bell Ellen infant–38
Bell William 54 farmer–40
Bell Sarah 48 wife–40
Ball Susan 6–40
Bell John 27–41
Bell William 40 storekeeper–41
Bell Jonathan 20–41

Bell Joshua 27 I–42
Bell Ellen 31–43
Bell Ernest 4–43
Bell Ethel 3–43
Bellamy E –9
Bellisco Joseph 28 lab. OP–30
Beloe Elizabeth 48 (married)–40
Benan Thomas 40–33
Bence Henry T –38
Bendall William 40–16
Bendall Sarah 30–16
Bendall Sarah 6–16
Bendall Samuel 11–16
Bengers Richard 21 labourer–20
Bengers John 20–20
Bengers Thomas 23 labourer–20
Bengne Mrs E 33 S–38
Bennet Thomas 24 labourer–20
Bennet Mrs 21–20
Bennet George 23 labourer–33
Bennett Christopher–11
Bennett James 32 miner–13
Bennett George–21
Bennett Mrs Thomasini 33–21
Bennett Thomas James 5–21
Bennett Edward Henry 3–21
Bennett Richard 2–21
Bennett John 19–21
Bennett M R 27 labourer–22sy
Bennett Mrs Tomasina 25–22
Bennett Absalom 20 labourer–23
Bennett J B –23
Bennett Samuel 33 labourer–23
Bennett Hannah 25–23
Bennett Mary 4–23
Bennett John G–1.1/2–23
Bennett Jonathan 27 labourer–24
Bennett John 28 labourer–27
Bennett Mr–27
Bennett Mrs–27
Bennett Mrs–28
Bennett Henry 22 labourer–30
Bennett Miss Elizabeth 16 S–31
Bennett Joseph 16 polisher–32
Bennett Miss Catherine 34–35
Bennett William 47–36
Bennett Eliza 42–36
Bennett N N 11–36
Bennett Albert 10–36
Bennett Maria 19–36
Bennetts William 14 miner–13
Bennetts John 22 labourer–22
Bennetts John 54 labourer–27
Bennetts Jane 52–27
Bennetts Nancy 17–27
Bennetts Susan 11–27
Bennetts William Henry 13 lab.–27
Benrose Austin 23 shoemaker–38
Benson Edward 28 bootmaker I–32
Bentley John 40 labourer–24
Bentley Mary A 2–24
Bentley Wright 33 labourer–24

Bentley William 37–24
Bentley Hannah 29–24
Bentley Ann 3–24
Bentley Thomas 23 labourer–33
Bentley Anne 20–33
Bergtholdt Louisa 33 OP–23
Bernard Daniel E 21–41
Bernett Simon 28 OP–43
Bernett Mary 28 OP–43
Bernett Louisa 7 OP–43
Bernett Rachel 5 OP–43
Bernett Rosen 3 OP–43
Bernett Betsy 1 OP–43
Bernett Isaac 1 OP–43
Bernie Elizabeth 22 spinster S–31
Bernston Davis 14 OP–13
Berry Helen 28 spinster–20
Berry Samuel 30–34
Berry Sarah 30–34
Berry James Wilson 24–37
Berry Isabel Jane 23–37
Berry Mabel 3–37
Berry Frank 1–37
Berry Robert 28 farmer–39
Berry E 21 mechanic–40
Berryman Thomas 16 labourer–20
Berryman James 25 labourer–35
Berryman John 37 labourer–35
Bert Frederick N 17 clerk–13
Bertram Mr 28 labourer–22
Bertram Adam 14 labourer–23
Besant Miss Jesse 18–23
Besi Pietra 26 OP–35
Bessey G W 54 bookseller–43
Best Ellen 27 servant I–32
Bestiwick William 61–34
Beswitherwick Anthony 19–29
Bethell Fanny 29–13
Bethell Sarah 3–13
Betinke Carl 39 OP–42
Betti Giovanni farmer OP–38
Bettie G 22 OP–26
Bettington Mrs adult–37
Bettington Emily 12–37
Bettington James 10–37
Bettington Ada 7–37
Bettington Joshua 3–37
Betz Adam 30 labourer OP–30
Beuttey Charles 34–28
Bevan J –9
Bevan John 22–28
Bevan William–28
Bevan Mrs 25–10
Bevan W J 3mths–10
Bevens Owen G 24 labourer–20
Beveridge Elsie 25 labourer S–21
Beveridge Jessie 22 S–21
Beveridge D 36 S–21
Beveridge James A–26
Beveron Elizabeth 40–20
Beveron John 8–20
Bewles Joseph 51 labourer–31

Beyer Miss-34
Bibo Acton 45 trader OP-40
Bibo Rosina 29 OP-40
Bibo Catherine 6 OP-40
Bibo Acton 3 OP-40
Bibo Elizabeth 1 OP-40
Bice Martin 22 miner-32
Bice Rebecca 22-32
Bice Catherine infant-32
Bickmann T W 27 labourer-25
Biddell Mrs Susannah-33
Biddell Susannah 9-33
Biddell Selina 7-33
Biddell Florence 5-33
Biddell Ada 2-33
Bielanski Antonio-9
Bielanski Cas-9
Bietz Johannah OP-42
Biggart Thomas junr 24 S-41
Bigger Thomas 22-29
Bigger John 19 labourer-31
Biggles William 22 labourer-22
Biggs Frederick 45 OP-42
Biggs St John A 20-43du
Binch F 35-40
Bindon Henry 30 labourer I-30
Binkell Clemens OP-41
Birch Mr-21
Birch Mrs-21
Birch Thomas 25-35
Birchall N -11
Bircher N OP-43we
Bird William 19 carpenter I-20
Bird Miss Mary 23 I-21
Birkway George 55 bag.minister-42
Birkway Harriet 52-42
Birkway Harriet 23-42
Birkway Leila 18-42
Birkway Joseph 19-42
Birkway Thomas 15-42
Birkway Ann 12-42
Birkway Walter 10-42
Birmingham John 24 joiner S-35
Birnie Miss S-31
Birrell Janet 19 spinster-27
Birrell George 17 labourer-27
Birrell Jeannie M 15-27
Birrell Elizabeth R 11-27
Birtwistle J 26 labourer-23
Bishof Frederic 30 trader OP-40
Bishop William 27 sawyer-21
Bishop John 21 labourer-26
Bishop Charles 18-27
Bishop T W labourer I-31
Bishop George 20-41
Bisley George Cox 13 labourer-35
Bispert Lorenzo 19 workman OP-38
Biss David 35 labourer S-26
Biss Arthur 21 labourer S-26
Biss Charles 20 labourer-31
Biss Charles 20 S-32
Bissett David 45 S-30

Bissett Mrs 40 S-30
Bitcon James 27 carpenter I-32
Bjonebye B OP-30
Black W -9
Black James 27 labourer I-21
Black Daniel 27 labourer-26
Black Mary 23-26
Black Andrew 3-26
Black Mary J 2-26
Black Isabella infant-26
Black Margaret 32 spinster-26
Black John 30 labourer S-30
Black Elizabeth 30 S-30
Black Alexander 7 S-30
Black Annie 5 S-30
Black John 2 S-30
Black Isabella infant S-30
Black Neil-32
Black Mrs E G -32
Black Archibald 8-32
Black Stewart G 5-32
Black Neil 3-32
Black Robert 35 I-36
Black Mary J 30 I-36
Blackburn John 51 engineer-40
Blackburn Joseph 45 I-40
Blacket Thomas 25 labourer-22
Blackew Joseph 24 labourer-30
Blackew Richard 21 labourer-30
Blackew Thomas 26 labourer-30
Blackey Johnston 27 labourer I-27
Blackey Joseph 24 farmer I-33
Blackey Johnston 21 I-33
Blackley James 25 labourer S-22
Blacklock John 43 miner-13
Blacklock John 15 miner-13
Blackmore Philip 25 labourer-13
Blackmore George 25 gardener-41sy
Blackwall Mrs Lucy 36-29
Blackwall Ada 8-29
Blackwell William 46 sawyer I-40
Blackwood J H -9
Blackwood Elizabeth C H 26 I-33
Blackwood Sophia 24 spinster I-33
Blackshaw Joshua-11
Blaern Amelia 24 spinster OP-37
Blainey Matthew 34 labourer-22
Blair Rev Hugh-11
Blair Mrs-11
Blake Edward-9
Blake F A 27 I-10
Blake John 29 labourer I-27
Blake Thomas 19 labourer I-37
Blakeney H -20
Blammer William-28
Blanchard Thomas 43 S-36
Bland James 30 labourer-24
Bland George 20 S-39
Blandford Charles 40-33
Blane Samuel 23 labourer S-26
Blaney John 28 miner-13
Blaubarn E OP-41

Blaymine James 47-43
Bleackley H junior-9
Blechmore Charles A 27-24
Blennerhassett James 26 lab. I-27
Blew Alfred-43
Bligh William H labourer-36
Blits L J 28 OP-33
Blits Leah 29 OP-33
Blits Sarah infant OP-33
Block Elizabeth 23-26
Block Henrietta 5-26
Blood Frederick 38-28
Blood Bridget 37-28
Blood John 20-28
Blood George 11-28
Blood Frederick 8-28
Blum Jacob 19 OP-38
Blumenthall Salamon 16 OP-13
Blundell Isaac 21 blacksmith-27
Blyth Adam 29 S-33ad
Blytheway John Thomas 28 miner-16
Boace George C -11
Boace A -11
Boake Barcroft 20-13
Boans James 27 labourer-25
Boans Henry 30 labourer-25
Boath Robert 30-28
Boazman Edward 34 labourer-25
Boazman Ann 32-25
Boazman James 8-25
Boazman Jno George 5-25
Boazman Mary 2-25
Boazman Sarah infant-25
Bocquet Alfred 26 labourer I-26
Bodel John 33 grocer I-33
Boden Richard 27-36
Bodgshun James-22
Bodgshun Mrs P -22
Bodshun Ellen-22
Body William 29 miner-11
Boid Edward 25 labourer I-30
Bolderstone Thomas 40 labourer-37
Boldicke R 21 OP-40
Bole James 27 labourer-23
Bolger John 18 labourer I-20
Bolitho Alfred 26 labourer-30
Bolitho Emily 33 servant-32
Bolitho Walter 21-32
Bolitho James 24 labourer OP-34
Bolitho Edwin 37 artisan S-38
Bolitho Jane 28 S-38
Bolitho Thomas 32 S-38
Bolitho Elizabeth 31 S-38
Bolitho Ellen 1 S-38
Bolitho William 27 farmer-38
Bolitho Anne 26-38
Bolitho Edwin 4-38
Bolitho Clara 2-38
Bolitho Ellen 1-38
Bolster Richard G 20 I-43
Bolton Marcus 35 labourer I-11
Bolton Matilda 26 spinster I-22

Bolton Joseph 20-29
Bolton Mrs Ann 40-41
Bolton Alice 14-41
Bolton James 11-41
Bolton Nancy 7-41
Bombay Maximilian-9
Bombardiere Gial 26 OP-35
Bombardiere Gio 30 OP-35
Bombardiero Pietro 29 OP-38
Bonappi Lunone 22 OP-40
Bonappi Andrea 22 OP-40
Bond Robert-11
Bonds Richard 41 miner-11
Bonham Patrick 32-34
Bonnford R C -32
Bonwick William E 22 lab. S-31
Book David 21 grazier OP-16
Book C W -28
Bookley William 30-24
Boomi M OP-42
Booth Hannah 28-29
Booth Mrs-31
Booth Mrs Maria 69-33
Booth Benjamin 17-36
Booth Thomas 16-36
Borechin William 42 miner S-35
Borechin Mrs 20 S-35
Borgen I C 35 OP-10
Borman John 20 labourer-24
Bornford P -32
Borren Stephen 35 farmer-40
Boson Lans S 23 labourer OP-27
Bosse Mrs Dina 27 OP-37
Bosse May 5 OP-37
Bosse Anna 3 OP-37
Bosse Henry 1 OP-37
Bosse Mrs Johanne 25 OP-37
Bosse Anna M 3 OP-37
Bosse (infant) OP-37
Boston Thomas Edward 21-27
Botham Mary 24 spinster S-30
Bothell J B B 19 labourer-22
Botterill George 29 engineer-13
Botterill Emma 29-13
Botterill Emily 2-13
Botterill James 32 engineer-13
Botterill Emma 29-13
Botterill Emma 3-13
Bottomley Joseph 55 labourer I-24
Bottomley Frederick-42
Bould Miss Jane 23-21
Boulster John 44 S-36
Boulter H -9
Boulton R -11
Bourham Major-36
Bourham Mrs-36
Bourke John 25 labourer-22
Bourke Joseph 30 labourer I-26
Bourke Patrick 21 labourer I-27
Bourke Andrew 25 labourer I-32
Bourke William H S 18-42
Bourne William labourer-25

Bousard Robert de-22
Bovey Thomas B 32-38
Bowden Robert-10
Bowden Miss Mary 50-36
Bowden Martin 31 I-36
Bowen Thomas-9
Bowen William-9
Bowen William 27-11
Bowen Charles J 27 I-32
Bowen John 34 labourer I-30
Bower Janet 50-10
Bower Mary A 25-10
Bower Eliza 20-10
Bower Sarah 18-10
Bower Walter 12-10
Bower Matthew 10-10
Bower Patrick 30 I-33
Bowers Miss Ellen 18 I-24
Bowers R B 28 miner-39
Bowke William 19-43
Bowler Joshua 46 labourer-23
Bowley Thomas-11
Bowley Thomas-43
Bowley Lucy-43
Bowley Charles 6-43
Bowley Thomas 4-43
Bowley Sydney infant-43
Bowwan Samuel 22 farmer-13
Bowman Robert 27 labourer-21
Bowman Jane 23-21
Bowman Sarah 1-21
Bowman C 28 spinster-27
Bowman John 35-34
Bowmer Francis 25-42br
Bowring Joseph-9
Bowring Mrs (& infant)-9
Box Miss Rebecca-21
Box Mr W D -28
Box Mrs-28
Box Charles V-30
Boyce Miss 25-24
Boyce H A spinster-30
Boyce Miss-30
Boyd Robert 27 mason-11
Boyd Mrs Susan 25 S-16
Boyd Margaret 1.3/4 S-16
Boyd Wilhelmina 1 S-16
Boyd William 20 farmer-21
Boyd William 32 labourer-26
Boyd William 16 labourer-27
Boyd Nicholas 18 labourer-27
Boyd William 17-34
Boyer Edward-9
Boyer T -9
Boyer William-9
Boyes James 21 labourer-23
Boyle Peter-16
Boyle Miss Lizzie 25-24
Boyle Patrick 17 I-35
Bracken Mr 24-16
Bracken Coghlin 2-16
Bracken Richard 1-16

Bracken Isabella 25 spinster-31
Bradbee Charles 27 labourer-35
Bradburne R H -9
Bradey James 35 farmer-16
Bradford Thomas 27 labourer-24
Bradford I R adult labourer-27
Bradford Annie S-39
Bradhand Watson 32-28
Bradley Michael 30 labourer-13
Bradley Hugh 30 policeman I-16
Bradley Francis 25 smith-21
Bradley Mary 26-21
Bradley Levi 35 labourer-21
Bradley Thomas 38 labourer-21
Bradley John L 14-21
Bradley Alexander-42
Bradley Margaret (& infant)-42
Bradman Catherine 33 spinster-22
Bradohan William 19 labourer-26
Bradshaw William 20-33
Bradshaw James 20-35
Bradshaw W 30 sailor-37
Bradshaw Capt G W 36-41
Brady John 24 labourer-22
Brady Edward 21-22
Brady Georgina 15 spinster I-28
Brady Margaret J 11-28
Brady Rose Eva 10-28
Brahm Samuel 30-10
Braidman Robert 21 labourer-20
Brain Thomas H 24 traveller-34
Bramwell Tom 35-29
Bramwell Sampson 23 bootmaker-31
Branch Benedict 31-16
Branch Christiana 27-16
Branch Charles 1-16
Brancker Benjamin-9
Brandwick William B 42-36
Brandwick Elizabeth 29-36
Brandwick Mainy 3-36
Branigan Michael 20-33
Branigan William 20 I-33
Brannon Michael 30 S-34
Branwell John-26
Branwell Mrs-26
Branwell Jessy 10-26
Branwell John 8-26
Branwell William 2-26
Brassey J -31
Brassey Master 8-31
Bratson William 34-42
Bratson Catherine 33-42
Bratson Ann 5-42
Bratson Eleanor 2-42
Braun N -9
Braun Joel 18 OP-43
Bravo Salvator 23 labourer OP-13
Bravo Guiseppe 17 labourer OP-13
Bravo Pietro 34 labourer OP-13
Bray James H 20 miner-13
Bray John 22 miner-32
Brayshaw William-9

Brazil John 22 smith I-10
Brazley Frances 15-35
Brazley Annie L 13-35
Brazley Henrietta 11-35
Brazley John 50-35
Brazley Harriet 52-35
Breading George-9
Breakell James 52-36
Breakell Hannah 40-36
Breakell Fanny 10-36
Breakell James 7-36
Breakell Sophia 5-36
Breakell Thomas 12-36
Breakell Sarah A 14-36
Breasley Johnson 19-34
Brebner James G 23 labourer S-27
Brebner Mary Ann 11 S-27
Brebner Jane 18 spinster S-30
Brebnor C labourer-28
Breen Daniel 22 I-28
Breen William 25 farmer-37
Bremner Jane 24 S-41
Brenan Edward 37-41
Brend George F 29-24
Brendenson L OP-30
Brennan Richard 22 farmer-16
Brennan Daniel 24 labourer I-21
Brennan Miss Mary 20 I-21
Brennan Frederick 28-25
Brennan John 25 labourer I-31
Brennan Timothy 38 plasterer-38
Brennard Thomas 28 labourer-21
Brent Thomas 21 labourer-22
Brereton James 45-38
Brereton Mary Ann 21-38
Breslan Margaret A servant-35
Bretherton Mrs Anne 27-16
Brevoney Mary 30 matron-20
Brevoney Mary Lucy 20-20
Brevoney Margaret 4-20
Brevoney Ellen 2-20
Brevoney (infant)-20
Brewer M N 56 labourer-28
Brewer John D 36-32
Brewer Peter 23 farmer I-32
Brewster William 24 labourer-34
Brewster Joseph C 23-38
Briad Mrs Eliza 38-21
Briad William P 10-21
Briad Edward 4-21
Brian Miss Ellen 19 I-24
Briarley Mr L-27
Briarley Mrs (& infant)-27
Brice Robert 35 labourer-29
Brice Mrs J 25-29
Brice Abigail infant-29
Brice Joseph 19 butcher S-35
Brick Patrick 30 labourer I-32
Brick J 25 I-40
Bridge Hannah 30-42
Bridge Thomas Edward 3-42
Bridgman Robert-21sy

Brien Edward 20 labourer I-22
Brien Francis 22 I-22
Brien John 25 labourer I-26
Brien Cornelius 30 labourer I-31
Brierley Charles 20 labourer-23
Brierley John 53 labourer-23
Briggs James 20 clerk-13
Briggs David 13 labourer-30
Briggs F -32
Briggs Mrs-32
Briggs Francis 18-32
Briggs Elizabeth 16-32
Briggs Charlotte 14-32
Briggs Maria 11-32
Briggs Clamina 10-32
Briggs Theodore 8-32
Briggs Robert 6-32
Briggs Hugh 4-32
Briggs Gertrude 2-32
Briggs Jennak 38 woolsorter-39
Bright Reginald-9
Bright Thomas 22 co.agent-10
Bright C H 35-24
Brighton Ann 20 spinster-30
Brighton Martha 18-30
Briglet Joseph 27 mariner I-42
Briglet Maria 26 I-42
Brigton Martha 60 widow-30
Brind Henry 28 labourer-20
Briscoe John-36
Briscoe Isabella-36
Briscoe Amy M 6-36
Briscoe John-37
Briscoe Isabella-37
Briscoe Ann Maria 6-37
Britt James 21 labourer I-23
Britten Joseph 45-33
Broad Thomas 37 gardener S-30
Broad Elizabeth 45 spinster S-30
Broad John 27 I-43br
Broad William 25 I-43br
Broad Charles 21 I-43br
Broadbent Agnes 48 ironmonger-10
Broadfield Miss 11-22
Broadhead George labourer-25
Broadhead Samuel 34 labourer I-26
Broadhurst Mary A I-21
Broadhurst Joshua 35 miner-21
Broadhurst Susan 25-21
Broadley Henry 33 spinner-37
Broadley Mary Jane 23-37
Broadshaw Agnes 22 spinster-13
Broadman James 43 labourer-27
Brock John 23 labourer S-24
Brock Robert 47 saddler S-37
Brock Thomas 21 S-37
Brock John 17 plumber S-37
Brock Robert 10 S-37
Brock Alexander 7 S-37
Brock James 5 S-37
Brock Catherine 19 S-37
Brock Jessie 14 S-37

Brock Alexander 29 S-43
Brock Thomas 37 S-43
Brock Marion 36 S-43
Brock Thomas 8 S-43
Brock (child) 7 S-43
Brockley Mrs Jane 32-21
Brockley Samuel 8-21
Brockley Alice 3.1/2-21
Brodie Henry 26-16
Brodie I L 24 labourer-24
Brodlay Mrs 29-30
Brodlay William 29-30
Brodlay John 10-30
Brodlay Helen 8-30
Brodlay Maggie 6-30
Brodlay Elizabeth 4-30
Brodlay (infant)-30
Brohan Edward 18-41
Bromley John-9
Bromley Edward 29 labourer-31
Bromley Mrs Martha 50-32
Bromley Sydney-32
Bromwich John 35 labourer-35
Bronchout Miss-20
Bronstein Solomon 29 S-35
Brood Patrick 22 labourer-27
Brooke G W 40-24
Brooke Seth 33 labourer-31
Brooke John 25 moulder-43du
Brooker Miss Elizabeth 25-21
Brooks Charles 31 I-32
Brooks Charles J 11 I-32
Brooks Edward 33-35
Brooks James 30-35
Brooks Jonathan 25-35
Brooks E P 23-40
Brookshaw Samuel 46-34
Brookshaw E 45-34
Broome T N-27
Brophy Thomas 33-41
Brosnan Thomas 20 labourer-26
Brotherston Andrew 20 brass S-16
Broughan Patrick 23-41
Brown A -9
Brown Miss-9
Brown W G -9
Brown W H -9
Brown C -9
Brown Charles-9
Brown William-9
Brown William-9
Brown Garnett-11
Brown Henry-11
Brown Jacob 35 farmer-11
Brown James 32 plasterer-11
Brown Mary 25-11
Brown John 30 miner-11
Brown Margaret spinster-11
Brown Matthew 26 draper I-11
Brown Daniel 27 farmer S-13
Brown Francis 32 miner-13
Brown John 44 miner-13

Brown Ann 44-13
Brown John 28 miner-13
Brown William 22 miner-13
Brown Robert 47 farmer-16
Brown Margaret 45-16
Brown Thomas 6-16
Brown Mrs Louisa 33-21
Brown Elisha 10-21
Brown Mary Jane 7-21
Brown Miss Jane 15-23
Brown Mrs Janet 35-23
Brown Jessie 8-23
Brown Mr-23
Brown Mrs-23
Brown Miss 5-23
Brown Miss 1-23
Brown Robson 24 labourer-23
Brown William 25 labourer-23
Brown Thomas 37 S-24
Brown Edward 20 labourer-25
Brown William 40-25
Brown James H 19 farmer S-27
Brown Henry A 27 labourer I-27
Brown James 24 labourer-27
Brown William M 34-28
Brown Catherine 32 spinster-30
Brown James 31 labourer S-30
Brown Ruth-30
Brown Paul surgeon-32
Brown Joseph 28-33
Brown John 18 farmer-35
Brown David 22 S-36
Brown George 23-36
Brown John 19 engineer-36
Brown John 25 farmer I-37
Brown Sarah 39 spinster I-37
Brown John 49 workman-38
Brown John-38
Brown Emma-38
Brown John potter-39
Brown Margaret 62-39
Brown Maria 20-39
Brown John 24-51
Brown William 24 enginefitter-42
Brown John 26 farm labourer-42
Browne John 23 farmer I-13
Browne Duncan 18 labourer-24
Browne Thomas 26 labourer S-24
Browne James 22-28
Browne M L I-43br
Brownlie Robert labourer-26
Browning Mrs Fanny 30-28
Browning Henry 2-28
Browning Mary 24 S-28
Browning Miss 28 S-28
Bruce A junior-9
Bruce George 23-26
Bruce Mrs Mary 50-26
Bruck George 35 shepherd-27
Bruen Mrs-9
Brumbel Thomas 35-13
Brumby Sarato 38 spinster-25me

Brunnel William 23-16
Brush S -36
Brush Miss-36
Bruson Caroline-32
Bryan Samuel 20 farmer I-13
Bryant J -9
Bryant Charles 35-29
Bryden John-29
Bryezinski A -9
Buchanan G -9
Buchanan George 37-10
Buchanan James-33
Buchuret A H 33 labourer-35
Buchuret Susan 23-35
Buchuret Elizabeth 3-35
Buchuret William 1-35
Buck Cornel 38 carter-40
Buck Margaret 33-40
Buck Hannah 4-40
Buck Andrew 2-40
Buck Ada 1-40
Buckell Francis 48 labourer-31
Buckell Emma 46-31
Buckell Fran G 18-31
Bucker Jean 24 I-20
Buckhorne Catherine 26 matron-25
Buckhorne Thomas 1.1/2-25
Buckingham William 21 fisherman-43
Buckle Mr-11
Buckley Thomas-11
Buckley John A 27 spinner-13
Buckley Robert 40 farmer-16
Buckley Miss Margaret 19 I-22
Buckley Patrick 17 I-22
Buckley Thomas 28 labourer-24
Buckley Mrs Harriet 38-32
Buckley Miss A 72 (died 5/4)-35
Buckley John Alfred 40-35
Buffa Guiseppe 18 OP-32
Buffa Lenardo 10 OP-32
Bull William 38 labourer-35
Bull Jane 39-35
Bull John H 7-35
Bull George E 5-35
Bull James W-35
Bullen J A -31
Bullen John A-33
Bullen Mrs-33
Bullock E -9
Bullock J -9
Bullow John 71 I-43
Bunch Joseph 26 labourer-24
Bunch Mary 23-24
Bunting Miss-21
Bundell William 60-34
Buppi Giovanni 33 OP-40
Burchfield James S-36
Burchitt William 42-24
Burdett Mr A-32
Burdett Mrs-32
Burdett R A 20 spinster S-32
Burdon Mrs Mary 45 1-41ho

Burgdoff Christian OP-39
Burgess Charles-9
Burk Henry 33 labourer I-24
Burke John 56 accountant I-10
Burke John 24 farmer-11
Burke James 35 labourer I-23
Burke Eliza 30-23
Burke Master 1-23
Burke James 30 I-29
Burke Margaret 25 I-29
Burke Thomas 21 I-29
Burke Edmond 22 labourer I-32
Burke Michael 30 I-32
Burke John 36 chandler-39
Burke Margaret 35-39
Burke John-42
Burkhart Samuel 23 farmer OP-38
Burley Robert adult labourer-20
Burley John 44 labourer-33
Burn J -9
Burnell Thomas-9
Burness Jonathan 16 labourer-24
Burnett Richard 24 labourer OP-26
Burns Daniel 28 shopkeeper S-10
Burns Pat 20 I-32
Burns James 24-41sy
Burns James 29 S-24
Burr Lena 22 spinster OP-27
Burra James 32-32
Burra Elizabeth 29-32
Burra Thomas 3-32
Burra Jane 2-32
Burridge Samuel 56 labourer S-30
Burridge Elizabeth 54 S-30
Burrows Esther 56 widow-26
Burrows Ellen 24 spinster-26
Burrows Josiah 19 miller-31
Burrows Isabella 38 S-38
Burstall B C -30
Burton R -34
Burton C -34
Burton Annie S infant-34
Bury Miss Fanny 18-21
Bush John 25 farmer S-20
Buss James 22 labourer-26
Bustable Mrs Mary 40-21
Butchart A 12-32
Butchart H 7-32
Butchart Master 8-32
Butcher Thomas 28 labourer-26
Butcher Alfred 33 I-33
Butcher A S 22 I-33
Butcher Jacob 39 S-36
Butcher Jane 39 S-36
Butcher Frances 6 S-36
Butcher Harry 4 S-36
Butcher Robert 21-43
Butler George 21 labourer-22
Butler Edward I-31
Butler William 22 labourer I-31
Butler Farnell 20-33
Butler George-34

Butler Mrs Harriette 24–37
Butler James spinner–37
Butler Mrs I–38
Butler Miss 28 I–38
Butler Master 17 I–38
Butliner J 21 labourer–22
Butliner Thomas 24–22
Butterment W C 35 S–32
Buttersfield Thomas 22 lab. I–26
Butterworth John L–29
Butterworths William 30–41ho
Buxton James H 23–10
Buxton Charles 40–24
Buxton Elizabeth 36–24
Buxton John R 17 labourer–34
Buxton R B 21–37
Buxton R R –41
Buxton Elizabeth–41
Buxton Elizabeth R 25 spinster–41
Buxton Mary Ann 19 spinster–41
Buzza Nicholas 25–32
Byers William 21 labourer–27
Byers John 35 farmer I–37
Byers Eliza 26 I–37
Byers Joseph 7 I–37
Byers Sarah 4 I–37
Byers Mary 2 I–37
Byne John 25 labourer I–32
Byrne Elizabeth spinster I–16
Bryne Michael 23 servant I–16
Byrne Michael 23 labourer–I–26
Byrne Mrs Margaret 30 I–29
Byrne John 10 I–29
Byrne Lizzie 8 I–29
Byrne Mary 5 I–29
Byrne Henry 4 I–29
Byrne James infant I–29
Byrne James 24 S–34
Byrne Catherine 24 S–34
Byrne (male child born 24/8)–34
Byrne Margaret 2 S–34
Byrne Francis 22–36
Byrne James 24 labourer I–37
Byrne Robert 32 miner–37
Byrne William 21 farm servant–37

C

Cabot Henry 43–42
Caddigan Michael 20 labourer I–16
Cadenhead A F 19 labourer S–26
Cadnichi Padole 21 OP–34
Cadwell Joseph 25–35
Caesar Julius 32–24
Caffery John 21 labourer I–31
Caffra John M I–43
Caffyn William 27–24
Caffyr William–21
Cahalane John 26 labourer–25
Cahill B 20 tailor I–10
Cahill John 28 I–29
Cahill William 23 saddler–31
Cahill Denis 29 I–32

Cain John 25 labourer–13
Cain John 40 miner–13
Cain Elizabeth 34–13
Cain William 22 coachmaker I–13
Cain W D farmer–39
Caine W –30
Caine John S–35
Cainini Guiy 20 OP–16
Cairney Thomas 40 labourer I–20
Cairney Margaret 25 I–20
Cairney James 1 I–20
Cains Mrs Ellen 39–16
Caird James–9
Cairns Emily 20 S–26
Cairns Elizabeth 19 S–26
Cairns Mr–26
Cairns Mrs–26
Cairns Grace 59–38
Calaghan John 28 agri.lab I–31
Calara Antonio 18 farmer OP–20
Calcutt Minnie 21 I–41
Caldecott T merchant–39
Caldecott E H 12–39
Caldwell Robert A 26–24
Caldwell Sarah J 24–24
Caldwell Mary A 22–24
Caldwell Jane E 24 spinster–41
Caley E –9
Caley Mrs–9
Calhane Andrew 18 labourer I–21
Calhoon Alexander 17 labourer–23
Calhoon Henry 14 I–23
Calhoon Margaret 18 I–23
Calhoon John 25 I–23
Callaghan J C 29 labourer I–22
Callaghan Mary servant I–35
Calvert Arthur 23 clothier–13
Calvert Margaret 20–13
Calvert Mary 23 spinster I–28
Calvin John 26 labourer–27
Calvin Margaret 24 labourer–27
Calvin Patrick 24 labourer I–31
Cameron Angus 31–10
Cameron Mrs 31–10
Cameron Isabella H 8–10
Cameron John 6–10
Cameron Adele 4–10
Cameron Margaret 2–10
Cameron Eliza 10mts–10
Cameron Mrs 25–20
Cameron Archibald 3–20
Cameron William 1–20
Cameron Mrs–21
Cameron Mr–21
Cameron Cyril–21
Cameron W R 28–24
Cameron Mary 19 spinster–25
Cameron William 18 labourer–25
Cameron Edwin S–28
Cameron Rev J 32 S–28
Cameron William 25 I–28
Cameron Hugh 55 labourer S–30

Cameron John 33 labourer–30
Cameron Miss M S–31
Cameron Saul S–31
Cameron Mrs George 22 S–34
Cameron Elizabeth infant S–34
Cameron R H –35
Cameron Mrs Catherine 24 S–41
Cameron Don 29 merchant S–41
Cameron Alexander 22–42
Cameron William S–42ot
Camerson Alexander 26 lab. S–16
Camerson James 40 S–29
Camerson Donald 18 labourer–33
Campbell A–10
Campbell William 28 mechanic–13
Campbell William 27 miner–13
Campbell Alexander 30 lab.S–21
Campbell Thomas 22 labourer I–22
Campbell Aug–23
Campbell D S 38–24
Campbell Mrs 36–24
Campbell Andrew 28 labourer–26
Campbell Margaret 22–26
Campbell Eliza 15–26
Campbell J L 22 labourer S–26
Campbell H M L infant S–26
Campbell Joshua 19 labourer–26
Campbell Mrs Mary 30 S–26
Campbell Lizzie 7 S–26
Campbell Kate 5 S–26
Campbell Albert 3 S–26
Campbell Alfred 1–26
Campbell Colin–28
Campbell Donald 25 S–28
Campbell Catherine 20 spinster–28
Campbell Finlay 22 labourer S–31
Campbell Frank labourer–31
Campbell John I 28 labourer S–31
Campbell James 25 carrier I–31
Campbell A N S–33
Campbell Duncan 22 I–34
Campbell Robert 18 I–34
Campbell James–34
Campbell Jane 43 gen.servant S–38
Campbell James 22–41
Campbell John–42
Campbell Elizabeth–42
Campbell Sarah 11–42
Campbell Mary–42
Campbell David 20–42
Campbell Peter 18–42
Campbell James 16–42
Campbell Mrs–42
Campbell Agnes 17–42
Campbell John 11–42
Campbell Mary 9–42
Campbell Alexander 7–42
Campbell Arthur 5–42
Campbell Jessie 2–42
Campbell Peter 45 S–42
Campbell Alexander 20 S–43ot
Campereh Elise servant–35

Campston P 33 builder-40
Campton Mary 23-30
Candriss Peter labourer-25me
Cane Michael 27 labourer-30
Canning James 24 farmer 1-40au
Canning Donald 22 I-40
Canningham James 39 labourer S-28
Canningham Alix 43-28
Cannon Samuel-9
Cannon James 26-41
Cannon Mary A 26-41
Cannon Michael 6-41
Cannon James 3-41
Cannon Eliza 1 41
Canova Giacomo 49 labourer OP-23
Cant Jessie 34 spinster-34
Cantisini Piesis 18 OP-35
Cantisini Dominici 22 OP-35
Cantlay John 21-31
Cantley Mrs 29-40
Cantley John 27-40
Cantledge Mary servant-31
Cantrell Joseph 34 storekeep I-32
Cantwell Johanna 20 spinster I-20
Canty Henry W 13-28
Capassi Graconi 39 OP-38
Capron E J -9
Caralli Fowziano 36 lab.OP-23
Carbey Henry 33-29
Card David I-38
Card Mary 10 I-38
Card Mary 8 I-38
Card Isabella 6 I-38
Card Henry 4 I-38
Card George 1 I-38
Cardinali A -9
Care William Rouch 53 labourer-31
Care William R miner-37
Carew Ellen 28 I-39
Carey Thomas 19 clerk-13
Cargett F A -27
Cargill Mrs-31
Cargill Miss-31
Cargill Miss-31
Carl John 21 labourer-30
Carlin Peter 30-34
Carlish John 24 I-31
Carlisle John-9
Carlisle Robert 51 miner-37
Carney Mary 3 I-20
Carmichael Archibald 27 farmer-35
Carmody Patrick 28 constable I-32
Carney George-9
Carnill John-9
Carnow T -9
Carothers John 21 labourer I-31
Carpenter H -9
Carpenter R 32-24
Carr M -9
Carr F B 23 S-11
Carr Matthew 35 miner-11
Carraghmore June 30-11

Carraghmore Thomas 7-11
Carraghmore Jane 6-11
Carraghmore John 1.1/2-11
Carrington John C 19 labourer-34
Carrogood John Man 23 labourer-27
Carroll Mrs Sarah 59-22
Carroll William 20 labourer I-22
Carroll Eliza 22 spinster I-22
Carroll Mrs Teresa 32 I-23
Carroll Catherine 11 I-23
Carroll Philip 9 I-23
Carroll Eliza 8 I-2
Carroll George 6 I-23
Carroll Mary 4 I-23
Carroll Thomas 2 I-23
Carroll female (born 21/3) I-23
Carroll John Man 39 labourer-27
Carroll Margaret 20 spinster I-28
Carroll Thomas 22 labourer I-31
Carroll Charles 14 I-33
Carroll James 50 I-33
Carroll Catherine 45 I-33
Carroll Andrew 11 I-33
Carroll Catherine 9 I-33
Carroll Miss Charlotte 32-35
Carroll Joseph-40
Carroll Mrs M B I-41
Carroll Patrick 21-41
Carron Charles James-21
Carruthers Robert 43 lab.I-22
Carruthers Mary 36 I-22
Carruthers Minnie 5 I-22
Carry John 28 I-42
Carsarotti Peter 44 miner OP-39
Carsarotti Ansdino 9 OP-39
Carson L -9
Carson Miss Grace 24 S-21
Carson James 18-27
Carson John 21 I-31
Carson James 24-31
Carson Sarah J 19 I-39
Carson Mary A 17 I-39
Carstairs G A -22
Carstairs Mrs-22
Carter Anne-9
Carter James-9
Carter George 30-16
Carter John 38 labourer-20
Carter Emma 35-20
Carter Emma 11-20
Carter Lydia 9-20
Carter David 7-20
Carter Caroline 5-20
Carter James 4-20
Carter George 11-20
Carter John 30-29
Carter T 30 servant-31
Carter Robert H 22 clerk I-32
Carter Joseph-34
Carter Henry 34-41
Carter Martha 40-41
Carter Charles Henry 12-41

Carter William 9-41
Carter Herbert 7-41
Carter Martha J 5-41
Carter Annie 3-41
Carter John 30-41
Carter Jabez 19-43
Carteret P Q de 27-43
Carthew Stephen 34 labourer-21
Carthew Thomas 21 labourer-21
Carthew William 29 labourer-23
Carthew Elizabeth 29-23
Carthy Michael 38 servant I-13
Cartin Michael 25 labourer I-20
Cartin Mrs 21 I-20
Cartwright Elizabeth 26-13
Cartwright Joseph 26 miner-13
Cartwright Thomas 21-13
Carty Mary-9
Carty Thomas 20 labourer I-32
Carvel John O 21 baker-40
Carver S-9
Carver William-11
Carwell Robert 23 farmer-13
Case James labourer-25me
Case Mar 19 spinster I-31
Casey James 60 labourer I-21
Casey Miss Margaret 17 I-21
Casey Pat 27 labourer I-24
Casey Mary 23 I-24
Casey Eugene labourer-25sy
Casey Mary Ann 36 spinster-25me
Casey Thomas 13-32
Casey William 33 labourer-32
Casey Mary 29-32
Casey John 4-32
Casey Mary 2-32
Casey Daniel 23 I-35
Casey Maurice 23 labourer I-39
Caspar Johann 18 labourer OP-29
Caspar Thomas 10 OP-29
Casquer John 21 I-31
Cass Francis 35-34
Cass Maud 26-34
Cass Eleanor 1.1/2-34
Cass Edward infant-34
Cass Edward 42-34
Cass Ann 35-34
Casta Pelis 16 labourer OP-26
Caster Henry 20 traveller-35
Castle William 21 farmer-27
Castle John 47-42
Caston Frank 19-29
Casy Patrick 28 I-43
Caterina Jean 19 OP-35
Catney Terence 26 labourer-25me
Catrina Colsin 17 OP-35
Catto John-42
Caugharty James 47 miner I-27
Caven Charles 23-10
Cazenon Mrs Margaret 37-13
Cazenon William 20 farmer-13
Cazenon Prescott 11-13

Cazenon Warren 9-13
Cazenon Pierce 6-13
Cazenon Lancelotte 1.1/2-13
Cecil William 45 ironmonger-10
Cecil Thomas 13-10
Cecil William 10-10
Ceeconelli Lorenzo 22 lab. OP-20
Cellar Marie 18 OP-38
Cenar Lorenzo 31 OP-38
Chadwick James-9
Chadwick William 27 farmer I-10
Chadwick James 44-16
Chadwick Bridget 21 spinster I-20
Chadwick James-23
Chadwick Mrs-23
Chadwick Richard 18 labourer-25
Chadwick Henry 48-29
Chadwick Mrs M 48-29
Chadwick Paulina 17-29
Chadwick Henrietta 15-29
Chadwick James 25-29
Chadwick William 36 labourer-35
Chadwick Elizabeth 33-35
Chadwick William 11-35
Chadwick Maria 7-35
Chadwick Julia 5-35
Chadwick Alice 3-35
Chadwick George 1-35
Challengeworth Edward 27 miner-38
Challengeworth Agnes 21-38
Chalmers John 35 tea dealer-21
Chambers Jonathan 18 lab.-25
Chambers Alice-34
Chambers Florence-34
Chambers Jane spinster-34
Chambers Edward 25 miner-16
Chambers James 21 labourer I-16
Chambers Sarah 28 spinster-22
Champion William 20-35
Chandler Thomas 16-41
Chandler James 25-41
Chandler Emily 25-41
Chandler James 1-41
Chandler John 32-41
Chandler Mary A 31-41
Chandler Emma 6-41
Chandler Clara 3-41
Chant Alfred 18 labourer-22
Chaplin Frederick 29 labourer-34
Chapman Frederick W 33 lab.-23
Chapman Emma 28-23
Chapman Miss-23
Chapman George 35-24
Chapman William C 24-34
Chapman David 22-34
Chapman James 21 S-38
Chapman Jonathan 29-39
Chapman Jane 34-39
Chappel Edward 25-11
Chapple Charles 19-34
Chard Arthur-23
Chard Henrietta-23

Charles David 34 mason-11
Charles Abraham 41-33
Charles Eliza 28-33
Charles Mary 12-33
Charles William George 3-33
Charles Emily 1-33
Charlesworth A -9
Charlesworth J -9
Charlton James 27 farmer-11
Charlton Isabella 25-11
Charlton Michael 11-11
Charlton John 2-11
Charlton Miss Elizabeth 19-23
Charlton Thomas 38 labourer-23
Charlton Elizabeth 39-23
Charlton Frances 11-23
Charlton Edward 9-23
Charlton William J 7-23
Charlton Ellen 5-23
Charlton Nathan 33 labourer-24
Charlton William 31-29
Charlton John 50 labourer-34
Charlton Elizabeth 46-34
Charlton Thomas 20-37
Charlton John 23-40
Charlton Martha 25-40
Cheasty James 24 labourer-26
Cheetham Mrs Sophia 30-22
Chenhall John 23 miner-32
Chenhall James 15-32
Chickolm Marcus 25 labourer S-22
Child William 25 miner-20
Childe Edward-9
Childe John-9
Chilton Elizabeth 30 matron-25
Chilton Mary A 7-25
Chisdal Robert 20-34
Chisholm Mr 33-24
Chojecki Stanley-9
Chown Edward-9
Chown H -9
Chown Lydia-9
Christey James 19 labourer I-22
Christian Robert J 22-30
Christian Emma 20 spinster-30
Christian G H -43sy
Christie Hugh 24 labourer-27
Christopher Thomas 40 labourer-35
Christopher Agnes 26-35
Christopher Charles 36-42
Christy David-9
Christy John-9
Chubbin Daniel labourer-30
Chubbin John 41 labourer-30
Chubbin Margaret 32-30
Chubbin Elizabeth 8-30
Chubbin Jessie 5-30
Chubbin Emily infant-30
Chubbin Matilda infant-30
Churchland Isaac 27-36
Churchyard Henry-43du
Churnside Miss-30

Clancey James 22 farmer I-11
Claney Henry 18 farmer I-10
Clapperton C J 29-24
Clark Bridget-9
Clark John-9
Clark George 33 labourer-22
Clark Sophia 35-22
Clark Elizabeth 3-22
Clark Harry 2-22
Clark Hugh 26 labourer S-22
Clark Robert 25 labourer S-22
Clark Hector 45 gardener S-27
Clark Mrs 48 S-27
Clark Betsey 17 S-27
Clark Georgina 17 S-27
Clark Gordon 15 gardener S-27
Clark Mrs G 55 S-30
Clark Margaret 22 S-30
Clark John 21 S-30
Clark George 18 S-30
Clark William 14 S-30
Clark Mrs Maria 53-34
Clark Alice 21-34
Clark Sarah A 20-34
Clark Robert 18-34
Clark Samuel 17-34
Clark Richard 22-35
Clark Richard 37 shoemaker-35
Clark George 22 labourer-36
Clark John 30-36
Clark James 23-36
Clark Eliza 29 I-39
Clark William-41
Clarke Elizabeth 24 S-10
Clarke H I 28-10
Clarke Joseph 53 rigger S-10
Clarke James-11
Clarke Reginald S 21 farmer-211a
Clarke Miss-22
Clarke Mrs-22
Clarke Captain-22
Clarke Arthur 22 labourer-24
Clarke Jonathan 35 labourer I-24
Clarke Margaret 36 I-24
Clarke Christopher 15 I-24
Clarke William 2 I-24
Clarke Robert infant I-24
Clarke Mary Ann 16 spinster-26
Clarke William 20-26
Clarke John 16 labourer-27
Clarke Mr-27
Clarke Mrs-27
Clarke Margaret spinster I-29
Clarke R 22 spinster S-29
Clarke Mrs Elizabeth 50-30
Clarke Elizabeth 23 spinster I-30
Clarke Frederick E 26 labourer-30
Clarke Robert labourer S-30
Clarke Miss Hannah 33-sy
Clarke Mr-32
Clarke Rev Charles 30-33
Clarke Eliza 30-33

Clarke Peter 23 labourer I-35
Clarke Miss Elizabeth 25-36
Clarke William-36
Clarke John-36
Clarke W T -37
Clarke William 40 I-40
Clarke Anne 45 I-40
Clarke James 42 S-41
Clarke Patrick 23 I-41
Clarke Miss 25-43
Clarkson G C -9
Claughton Luke 30 labourer-22
Clavel George-35
Clay Thomas jun 22 joiner-11
Clayton Joseph-9
Clayton Dinah 34 labourer I-31
Clayton William 58 S-32
Clayton Charlotte 49 S-32
Clayton John Bell 34 farmer-37
Clayton Hannah 32-37
Clayton Lilly Jane 7-37
Clayton Minnie N 4-37
Clayton Joseph 26-42
Cleary James 18 labourer-24
Cleary Patrick 56 labourer-25
Cleary James 26 labourer I-32
Clegg J A -9
Clegg Richard 25 labourer-23
Clegg Henry 24 labourer-26
Clegg John T 20-38
Clement James 38 baker S-42
Clement John 35 S-42
Clements Thomas-9
Clements John 40-39
Clementson Mrs Elizabeth 20-23
Clementson Joseph 23 labourer-23
Clementson William 21-23
Clementson Matthew 28 labourer-23
Clementson Ann 21-23
Clementson Elizabeth 2-23
Clementson Emma 1-23
Clementson Michael 25 labourer-23
Clementson William 28 labourer-23
Clemmons William 23 labourer-25
Clenson Henry-21
Clerk John 41 publican-13
Cleve Elizabeth 45-43
Clifford Jane 25 spinster I-30
Clifton Mrs A B 25 S-33
Clifton Beatrice M 4 S-33
Clinton Thomas 22 labourer I-30
Clinton William 21 labourer-30
Clinton Elizabeth 20-30
Clive Daniel 35-27
Cloggner Charles 32 labourer-25
Cloghessy Bridget 18 servant I-42
Cloth W J 25 labourer-20
Cloth John 19 labourer-20
Clucas Hugh 19-38
Cluckey Miss Sophia 17-22
Cluiton James 26 labourer I-26
Coade W 27 miner-10

Coade I 21-10
Coate Capt A-35
Coates James I 21 farmer-20
Coates Robert 40 labourer-24
Coates Mrs Elizabeth 38-36
Coates Walter-36
Coates Mrs-36
Coates Walter J-36
Coates Isaac 30-40
Coburn John 55 farmer-16
Coburn Maria 50-16
Coburn Johnstone 24-16
Coburn William 22-16
Cochlan Thomas-35
Cochran Richard 37 labourer S-31
Cochrane David 24 farmer I-31
Cock Charles 50 labourer-34
Cockburn George 28 clerk-13
Cockcroft George 38 labourer-30
Cockfield David 34 labourer I-22
Cocking Samuel 19 labourer-22
Cocking James 23 miner-42
Codd Edward 20 labourer-27
Codd James 23 labourer-27
Code John 36-41
Code Annie 31-41
Code Julia 10-41
Code George 3-41
Cody Michael 18 labourer I-13
Cody Nicholas-38
Cody Margaret-38
Cody Edward 34-38
Coffee Michael 54 farmer I-32
Coffee Susan 43 I-32
Coffee Susan 14 I-32
Coffey John-35
Coffey Mrs Mary Jane 45 I-35
Coffey Elizabeth 18 I-35
Coffey Isabella 10 I-35
Coffey James 6 I-35
Coffin I P -26
Coghlan William-9
Coghlan Honora 30 spinster I-28
Cogle C M -20
Cogley Francis 45 farmer-20
Cohen S -9
Cohen S adult-10
Cohen Mrs adult-10
Cohen Mark-16
Cohen Mrs Clara 27-22
Cohen Rosa 9-22
Cohen Ena 7-22
Cohen Edward 4-22
Cohen Henriech 16 labourer OP-22
Cohen Miss Caroline 25-23
Cohen Sigmond labourer-25
Cohen Joseph 23 labourer I-26
Cohen Samuel I-29
Cohen Mrs I-29
Cohen Amelia 6 I-29
Cohen Arthur 4 I-29
Cohen Hannah 2 I-29

Cohen Montefere infant I-29
Cohen Calsave 16 labourer OP-30
Cohen Morris 15-38
Cohen Henry 52-42
Cohen Elizabeth 42-42
Cohen Sarah 22-42
Cohen Leah 14-42
Cohen Esther 12-42
Cohen Fanny 10-42
Cohen Anley 8-42
Cohen Sydney 7-42
Cohen Alfred 5-42
Cohen Percy 3-42
Cohen Constance infant-42
Coher John 29 labourer I-24
Cola Erigo 14 labourer OP-20
Colban Thomas 60-42
Colbourn Henry 28 labourer-24
Colburn Eliza 39 I-10
Colburn Henry 13 I-10
Colburn Eliza 11 I-10
Colburn John 10 I-10
Colburn Thomas C 9 I-10
Colburn Robert 8 I-10
Colburn Louisa R 3 I-10
Colburn Rebecca 2 I-10
Coldbrick George 22-41
Coldbrick Mrs M A 17-41
Cole Miss Bridget 30 I-23
Cole Joseph 27 S-32
Cole Ellen spinster-34
Cole Richard 17-36
Cole George 16-36
Cole William-36
Coleman William C 21 labourer-24
Coleman William 40 labourer-25
Coleman Mary 35-25
Coleman Miss H-32
Coleman James 27 constable I-32
Coleridge Mrs-36
Coleridge E -36
Colerin Robert 40 I-30
Colerin Marian 26 I-30
Coles H J -9
Coles Samuel H 30 labourer-27
Coles Halstaff 6-27
Coles Henry 28-41
Colgan Joseph Henry 19 I-41
Coll William 33 I-40
Collen Thomas 19 labourer-25
Collet George 20 labourer S-35
Collie Henry 28 labourer-20
Collier James-9
Collier A -9
Collier James B 22-35
Collin Margaret 20 spinster-16
Collins I 25 miner-10
Collins Henry 30 miner-11
Collins Henry jun 19 mason-11
Collins Henry-11
Collins Francis-13
Collins Mary-13

Collins Amelia servant-27
Collins John I-28
Collins Mrs I-28
Collins John B 22 labourer I-30
Collins Timothy 26 labourer I-30
Collins Patrick 26 carpenter I-31
Collins Miss Catherine 28-32
Collins Joseph 36 farmer I-32
Collins Mrs Sophie 33-33
Collins Marie 11-33
Collins Tom 9-33
Collins Susan 7-33
Collins Sophie 5-33
Collins William 25 labourer-34
Collins John 26-35
Collins James 20-41
Collins Martin 20-41
Collins William 35 mechanic-42
Collis Edwin John 18-42
Collon George 38 labourer S-24
Collon Emma 37 S-24
Collon Eliza Ann 5 S-24
Collon Sampson 35 S-24
Collon Emily 9 S-24
Collon Lucy 7 S-24
Colorhey Daniel 23-34
Colthurst Henry-29
Colville James 26-37
Coman John 29 labourer I-31
Coman Catherine 23 I-31
Coman Denis 1 I-31
Combellac John 32 merchant-11
Comber J F -33
Comberballick Thomas 27 miner-10
Combes James 24 farm servant I-37
Connebe Rev Richard-29
Connebe Mrs-29
Conch Mary Ann 21 spinster-25
Condon Patrick 24-34
Condon John 24 I-36
Coney P G 25-10
Conlow Thomas-9
Connelan Patrick 30 labourer I-31
Connell Henry 29 labourer-22
Connell Albert 23-22
Connell Thomas 24 labourer S-22
Connell Edmund 21-27
Connell Jonathan 24-28
Connell John I-28
Connell Thomas 38 I-33
Connell John 30 I-34
Connell Maria 30 I-34
Connell Margaret 9 I-34
Connell James 7 I-34
Connell Maria 5 I-34
Connell John 3 I-34
Connell Nancy 1 I-34
Connell Joseph 35 farmer I-37
Connell Margaret 32 I-37
Connell M A 19 I-42
Connelly Miss Catherine 24 I-24
Connolly John-9

Connolly Miss Julia 20 I-24
Connolly Thomas 26 servant I-37
Connolly Hugh 19 I-42
Connor Matilda 24 I-10
Connor Patrick 40 sailor I-13
Connor John 11 I-13
Connor James 18 farmer I-16
Connor John 20 labourer-16
Connor Jeremiah 30 I-33
Connor Michael 35 farmer I-41
Connor Patrick 37 I-43
Connors Michael 30 I-28
Connors John 21 I-32
Conole James 24 I-32
Conrad Dida 45-43
Conrie Annie 21 spinster S-30
Conroy Patrick 27-41
Considine John 18 I-28
Considine Michael 20 I-28
Considine Patrick 18 I-28
Considine Thomas 30-41
Constani Christine 24 OP-40
Constani Bertha 18-40
Constantine Demetrius 16 OP-38
Conteleo Henricho 36 lab.OP-30
Conway Michael 24 I-28
Conway John 21 labourer I-31
Conway Thomas 19 I-31
Conway Miss Alice J 17 I-32
Conway Thomas 25 I-32
Conway Mrs Catherine 39 I-39
Conway Mary 15 I-39
Conway Ellen 11 I-39
Cook Robert 34 confectioner-10
Cook Mrs 24 (& infant)-10
Cook Edward 27-16
Cook Harriet I 22-16
Cook Mrs H J 25-23
Cook H B 1-23
Cook John 18 labourer-26
Cook Emily 20 spinster-26
Cook Jessiah 24-28
Cook William 20-28
Cook John R 35-29
Cook Mrs M 20-29
Cook Mrs Catherine-32
Cook Thomas 18-33
Cook John 18 labourer-34
Cook James S-35
Cook Jane S-35
Cook Michael 24 I-35
Cook Thomas 24-41
Cook John 36 gardener S-43
Cook Mary 20 S-43
Cooke G A 20 labourer-24
Cooke Arthur 24-26
Cookworthy J -40
Cooney James 24 I-33
Coony Michael 22 labourer I-22
Cooper Gell -9
Cooper Edward 34 farmer-16
Cooper Victoria 34-16

Cooper Herbert 11-16
Cooper Alice 5-16
Cooper Ellen G 16 spinster-16
Cooper John 28 labourer-20
Cooper Michael 20 labourer I-21
Cooper Thomas 60 labourer-21
Cooper Ann 57-21
Cooper Daniel 19-21
Cooper Mary 15-21
Cooper William 23 labourer-25
Cooper Benjamin 22 labourer-29
Cooper W -32
Cooper Charles 25-36
Cooper Thomas 38-36
Cooper Emma 36-36
Cooper John 44-38
Cooper Emma 37 servant 41-1y
Cooper Thomas 16-43
Cooss Michael 31-34
Cooss John 19-34
Cope James 32 labourer-25
Copeland Hugh 21 labourer-22
Copeland Miss Eliza 24-23
Copeland William 31 miner I-37
Copeland Elizabeth 30 I-37
Copeland Agnes 9 I-37
Copeland Ellen 7 I-37
Copeland Joseph W 5 I-37
Copland Alexander 19 servant S-31
Coppack Joseph 17 servant-10
Corbett Josh 19-10sy
Corbett William 20 labourer-25
Corbett John 22 I-35
Corbett Fanny 38 I-42
Corbett Frederick 15 I-42
Corbett Emma 11 I-42
Corbett Percy 10 I-42
Corbett Mary 8 I-42
Corcoran Ellen 30 I-39
Cordisson Frederick-9
Cordner Henry-9
Cordo Matromani 24 OP-43
Cordy Michael 22 farmer I-13
Cordy Edmond 22 I-29
Cordy Thomas 21 I-29
Corgrave Richard 24 labourer I-26
Corkaum Charles 20 clothier-13
Corkhill William 37-35
Corkoki Guiseppe 20 lab.OP-26
Cormack James 22-41
Cormack Joseph 20-41
Cornall James 42 miller-38
Cornall James 20-38
Cornall Ralph 17-38
Cornall Joseph 10-38
Cornall Matthew 5-38
Cornall John 40 miller-38
Cornall Maria 40-38
Cornall James 11-38
Cornall Robert 10-38
Cornall Joseph 42 miller-38
Cornall Maria 38-38

Cornall Maria 11-38
Cornall Margaret 3-38
Cornall Elizabeth 21-38
Corner Edward adult labourer-27
Cornish John 33 butcher-11
Cornish Thomas 40 miner-11
Cornish Richard 28-11
Cornish Edwin 20-11
Cornish Thomas 46 clerk-13ho
Cornish Elizabeth 46-13ho
Cornish George 15 clerk-13ho
Cornish Elizabeth 16-13ho
Cornish Ellen 6-13ho
Cornish Louisa 4-13ho
Cornish Caroline 1-13ho
Cornius J T -9
Cornochan Peter 36 joiner-20
Cornwall Richard 30 labourer I-27
Cornwall Mary Ann 24 I-27
Corrall Fredericks 23 labourer-26
Corran Charles S-40
Corrigan Mrs Susan 34 I-21
Corrigan Henry 11 I-21
Corrigan Susan 7 I-21
Corrigan Jane 5 I-21
Corrigan James 26 I-29
Corrigan Thomas 29 I-35
Corrigan Catherine 29 I-35
Corrigan Michael 5 I-35
Corrigan John 3 I-35
Corrigan Ann 1 I-35
Corrigan Law infant I-35
Corry Arthur 35 agri lab I-31
Corry Mary A 34 I-31
Corry James 24 farmer I-31
Cortissas F 45 jeweller-10
Cortissos R -9
Cosgram Henry 20 labourer I-20
Cosgrave Patrick 20 labourer I-26
Cosgrieve Mary 17 I-33
Cosgrove Andrew 24 farmer I-41
Cosgrove Thomas 26 I-41
Cosgrove James 21 labourer I-40
Coshen Richard 23-28
Cossage H 39 labourer-26
Cossage Mrs 37-26
Cossage Mary 7-26
Cossage Catherine 5-26
Cossage Charles 2-26
Cossage Alfred infant-26
Costigan Matthew 23 labourer I-31
Costigan John 18 I-31
Costigan William 21 I-35
Coston John-41
Cotes Jeremiah 22 labourer S-31
Cotter Miss Bridget 25 I-22
Cotterall John B S-32
Cottier Robert 19 labourer-27
Cottier Robert 45 labourer-27
Cotter William 25 I-29
Cottier Robert 38-43
Cottier Walter 11-43

Cotton Mrs Mary 23-13
Cotton Sarah Ann 1-13
Cotton Robert 25 labourer-23
Cottrell Ellen 33-16
Cottrell Charles 13-16
Cottrell Walter 11-16
Cottrell Ellen 7-16
Cottrell Samuel 20-34
Cottrier Miss 30-41
Coubrough William clerk-33
Coudon Bridget 19 servant I-42
Couglan Patrick 37-41
Couglin Patrick 21-41
Coulson Joseph 25 miner-11
Coulson Mark 19 labourer-24
Coulson Carry 42 labourer I-31
Coulson Elizabeth 34-42
Coulston Thomas 24 farmer-21
Coulter Samuel 24 labourer I-22
Counor Michael 24 labourer I-23
Counsell James 32 I-28
Couper Peter 30 engineer S-33
Court John 26 labourer-22
Court James 25-22
Court Harriet 29 spinster-22
Court Thomas 30-33
Court Jane 33-33
Court Ellen J 12-33
Court John 9-33
Court Catherine Ann 1-33
Courtenay P A -22
Courtney Mrs-42we
Cousidine Denis 27 labourer I-21
Coutauche D -9
Cowan Joseph 23 farmer-13
Cowan W A 29 I-33
Cowell Elizabeth 23-43
Cowie James C 36-28
Cowie Margaret 35-28
Cowlan Edward 36 miner-13
Cowle Philip 24 engineer-32
Cowley G E -9
Cowley John 18 labourer-26
Cowley James 25 labourer-26
Cowper George 20-36
Cox Thomas 22 labourer-23
Cox Amy M 22-23
Cox E 22 spinster-27
Cox Anne Sophia 3-27
Cox Henry B 30-30
Cox Michael 18-34
Cox Patrick 25 I-35
Cox Ambrose 29-36
Cox Samuel 23-36
Cox Samuel R -23
Cox Teresa 18-36
Coxon Michael 46 labourer-21
Coyle Mrs C 30 I-24
Coyle Matthew 26 I-28
Coyle Patrick 26 labourer I-31
Coyle Rose 27 I-31
Coyle James 6 I-31

Coyle Bernard 4 I-31
Coyle Peter 1 I-31
Coyle (female born 19/12) I-31
Coyle John 21-42
Crace Edward-33sy
Crace Henry S-35
Crace John T S-35
Cragey Richard 25 labourer-22
Cragg Edward B 36 merchant-42
Cragg Mary 36-42
Cragg Thomas 10-42
Cragg Mary 7-42
Cragg Mable 4-42
Cragg Georgina 2-42
Craghill Jonathan 29 lab.-25me
Craib George-29
Craig Robert-9
Craig Thomas O 21 druggist S-11
Craig William 21 miner-11
Craig Frederick 26 labourer-21
Craig Miss Jane 20 S-23
Craig Andrew 30 labourer-24
Craig Sarah 35-24
Craig Jacob 27 labourer-24
Craig John G 27-29
Craig Mrs Mary A 28 S-30
Craig Alexander 35 S-32
Craig Charles W 25 warehouseman-37
Craig John I-37
Craig Mrs I-37
Craig Thomas R 2 I-37
Craile Maria 30 spinster-22
Cramp Daniel 20 quarryman-11
Crampton Joseph 25 farmer I-31
Crampton Nathaniel 20 I-31
Crane William 24 labourer-20
Crannie Giovanni 19 OP-28
Crannie Catare 17 OP-28
Cranston George 24 plumber-11
Crass John I 22 labourer-31
Craven Eliza 42-20
Craven Susannah 24-20
Craven Elizabeth 1-20
Craven John 25-35
Crawford E adult spinster-20
Crawford Thomas 24 labourer-22
Crawford Rev A -23
Crawford William J 20 lab.-25me
Crawford John 28-33
Crawford Samuel 21-36
Crawford John 36 artisan I-37
Crawford Robert 24 farmer S-37
Crawford A 25 I-43
Crayton Miss 30 I-20
Creedon Timothy 24 labourer I-16
Creeth James-9
Creeth Richard 28 I-10sy
Crellin William 38-32
Crellin William-32
Cremer Thomas 24 labourer-25me
Cresser Henry 40 labourer-22
Creson Mrs-22

Creswell Sarah 50 spinster I-27
Creswell Joseph 24 labourer I-27
Creswell Eliza 20 spinster I-27
Creswell John 11 I-27
Creswell Annie 9 I-27
Critchell Frances G spinster-21
Critchley Moses-9
Crithani Emmanuel 38 OP-38
Crockett Latham 23 I-31
Croft James 28 farmer-11
Crofts Henry 26 blacksmith-13
Crofts Joseph S farmer-39
Croker Thomas 30 miner-13
Croker Mrs Emily 32-23
Croker Eliza A 8-23
Croker Robert 29 I-32
Croker Mary A 25 I-32
Croker Mary 4 I-32
Croker Elizabeth 3 I-32
Croker Francis 1 I-32
Croker John Arthur 19 artisan-37
Crokker Margaret 35-11
Crokker Eleanor 5-11
Crokker John 2-11
Cromer Henry J 26 S-41
Cromer Sarah 21 spinster S-41
Cromie John 25-33
Cromie Mary 18-33
Cromie William 22 I-42
Crompton William P 20-13
Crompton Mrs Jane 35-23
Crompton Thomas 17-23
Crompton Betty 7-23
Crompton James 1-23
Crompton Thomas 24-35
Crone Joseph R 24 labourer-30
Cronican Bridget 47 I-43
Cronican Bridget 15 I-43
Cronie Marcus 25 farmer I-39
Cronin Miss C 25-24
Cronin Dennis 25 S-24
Cronin Mary 21 spinster-40
Crook Archibald 38 bootmaker S-32
Cropley Simeon 25 clothfuller-13
Cropley Isabella 26-13
Cropley William-38 clothfuller-13
Crosbie James J 21 S-29
Crosbie Piera 24 OP-29
Cross Jessie spinster-11
Cross Richard-22
Cross William 21 labourer-24
Cross Thomas 24-24
Cross James 37-34
Cross James B 11-34
Cross Mary A 10-34
Cross William 27-41
Crosse Hugh B -37
Crosse C Lyon I-37
Crossey W A 24 I-40
Crossley Miss Elizabeth 28 I-26
Crossley Catherine 20 spinster-29
Crossley W J 24 pawnbroker S-39

Crosthwaite Alexander 15-24
Crother James 21-41
Crothers Joseph 45 labourer-27
Crothers Eliza 40-27
Crouch Emma 31 spinster I-29
Crouther John 30 labourer S-28
Crowley John 22 labourer I-16
Crowley Jeremiah 16 I-16
Crowley Cornelius 20 lab.I-24
Crowley Jeremiah 22 labourer I-26
Crowley James 20 I-26
Crowley John-29
Crowther Thomas 26-10
Crowther William 30-10
Crowther John 35-10
Crowther Thomas 22-41
Crowther Samuel 54-42
Crowther Eliza 52-42
Crowther Eliza 4-42
Crozier William-9
Cruckshank John S-43
Cruckshank Mrs S-43
Cruickshank George 24 lab.S-22
Cruickshanks Charles-33
Cruise Thomas 19 labourer I-32
Crump Cresswell 30-24
Cuddyford James H 24 farmer S-16
Culer Henry 25 cooper-11
Cullen Malcolm 24 clerk S-13
Cullen J W 21 labourer I-22
Cullen Denis 25 labourer I-24
Cullen Peter 70 groom I-31
Cullen John 20 labourer I-35
Cullen Michael 23 I-35
Cullen William-35
Cullen Mrs E -35
Cullen Isabella-35
Cullen John 47 miner S-39
Cullen John 21 S-39
Cullen M 44 I-40
Culonday George-28
Cultricott John 37-36
Cummier M M E 32 labourer I-32
Cummier Richard 3 I-32
Cumming Alex adult engineer-40
Cumming Mrs E 32-42
Cumming Andrewena 4-42
Cumming Thomas 2-42
Cumming John infant-42
Cummins Philip 27 labourer-27
Cummins Edmond 18 I-32
Cummins Honora 14 I-32
Cummins Robert 22 labourer S-35
Cunningham Margaret 25 (& inf)-10
Cunningham Thos.45 carpenter I-10
Cunningham William 22 I-10
Cunningham John 19 I-10
Cunningham William 26 farmer S-11
Cunningham Ann 24 servant-11
Cunningham Philip 22 farmer-13
Cunningham James 26 labourer-26
Cunningham Miss Margaret 24 S-26

Cunningham Miss 14-31
Cunningham Agnes 13-31
Cunningham Robert 19 labourer-33
Cunningham William 17-34
Cunningham James 25 labourer-35
Curle Eleanor 38-34
Curly Thomas 24 labourer-26
Curly Michael 19 labourer I-27
Curnow Stephen-9
Curren Miss-9
Curren Michael 27 I-32
Currie James W 36 labourer S-22
Currie Ann 38 S-22
Currie Ann 6 S-22
Currie Emelia 4 S-22
Currie Mary A 2 S-22
Currie James 1 S-22
Currin N 42 labourer I-24
Currin Miss Matilda 20 I-24
Currin Miss Priscilla 18 I-24
Cursteins Hans 35 labourer OP-27
Curtayne I -38
Curtin Bartholomew 25 labourer-21
Curtin Thomas 22-21
Curtin Miss Mary 20-21
Curtis William-11
Curtis Alfred P 25 labourer-22
Curtis William 30 labourer-24
Curtis Henry 21 labourer I-26
Curtis Kate 24 I-38
Curtis Anne 1 I-38
Curyoline Domeneco 21 OP-40
Cusack Mrs Maria 30-32
Cush Mary 28-20
Cush James 5-20
Cush Ellen 4-20
Cuthbert William 32 miner-13
Cuthbert Betsy 25 servant-30
Cutts Thomas 20-36

D

Dabondi Filipa 41 OP-40
Dabondie Bernard OP-43
Dadd Alice-34
Dagge William 33 policeman-42
Daglis Miss Margaret 19 S-35
Daglish Miss Hannah 50-35
Dagnall Josiah 28 S-36
Daiyanite Matthew 22 OP-16
Dalby John-41
Dale Thomas 27 smith-13
Dale John 19-28
Dale George 18-33ad
Dallachy John 36 S-43
Dallas John 20 joiner S-43
Dallen Mrs-22
Dally W B -22
Dally John Richard-22
Dally James 20 engineer S-35
Dally Mary 20 S-35
Dally Thomas 3 S-35
Dally James 1 S-35

Dally William S infant S-35
Dally Charles-41
Dally Margaret-41
Dalrade Bernardo 33 OP-40
Dalrymple H -9
Dalrymple D 21 labourer-22
Dalrymple Mrs A 41 I-39
Dalrymple Mary 19 I-39
Dalrymple James 47 I-39
Dalton Mary 32 spinster-20
Dalton John 23 labourer-26
Dalton Rev M I-28
Dalton Mary 39 spinster I-31
Dalton Johanna 19 spinster I-31
Dalton Patrick 15 I-31
Dalton Bridget 9 I-31
Daly Mrs Mary 46 I-28
Daly Moses 22-28
Daly Richard 20-28
Daly John 21 labourer I-31
Daly Timothy 20 labourer I-31
Daly Francis 14 I-32
Daly Patrick 55-36
Daly Honora 50-36
Daly Robert 29 I-38
Daly John 21 farmer I-40
Damenco Pianta 21 OP-38
Damington Henry 32 labourer-23
Damon Ned 12 OP-40
Dance Edmund 25-27
Dance George 22-27
Dance Robert 17-27
Danckest Henry 22 I-16
Dane Capt J -23
Dane Mrs-23
Dane Juliana-23
Dane Mary-23
Dangerfield John 30 labourer-28
Daniel Kate-42
Daniels William 56 OP-36
Daniels Ann 34 OP-36
Danks Samuel 38 labourer I-32
Danks John 74 S-33
Danks Ann 45 spinster S-33
Danks Sarah-39
Danscombe J M -29
Danzigar-9
D'Arville C -9
Darcey John 22 I-34
Darcey James 20-41
Darey Thomas H 23-27
Dargaer Lorenzo labourer-25sy
Darling Grace 24-39
Darling Alex 24 S-40
Darnell B S-36
Darnell Mrs S-36
Darnell Elizabeth 11 S-36
Darnell Florence 10 S-36
Darnell Launcelot 8 S-36
Darnell Rosalie 7 S-36
Darnell Cuthbert 5 S-36
Darnell Henry 3 S-36

Darnell Lucy 2 S-36
Darnert Henrich 23 labourer OP-23
Dauldrey Robert 55-43
Dauppe Gio 25 OP-40
Davenport John 25 I-36
Davern John 21-41
Davern Michael 23-41
Davey John-9
Davey James 38 labourer-20
Davey Mrs Ann 35-21
Davey Stephen 9-21
Davey Jane 18-21
Davey John 12-21
Davey Elizabeth 16-21
Davey Miss Louisa 16-21
Davey William Henry 21-21
Davey George 45 labourer-26
Davey Mrs 38-26
Davey Mary 2-26
Davey John 25 miner-35
Davey James 23-35
Davey Henry 54 I-39
Davey Sarah 54 I-39
Davey Thomas 40-40
Davey Mrs I 24-40
Davey Beatrice 6-40
Davey infant-40
Davey Elizabeth M 17-40
David Alexander 28 labourer S-27
Davidson John 39 miner-20
Davidson Thomas 38 labourer-22
Davidson Elizabeth 43-22
Davidson William 28 labourer-22
Davidson Joseph 19 OP-33
Davidson Thomas 21 S-33
Davidson Elizabeth 20 S-33
Davidson Thomas 1 S-33
Davidson J M 30 S-40
Davidson Thomas-41
Davies E -9
Davies William-9
Davies William-9
Davies H junior-9
Davies Henry E 23-10
Davies C M 20-10
Davies E 19-10
Davies John T 25 farmer-11
Davies Miss-11
Davies William 26 cooper-16
Davies Sophia 21-16
Davies Mrs Catherine 29-21
Davies Ruth 6-21
Davies Richard 4-21
Davies Mrs Mary 35-21
Davies Ann 10-21
Davies John 7-21
Davies David 30 labourer-23
Davies Catherine 3-23
Davies Robert 32 labourer-23
Davies Ann 19-24
Davies Daniel W 17 labourer-24
Davies Thomas 21 labourer-25

Davies Thomas 29-28
Davies Andrew 30 labourer I-31
Davies John 28 labourer I-31
Davies David 27 labourer I-32
Davies E John 19 labourer S-32
Davies Miss Ann F 25-36
Davies John 20-36
Davies Jane 31-37
Davies Ann Jane 8-37
Davies Elizabeth Ellen 6-37
Davies Catherine 3-37
Davies Elizabeth 22 spinster-38
Davies Esther 38-38
Davies Sydney 21-38
Davies Anne 23-39
Davies David 32 grocer-39
Davies Edward 21-40
Davies Llew 19-40
Daviman Henry 20 labourer I-24
Davine Miss Kate 22-21
Davis G 35 labourer-10
Davis Isaac 21 farmer OP-10
Davis George 38 upholsterer-11
Davis John 29 sailor-13
Davis James 35 labourer-20
Davis Mrs Mary 36-21
Davis Angelina 14-21
Davis John 12-21
Davis Mrs Ann 45-23
Davis Edward 16-23
Davis Jane 11-23
Davis David 9-23
Davis Elizabeth 38-41ly
Davis George 25-41
Davis Thomas 36-41
Davison Walter 29 labourer-26
Davison Francis 37 OP-33
Davy William 35 labourer-20
Davy Miss 7-20
Davy Ellen 27 spinster-28
Davy John 20 labourer-35
Davy William 26-35
Dawbar William 27-36
Dawman William 40 labourer-24
Dawman Ann 30-24
Dawson W 19-10
Dawson William 36 labourer I-20
Dawson Michael 30 labourer I-22
Dawson John 28 farmer-27
Dawson Mrs Phoebe 40 I-37
Dawson Capt-42
Day Benjamin 20 stonemason-11
Day John 49-34
Day Emma 47-34
Day Andrew 20-34
Day Alfred 21-41
De Castella Herbert-22
Deakin George 27 carpenter-11
Dean John-9
Dean Joseph 28-33
Dean Hargreaves N 22 labourer-38
Dean Eliza 24-38

Dean James–41
Dean James (2nd class)–41
Dean George 24–42
Deane William 27–34
Deane Edward 40 I–41
Dearden George 27 labourer S–35
Dearmond William 31 clerk–13
Deasey Jeremiah 46–16sy
Deasey Jeremiah 11–16sy
Deasey Mary 8–16sy
Deasy James 24 labourer I–27
Deayall Miss Catherine 31 S–27
Deegan Michael 32 labourer–27
Deehan A spinster–31
Deehan Margaret 29 spinster I–38
Deehan Henrietta I–39
Deely Stephen 27 labourer–27
Deely Catherine 23 spinster–27
Deer John 38 miner OP–16
Deking Enos 36 miner–16
Delaney Bridget 13 I–22
Delaney John 50 labourer I–22
Delaney Judith 20 spinster I–22
Delaney Ellen 17 spinster I–22
Delaney Matthew 20 labourer I–27
Delaney John 36 labourer I–31
Delaney Eliza 38 I–31
Delaney William 16 labourer I–31
Delany Daniel 45 I–42
Delbridge William 25 labourer–26
Dell Margaret–9
Delmore Margaretta 25 OP–36
Delyshine James 30 labourer–20
Demiston Robert B 33–42ot
Demiston Maria 32–42
Demorco Prospero 9 OP–32
Dempsey James A 26 farmer–35
Dempsey William J 21–35
Dempsey James A 27 farmer I–37
Dempsey William 24 farmer I–38
Dempsey Bridget I–41
Denham Mr 28 S–16
Denholm Robert 21 S–29
Denholm Allison 28 S–43
Dening J spinster S–31
Dennis Charles 26–29
Denniston F 35–42
Denniston Emma 32–42
Denniston Charles 4–42
Denny Mrs Jane–37
Dent George 26 farmer–11
Dent John 26 labourer–22
Dent George 40 farmer–27
Dent Ruth 33–27
Dent Henry 42–33
Denton James 20 labourer–31
Deprappe Pietro 22 OP–40
Derasson John 20 miner–31
Derasson Mary A 26–31
Derasson (male) born 6.2.1868–31
Dereton Benjamin 22 miner–31
Dereton Harriet 28–31

Dereton Sarah 1–31
Derhety Jonathan 19 labourer I–24
Dermott William 30 I–33
Derry Joseph–28
Dessause Louis W OP–26
Destin Joseph 38 labourer I–30
Devensmein Miss Christina 51–34
Devereux Henry 20 labourer–31
Devine John 29 merchant–11
Devine Patrick 27 I–28
Devine J 26 S–33
Devis Ellen 36 I–43
Devis William 10 I–43
Devis Margaret 3 I–43
Devis Ernest 2 I–43
Devis Violet infant I–43
Devislish Gio 35 OP–35
Devon Michael 20–labourer I–23
Devyer John 24 labourer I–20
Dewar Thomas 22 labourer S–27
Dewar George 34 labourer–31
Dewer Thomas 20 S–36
Dewild William 22 sawyer–10sy
Dewhurst John 18 labourer–30
D'Horty Daniel 22 clerk OP–13
Dible Mary 20 spinster I–22
Dick Robert S–33
Dicken Henry 39 labourer–31
Dicken Mary 46–31
Dicken Henry 10–31
Dicken Thomas 7–31
Dicken Mary 62 spinster–31
Dicken Henry 19 mechanic–40ly
Dickenson Mrs–9
Dickenson Thomas–9
Dickenson Thomas 22 labourer–22
Dickenson Thomas C 21–42
Dickinson William 17–11
Dickinson William 24 labourer–23
Dickinson James 27 labourer–24
Dickson C –9
Dickson David 20 labourer I–22
Dickson James 36 labourer–24
Dickson Ann 34–24
Dickson Miss 20–26
Dickson Robert 30 labourer I–30
Dickson Mr & Mrs–34
Diebels Mrs OP–34
Diebels Miss OP–34
Diebels Jacobs OP–34
Digby William T 24–24sy
Dillon James 24 I–40
Dillow Richard 20 labourer–21
Dillow Thomas 18 labourer–21
Dincess Charles 23–25
Dinetti Acqualini 35 OP–36
Dinetti Martini 30 OP–36
Dinetti Bridget 8 OP–36
Dinetti Lorenzo 10 OP–36
Dingey Peter S 22 engineer–38
Dingey Lilly 21–38
Dingwall Alexander 49 I–34

Dingwall Elizabeth 47 I–34
Dingwall William 11 I–34
Dingwall Elizabeth 8 I–34
Dingwall Robert 14 I–34
Dinkworth Henry 26 shoemaker–41
Dinon James 18 labourer–23
Dinning M 19 spinster–28
Dittinon Mrs 57 OP–22
Divantor Fanny 24 spinster–25
Dixon Samuel–9
Dixon E 21–10
Dixon Matthew 25 miner–11
Dixon Thomas 28–11
Dixon Francis 30 stoker–13
Dixon John 45 labourer–20
Dixon Jane 36–20
Dixon John 5–20
Dixon William 2–20
Dixon Mrs Jane 38–23
Dixon John 15–23
Dixon George 12–23
Dixon Elizabeth 6–23
Dixon Thomas 29 labourer–23
Dixon George 28 labourer I–24
Dixon John 30 labourer I–26
Dixon George 40 stewart–27
Dixon Ralph 20 labourer–27
Doad George–9
Dobbin Sarah 28–42ad
Dobbin Edward 6–42ad
Dobbin Ann 4–42ad
Doberer Miss Catherine 33 OP–33
Dobin James W 28–37
Dobinson Thomas 40–24
Doble James 24 miner–11
Doble William 49 miner–13
Doble James 33 labourer I–24
Doble Jane 30 labourer I–24
Doble James infant I–24
Doble Jane 12–34
Doble Bessie K 11–34
Dobson William 34 labourer–22
Dobson Mary 33–22
Dobson Ann 7–22
Dobson Jane 4–22
Dobson John 2–22
Dobson Robert labourer–25
Dobson Mary Jane–25
Dobson Martha Ann 14–25
Dobson Anderson 11–25
Dobson Sorato 9–25
Dobson Margaret 7–25
Dobson John 5–25
Dobson Rebecca 4–25
Dobson William 2–25
Dobson Ann infant–25
Dobson Anderson 28 labourer–27
Dobson Miss Alice 23–32
Dobson Miss Sarah 60–32
Dobson John–36
Dobson Mrs Johana 25–37
Dodd Joseph–9

Dodd Benjamin 26 butcher-13
Dodd Mary 20-13
Dodd Mary infant-13
Dodd Josh 27 labourer S-27
Dodd Miss-31
Dodds James 14 labourer S-23
Dodds Miss Betsey 16 S-23
Dodson George-9
Dogett Thomas 32 labourer-27
Dogett Rose 35-27
Dogett Charlotte 26 spinster-27
Doherty Mrs Ann-26
Doherty Henry 10-26
Doherty Hugh 8-26
Doherty Anne 5-26
Doherty William J 2-26
Doherty Michael 30 labourer I-26
Doherty Denis carrier I-39
Doherty John 30-41
Doherty Martha 25-41
Doherty William 4-41
Doherty James 2-41
Doig Alexander 26 labourer-27
Doig Peter 21 I-28
Doig Alexander 69 boilerman S-43
Dolan John 21 farmer I-16
Dolan Miss Ann-36
Dolne David 21 labourer S-26
Dolphin Herbert 21-43ne
Domenica Conteson 21 OP-33
Domerthane Elizabeth 24-29
Domgoole James 19-41
Donnelly Ann 16 spinster I-26
Donagley Jane 20 spinster-25
Donald Matthew 24 labourer S-21
Donaldson Margaret-9
Donaldson John 25 labourer S-26
Donelly James adult farmer I-40sy
Donelly Mary adult wife I-40sy
Donelly Mary 6 I-40sy
Donelly John 4 I-40sy
Donelly Ellen 2 I-40sy
Donelly Thomas 1 I-40sy
Donnehough James 20 farmer I-13
Donnelan Miles 37 labourer I-31
Donnelan John 14 I-31
Donnelly James 21-32
Donnely James 28 labourer I-27
Donnie James 19-30
Donoghue Daniel 20 labourer I-24
Donohoe John 21 labourer I-22
Donohoe James labourer-23
Donovan Miss Sally 19 I-21
Donovan Patrick 24 labourer I-22
Donovan James 20-22
Donovan Miss Ann 24-24
Donovan John 22 labourer-25
Donovan Miss Catherine 38 I-28
Donovan John 25 labourer I-32
Donovan Michael 39 I-36
Donovan Ellen 38 I-36
Donovan William 10 I-36

Donovan Patrick 8 I-36
Donovan Mary 3 I-36
Donovan Alice infant I-36
Donro William 36 labourer-24
Doolan Maurice 22 I-16
Doolay Annie 18 I-43
Dooling Michael 18 labourer I-31
Dooning Joseph 26-30
Dorizze Guiseppe 16 lab. OP-26
Dorley Thomas 27-16
Dorman Frank 11-29
Dorney Thomas P 22 labourer I-21
Dorney James 20 I-21
Dorney Thomas 18 I-21
Dorsa Catarina 40 OP-38
Dorsa Catarina 2 OP-38
Dorso Pietro 31 labourer OP-31
Doucet Samson 27-29
Douchy Timothy 30 agri.lab I-31
Douchy Nancy 25 I-31
Douchy Tim 6 I-31
Douchy Cornelius 4 I-31
Doud Mary 27 servant I-11
Dougall Patrick 17 S-33
Dougall Jane 34 servant-38
Dougall Robert 18-41
Douglas Mary Ann 29 laundress-16
Douglas Miss Ann 30-21
Douglas Jonathan 24 labourer-24
Douglas James 21 labourer-25
Douglas John 25 labourer-25
Douglas John 38 labourer I-26
Douglas Alexander 26-36
Douglas John 30 S-41
Dourneen James 34 I-32
Dourneen Elizabeth 33 I-32
Dourneen Elizabeth 11 I-32
Dourneen Catherine 8 I-32
Dourneen Alice 5 I-32
Dourneen Hugh 4 I-32
Dourneen Jane 2 I-32
Dourneen James infant I-32
Douthwaite Walter 25-36
Dove Emilia 22 servant S-38
Dovell William 50-28
Dovizzo Guiseppi 50 OP-35
Dovizzo Tomasio 18 OP-35
Dow James 25 engine fitter-13
Dowdale Frederick 35 mariner S-35
Dowdall Mary 22-43
Dowey Patrick 27 farmer I-31
Dowling Michael 22 blacksmith I-31
Dowling William 38 I-32
Dowling Julia 35 I-32
Dowling Henry 16 (died 21/7)-32
Dowling Julia 14 I-32
Dowling Bernard 8-32
Dowling James 23 I-33
Dowling John 23 I-35
Downee Francis 24 labourer-21
Downer Robert 26 labourer-25
Downes John 23 labourer I-30

Downey John 18 I-40
Downie John 25 miner S-32
Downs John 28-41
Downs Marcella 20-41
Dowvan Thomas OP-42
Dowys Jacomo 40 labourer OP-26
Doyle John 27 farmer I-10
Doyle Mrs 19 I-10
Doyle Kate 1 I-10
Doyle M 29 butcher I-10sy
Doyle Matthew 32 miner-11
Doyle John 18 sailor I-13
Doyle Thomas 45 labourer-22
Doyle Catherine 40-22
Doyle Louisa 14-22
Doyle Sarah A 11-22
Doyle John C 9-22
Doyle William 8-22
Doyle Frank 6-22
Doyle John 40 labourer I-26
Doyle Patrick 21 labourer I-30
Doyle Miss Margaret 38 I-35
Doyle David 19-36
Doyle Eliza 60 widow-37
Doyle Judith 22 spinster I-37
Doyle Bridget 19 I-41
Doyle John 30-41
Doyle Anne 26-41
Doyson William Henry-42
Dradman Louis 25 glazier OP-16
Drake Elizabeth 30-11
Drake Emma 25-11
Drake infant-11
Drake Victoria 26 spinster-30
Draper Miss C 33-29
Draper Thomas 18 labourer S-32
Dreher Bernard 36 OP-37
Dreman Michael 28 labourer I-26
Drew Charles-11
Drewe Ann 40 spinster-28
Drione Mrs Ann M 54-30
Dripps Thomas 21 I-37
Driscoll Ellen 21 spinster-25
Driscoll G C 34 I-42ot
Driscoll Margaret 50-43
Driscon Launcelot-43ot
Driscon Mrs-43ot
Driscon Laura 15-43ot
Driscon Ernest-11-43ot
Driscon George 9-43ot
Driscon Henry 6-43ot
Driscon Septimus 1-43ot
Driscon William G 18-43ot
Driscon Launcelot 13-43ot
Driscon Hugh 13-43ot
Drowsell Emily 27-42sy
Druck Sophia 23 spinster-25
Druck Pauline 25 spinster-25
Drummond William 23 labourer S-23
Drury Catherine-9
Dryce George 27-41
Drysdale William 39 labourer-34

Drysdale Isabella 39-34
Drysdale Isabella 11-34
Drysdale George 5-34
Drysdale John 1-34
Drysdale Henry 1-34
Drysdale James A 14-34
Drysdale Benjamin 16-34
Drysdale William G 20-34
Dubedat Mrs E 21 I-28
Dubedat Francis infant I-28
Duck Thomas 30-36
Duck Susanna 35-36
Duck Elizabeth 9-36
Duck Samuel 8-36
Duck Thomas 5-36
Duck Priscilla 2-36
Duck Susan E infant-36
Duckworth Susannah 24-42 1y
Duckworth Sarah Ellen infant-42 1y
Dudley Thomas I-36
Duerdon John R-30
Duff Mrs Elizabeth 36 S-29sy
Duff Sidney 2 S-29sy
Duff Thomas infant S-29sy
Duffett Mr-9ca
Duffett Mrs-9ca
Duffey John 35 I-43
Duffy Francis 18 labourer I-27
Duffy Edward 14 labourer I-27
Duffy Patrick 25 I-28
Duffy James 14 labourer I-31
Duffy John 36 farmer I-40
Duffy Edward 20-41
Duffy Elizabeth 30-43
Dufton John 20 I-26
Dufty F H 40-32
Dufty Alfred 10-32
Dugdale James 29 labourer-20
Dugdale Henry 22-21
Dugdale Mr 21 labourer-22
Dugdale E R 18-36
Dugnall Richard 35 boilermaker-13
Duke John 53-42
Dukes Miss Mary-36
Dulles Miss Mary 35-24
Dulmano Giovanni OP-38
Duncan John-11
Duncan John-22
Duncan William 24 labourer S-23
Duncan James 26 labourer-25
Duncan William 19 labourer-25
Duncan John 38 labourer I-32
Duncan Henry 50 bootcloser-40
Duncan John 43-42
Duncan John S-43
Dunford Patrick 29 labourer I-38
Dunford Michael 13 I-38
Dunlea John 28 farmer-16
Dunlop Robert W merchant S-41
Dunn James-9
Dunn Thomas 24 farmer-11
Dunn Richard 33 farmer I-13

Dunn Laurence 24 labourer I-22
Dunn Thomas M 32 labourer-26
Dunn J C M 29 clerk-32
Dunn Frank 22 I-40
Dunn James 51-41
Dunn Margaret 38 (2nd class)-41
Dunn Gerald 16 (2nd class)-41)
Dunn Thomas 14 (2nd class)-41
Dunning Denis 28 I-32
Dunning Mary 28 I-32
Dunning Catherine 3 I-32
Dunning Michael 1 I-32
Dunning female(born 19.8.1868)I-32
Dunstan James 68 labourer-27
Dunstan Emma 27-40
Dunstan Sean 6-40
Dunstine Mr 39 labourer-20
Dunstine Jane 46-20
Dunstine Lette 7-20
Dunstine Mary 42-20
Dunstine Edward 16-20
Dunstine Mary 13-20
Dunstine Elizabeth 10-20
Dunstine Jane 14-20
Dunstine William 6-20
Dunston John 35 miner(died sea)-11
Dunston Charles 27 miner-39
Dunston Elizabeth 23-39
Dunstone John 24 labourer-22
Durham Martin 25 labourer I-34
Durham Margaret 19 I-34
Durham M E 1 I-34
Durham Thomas 27-36
Durham Mary 28-36
Durham Jane 7-36
Durham George 4-36
Durham Joseph 2-36
Durham Martin infant-36
Durmersig Capt-22
Durmersig Mrs-22
Durmersig Miss-22
Durmersig Mr-22
Durose Edwin 21 labourer-22
Durose James 28-22
Duross William 15-30
Durston John 21 miner-31
Dutton Dorothy 16-36
Dutton H M D -39
Dwan Martin 27-41
Dwyer James 30 I-10
Dwyer James 22 labourer I-22
Dwyer Peter 40 labourer I-30
Dwyer Edmund 23 labourer I-31
Dwyer William 21 I-31
Dwyer Nans 20 labourer I-32
Dwyer Miss Ellen 22 I-32
Dwyer Richard 29 I-32
Dwyer Michael farmer I-33
Dwyer Denis 25-41
Dwyer Ellen 27-41
Dyer Herbert 35-28
Dyer Mrs C 34-28

Dyer Cecil 3-28
Dyer Percy 1-28
Dyer Patience infant-28
Dyer R W B 35-31
Dyer Mary B 33-31
Dyer William 8-31
Dyer James R A 4-31
Dyer Alfred E J I-31
Dynon John 40-29
Dynon Mrs-39
Dynon James 16-39
Dyson E spinster-20sy
Dyson Watts 38-39
Dyson Maria 35-39

E

Eadia Ant 26 labourer OP-26
Earl John 21-28
Earnet John 30 labourer OP-23
Earnet Mrs 25 OP-23
Eason Samuel 20 I-35
Eastman Thomas 20 miner-32
Eastmoor Joseph 40 labourer I-35
Easton Miss Sarah 32-21
Eastwood James-9
Eastwood Alfred 21 labourer-25
Eastwood F 16 labourer-25
Eaton Thomas 35 labourer-22
Eaton Annie 23-22
Eaton Annie 5-22
Eaton Frederick W 2-22
Eccles Sarah A 41-20
Eccles Leaha 18-20
Eccles Charles 14-20
Eccles Michael 28 farmer-27
Eddongton John F 19-26
Edelston Samuel 29 baker-11
Edelston Elizabeth 25-11
Edelston William 2-11
Edelston Samuel infant-11
Edgar Jessie 30 spinster-26
Edgar William 25 labourer-26
Edgar Agnes 50 spinster-30
Edgar Jane 40 spinster-30
Edgar Robert 24 farmer I-38
Edgar Catherine I-43
Edge Martha 33 spinster-25
Edge John Henry 38 I-32
Edge Martha 35 I-32
Edge James 22 labourer S-35
Edge John 20 S-35
Edington Francis 28 S-43
Edler David 40 labourer-26
Edmonds Richard 22 farmer-13
Edmonds William-41
Edmund William 21-28
Edwards Mr-9
Edwards Mrs-9
Edwards (3 children + infant)-9
Edwards Edward-11
Edwards Nicholas 25 miner-11
Edwards John 28 miner-13

Edwards Jane 26–13
Edwards Levi 27 farmer–16
Edwards Mrs Lavinia 34–23
Edwards William 28 labourer–24
Edwards Louis 35 labourer–26
Edwards John 17 labourer–28
Edwards Elizabeth 30 spinster–31
Edwards Miss Margaret 26–32
Edwards Caroline 13–33
Edwards Eliza 12–33
Edwards Henry J K 38–33
Edwards Caroline 34–33
Edwards Henry 9–33
Edwards Frederick 8–33
Edwards Albert 6–33
Edwards Lavinia 2–33
Edwards Alice 1–33
Edwards Eveline infant–33
Edwards Ellen 54–34
Edwards Richard 11–34
Edwards John 21–34
Edwards George 18–34
Edwards William 15–34
Edwards Henry 30–35
Edwards Catherine 22–35
Edwards William 25–36
Edwards Martha 32–36
Edwards Thomas 42 saddlemaker–38
Effey Charles 30 labourer–25
Egan John 22 labourer I–21
Egan Edward 20 I–21
Egan Michael 24 labourer I–21
Egan Thomas 16 labourer I–30
Egan Tim 14 labourer I–31
Egan Timothy 18 labourer I–32
Egan Margaret 21 I–33ad
Egan James 23–41
Egart Robert 22 labourer–35
Eggleson James 34–40
Egremont John 26–42
Ehlers Ernest–33
Ehrman Samuel 17 labourer S–31
Elder W C –28
Elder Robert B 35 farmer I–38
Eldridge John 24–41
Eldridge Eliza 25–41
Eldridge Mary A 4–41
Eldridge Alfred 3–41
Eldridge Sarah 1(died at sea)–41
Elias Alfred 17–24
Elins Edwin 36 artisan–38
Elins Anne 35–38
Elins Alfred E 2–38
Elkin Miss Catherine 23 I–23
Elkin Miss Mary 25–23
Elliman John 32–41
Elliot Robert 32 I–32
Elliott J H –9
Elliott Joseph 37 baker–11
Elliott Miss Eliza J 14–24
Elliott Miss Hannah 32–24
Elliott Harry 27–28

Elliott James 23 miner–31
Elliott Thomas P 37–37
Elliott William 28–37
Elliott Joseph 14 ropemaker–38
Elliott William 28 labourer–41
Elliott James 20–41
Ellis William–9
Ellis William J 23 surveyor–13sy
Ellis Matthew 32 seaman–21
Ellis Robert 26–27
Ellis Elizabeth J 27–27
Ellis Francis E infant–27
Ellis Miss–30
Ellis Pascoe 45 miner–32
Ellis Robert H–33
Ellis Jane–33
Ellis Arthur 19–42
Ellis Charlotte 58–43
Ellison Robert–29
Ellott George 40 I–40
Ellwood Thomas E 21 labourer–22
Ellwood Andrew 23(died at sea)–41
Elston James 32 seaman–37
Elston Henry 25 seaman–40
Eltoft John 22 grocer–39
Elwick Frederick W 18 S–35
Elworthy Edward–41ly
Elworthy Sarah–41ly
Elworthy A Maud 6–41ly
Elworthy Edith 4–41ly
Elworthy Edward 2–41ly
Elworthy Frederick infant–41ly
Emerson James 44 labourer–27
Emerson Thomas 17 labourer–34
Emmerson Thomas C–34
Enders Christian 28 lab.OP–29
Enders Frederike 33 OP–29
Enders Christian infant OP–29
Endey James 34 labourer–20
Endey Abel 40 labourer–20
Engall George J 51–41
Engall Mrs 62–41
Engall Henry Alex 25–41
England Edward–11
England Edward 21 miner–11
England William 19 smith–11
England William 39 engineer–43ot
England Jane 27–43ot
English Pat 22 labourer I–24
English Robert 40–29
Ennis Mr & Mrs–10
Ennis James 48 carpenter–38
Ennis Mary 43–38
Enraght Rev 60 I–30
Enraght William 22 labourer I–30
Enright Maurice 30 labourer–23
Erwin John 20 labourer–27
Esnouf Philip 37 labourer–20
Esnouf Emma 27 labourer–20
Ester John 23 draper I–35
Ethersby James 49–23
Ettenbank John–20sy

Ettols Thomas J–41
Ettols Mary Helen 9–41
Ettols Frances 51–41
Eustace Charles 39–43
Evans George–9
Evans W 18–10
Evans Charles 30 labourer–11
Evans William 27 miner–13
Evans Mrs Mary 60–21
Evans John 19–21
Evans Walter 17–21
Evans Mr–21
Evans Mrs–21
Evans Robert 18 labourer–22
Evans David 35 labourer–23
Evans John 35 labourer–23
Evans Mrs–23
Evans Morris 34 labourer–23
Evans Thomas 21 labourer–23
Evans Ann 21–23
Evans David D 20 labourer–24
Evans Elizabeth 20–24
Evans Mary infant–24
Evans John B 55 labourer–24
Evans William 26 labourer–24
Evans Ann 25–24
Evans William 3–24
Evans David infant–24
Evans Joseph William labourer–28
Evans John 20 labourer S–32
Evans Elizabeth–33
Evans Jon C 19 S–33
Evans John L–37
Evans David 50–39
Evans R P adult I–40
Evans Francis 45–42
Evans Dora 33–42
Evans Alice 11–42
Evans James 5–42
Evans Mary 2– 2
Evans Charles 1–42
Evant William 34–35
Evant Martha 30–35
Evant Joseph 8–35
Evant Maria 7–35
Evant Emily 5–35
Evant William 3–35
Evant Martha 2–35
Ever Michael 37 miner–11
Everard Robert 17 clerk I–32
Everard George 14 I–32
Everingham Frederick–21
Everitt John 22 farmer OP–16
Everitt B J–33
Ewant Mr–11
Evert William 17 clerk–13
Ewant Mr–11
Ewart James 25 labourer–32
Ewart Jane 32–32
Ewart Elizabeth M 4–32
Ewart John H 2–32
Ewart Jane infant–32

Ewart Mrs Margaret 55–32
Ewins William 26 printer I–11
Exelby Thomas 32 blacksmith–37
Exelby Jane 30–37
Eyes Charles–9
Eyre Frederick 24 clerk–13
Eyres Robert 31–35
Eyres Frances 20–35
Eyres male (born 5.4.1870)–35
Eyson Thomas 37 labourer S–32

F

Fagan James 29 labourer I–26
Faiend Mr W S–20
Faiend Mrs–20
Faiend Owen–20
Fairbain Thomas 27 shepherd–10
Fairbain George–20
Fairbain Mrs–20
Fairbain George–20
Fairbain James–20
Fairbain Charles–20
Fairbain infant–20
Fairbarn Miss 21–26
Fairbarn Jessy 19–26
Fairbourne James 35 butcher–13
Fairbrother Laurimas 35 lab.–13
Fairbrother Elizabeth 35–13
Fairburn Miss–29
Fairfax John–28
Fairfax Mrs–28
Fairfax Miss–28
Fairhurst M –9
Fairhurst James 24–35
Fairhurst Ellen 23–35
Fairless William 40 labourer–26
Fairley Isabella 15–33
Fairley Sarah 17–33
Fairley Thomas 13–33
Fairley John 46–33
Fairley Rebecca 40–33
Fairley Jane 4–33
Fairley Robert 2–33
Fairley Samuel infant–33
Fairman John 18 mechanic–35
Fairman Maria 19–42
Fairman Cassie 17–42
Fairman Robert 22–42
Fairman Anthony 20–42
Falk Aldred 18 labourer OP–28
Falkiner Elizabeth 30 I–40
Falkiner Edward 9 I–40
Falkiner Ormond 6 I–40
Falkiner Samuel 32 I–40
Falkner James 30–29
Falkner Charles 25–33
Falkner Frederick 17–33
Falkner Thomas 18–33
Fallan Benjamin 30 labourer–27
Fallon James 30–41
Fallon Mary 30–51
Fallon Thomas 13–41

Fallon Patrick 5–41
Fallon Mary 2–41
Fallows Enoch 24–39
Falls James 34 labourer–24
Falls Jane 34–24
Falls John 12–24
Falls Mary Ann 10–24
Falls Jane 9–24
Falls Elizabeth 7–24
Falls Thomas 5–24
Falls James 3–24
Falls Sarah 2–24
Faran Albert 32–37
Farbon Mary Ann widow–37
Farbon Mary Ann 13–37
Farbon Emma 11–37
Fard Miss Julia 18–24
Fardill J–9
Farish Christopher 28 labourer–27
Farley Lewis 24 I–30
Farley Lionel 16 I–30
Farley Charles J 18–34
Farley Herbert 11–34
Farmer James 25 labourer I–21
Farmer Henry 25 farmer I–38
Farmer John 20 I–38
Farmer Jonathan 60 workman–38sy
Farmer Harriette 61–38sy
Farmer George 22–38sy
Farmer Elizabeth 30–38sy
Farmer Sarah 18–38sy
Farmer Susan 16–38sy
Farnell Thomas 30 labourer I–24
Farnell Miss Bridget 20 I–24
Farrant Quayle–23
Farrant Robert–27
Farrar T W –13
Farrar Capt R–23
Farrar Spawforth S–36
Farrar Henry Wm 64 merchant–39
Farrar Elizabeth 59–39
Farrar Emma 31–39
Farrar Sophia C 20–39
Farrar Edward 18–30
Farrier H W 30–24
Farrier Mrs 28–24
Farroll Mrs I–38
Farroll Miss I–38
Farroll Eva 11 I–38
Farroll Flora 9 I–38
Farroll Frederick 7 I–38
Faulding Mr–29
Faulding Mrs–29
Fauless William 25 farmer–11
Faulkner Samuel 23 labourer–23
Faull Mrs Jane 46–41
Favage Francois 20 labourer OP–22
Fawcett Miss A K 25–24
Fawthorpe Jabez 25 labourer–26
Fay Edward 25 miner–10
Fayrer Henry 20 OP–10
Fazakerly Joseph 27–37

Fead Robert 23–16sy
Feader George L 38 labourer I–31
Feake Alfred T 28–41
Fearnley E B 28–11
Fearnley Charlotte 27–11
Fearnley Charles B infant–11
Fearow William 37 labourer–28
Feasson David 35 labourer–22
Feasson Phoebe 31–22
Feasson John F 5–22
Featherstone Joseph N 43 lab.–23
Featherstone Ann 36–23
Fedden A –9
Fedden O –9
Fee James 21–36
Feeley H P –9
Feeney Mrs A 35 I–41
Feeney Peter 13 I–41
Feeney John 11 I–41
Feeney Daniel 19 I–43
Feenon Elizabeth 20 spinster I–26
Fehrenback Sebastian 49 lab. OP–21
Fehrenback Caroline 44 OP–21
Fehrenback Caroline 2 OP–21
Feldheim Mr–20
Feldheim Mrs–20
Felix Henry labourer–35
Felixpani Masinio 17 OP–37
Felkin Miss Elizabeth–21
Fellores Thomas H–37
Fellows C J –43
Fenally Andrew 36–41
Fenally Ellen 32–4
Fenally Jane 8–41
Fenally Mary 6–41
Fenally Andrew 2–41
Fenelly George 50–39
Fenigan James 24 labourer I–24
Fenton James–20
Fenton Mrs–20
Fenton infant–20
Fenton James–20
Fenton Eleanor–20
Fenton Louisa–20
Fenton Sarah 26 spinster S–27
Fenwick O –9
Fenwick Charles L C–23
Ferguson A S 22 labourer–21
Ferguson Mrs 60–22
Ferguson Lillias 30 spinster–22
Ferguson John 22–22
Ferguson James 23 labourer S–23
Ferguson Isabella 30 S–23
Ferguson Agnes 11 S–23
Ferguson Jonathan 18 labourer I–24
Ferguson William 34 labourer–25
Ferguson Jean 30–25
Ferguson William 4–25
Ferguson Robert 2–25
Ferguson John 15 labourer I–28
Ferguson Nathaniel 19–28
Ferguson Alexander 28 carrier S–31

Ferguson John 22 S-31
Ferguson Patrick 20 S-31
Ferguson Samuel J 32 I-32
Ferguson Elizabeth 27 I-32
Ferguson Mrs S-33
Ferguson Miss Helen S-35
Ferguson John Adam S-35
Ferguson Hugh 52 mason S-38
Ferguson Janet 47 S-38
Ferguson Margaret 21 S-38
Ferguson John 19 S-38
Ferguson James 16 S-38
Ferguson Gilbert 12 S-38
Ferguson Janett 9 S-38
Ferguson John 20 I-39
Ferguson Rachel 20 I-39
Ferguson Elizabeth 40-43
Ferguson Mary 10-43
Ferguson George E 8-43
Ferguson Robert 6-43
Ferguson Herbert 4-43
Ferguson Elizabeth infant-43
Ferrall A jnr-11
Ferrari Carlo 27 OP-35
Ferrars Giovanni 21 OP-38
Ferrie William 45-42
Ferrie Mrs 43-42
Ferris Thomas-9
Ferris Alexander 40 labourer I-32
Fers Thomas 18 labourer-26
Fers Alice 17 spinster-26
Fethergill William 29 bricklayer-11
Fethergill Dinah 27-11
Fethergill William 3-11
Fethergill John J 5-11
Fethergill Dinah infant-11
Fettling Peter 24-36
Feynson Robert 29 labourer I-24
Field Edwin-11
Field John 18-33
Fielding John 28-42
Fielding Maria 24-42
Figg Edward J -26
Figg Miss 11-26
Fildes William-42
Filey George E 35 labourer-25
Filey Thomas 11-25
Finberg John 32 miner-21
Findlay George 36 labourer-24
Findlay Jessie 32-24
Findlay Jane 9-24
Findlay George 7-24
Findlay James 5-24
Findlay Alexander 2-24
Findlay Miss Mary H 25 S-32
Findley William L 18-27
Finerty Anne 13 I-32
Finerty Pat 35 agri.lab I-32
Finerty Bridget 34 I-32
Finerty James 11 I-32
Finerty Pat 10 I-32
Finerty Margaret 8 I-32

Finerty Mary 7 I-32
Finerty Bridget 4 I-32
Finerty David 2 I-32
Finerty Catherine infant I-32
Finlay Margaret 8 S-26
Finlay James 35 S-26
Finlay James 18-36
Finlay Michael 30-36
Finn Richard 20 labourer I-22
Finn S G 45 labourer-23ad
Finn Thomas 28 labourer-23
Finnamore Catherine 48 I-10
Finnan Edward 23 I-35
Finnigan James 16 labourer I-31
Fiowitt D -9
Firth Aquila 41-33
Firth Mary 41-33
Firth James 10-33
Firth John 7-33
Firth R G Joseph 16-33
Firth Sarah A 19-3
Firth Mary 19-33
Firth Edwin 22 merchant-42
Fischer Dorothea 22 OP-40
(married Ned Wurn at sea)
Fishco George 25 labourer OP-30
Fisher George 42 merchant-13
Fisher Emma 32-13
Fisher Mary spinster-25
Fisher Frederick 28 labourer I-26
Fisher Peter 60 labourer-34
Fisher Mary A 60-34
Fisher Elizabeth 30-34
Fisher Mary G 28-34
Fisher Betsey G 50-34
Fisher Robert 36 workman I-40
Fisher Sarah 60 nurse-42
Fitch Mrs (& child)-28
Fitzgerald Ellen 21-10
Fitzgerald Mary E 19-10
Fitzgerald Joseph 23 clerk I-10
Fitzgerald James 25 I-11
Fitzgerald Eliza 50 widow I-13sy
Fitzgerald John 11 I-13
Fitzgerald Margaret 14 I-13
Fitzgerald Eliza 50 widow-16
Fitzgerald John 21 labourer I-22
Fitzgerald Matthew 40 I-22
Fitzgerald Francis 16 labourer-23
Fitzgerald William 22 I-23
Fitzgerald Alice 20 spinster I-23
Fitzgerald William 22 lab.-25
Fitzgerald James P 21 labourer-26
Fitzgerald Pat 20 labourer I-26
Fitzgerald John 18 I-26
Fitzgerald Mary spinster I-30
Fitzgerald Mary 20 spinster S-31
Fitzgerald Miss Teresa 40 I-32-ho
Fitzgerald James 27-34
Fitzgerald Mary Ann 45 spinster-37
Fitzgerald Wm J 29 civil eng. I-37
Fitzgerald Lillie 28 I-37

Fitzgerald Michael 1 I-37
Fitzmaurice John 21 labourer I-20
Fitzmaurice Miss Margaret 18-36
Fitzmaurice A J 41 corndealer I-39
Fitzmaurice Maria 42 I-39
Fitzmaurice Maria 3 I-39
Fitzmaurice Marian 2 I-39
Fitzmaurice Robert 1 I-39
Fitzpatrick John 22 labourer-23
Fitzpatrick Miss Sarah 23 I-24
Fitzpatrick Henry 20 labourer-26
Fitzpatrick Henry 47 lab.I-35
Fitzpatrick Mary 50 I-35
Fitzpatrick William 16 I-35
Fitzpatrick Hannah 18 I-35
Fix John 22 labourer-31
Fix William 25-31
Fizzell Samuel labourer I-28
Fizzell Kate-28
Fizzell Sarah J 3-28
Fizzell Kate 2-28
Fizzell Mary infant-28
Flanagan Joseph 36 clerk I-10sy
Flanagan Ann 30 I-39
Flanagan Sarah 10 I-39
Flanagan Michael 8 I-39
Flanagan John 6 I-39
Flanagan Patrick 1 I-39
Flannary Michael 26 labourer I-21
Flannary James 19 I-32
Flatow Joseph 36-33
Flavell Rev Thos-33
Flaver Joseph 45 labourer-27
Fleming Vadelia 25 spinster-22
Fleming Robert 35-24
Fleming Margaret 26-24
Fleming Richard 11-24
Fleming Robert 6-24
Fleming William 4-24
Fleming Jonathan 3-24
Fleming Margaret infant-24
Fleming James 26 I-28
Fleming Mrs-28
Fleming George 22 agri.lab S-32
Fleming John 44-34
Fleming Harriet 43-34
Fleming Elizabeth 16-34
Fleming Cathering 4-34
Fleming Harriet 1-34
Flenigan Pat 21 labourer I-23
Fletcher Mrs-9
Fletcher W S -9
Fletcher George labourer-25
Fletcher Robert 27 labourer-25
Fletcher Joseph 22 I-28
Fletcher Thomas 20 I-28
Fletcher George 36 I-36
Fletcher George 48-38
Fletcher Helen 44-38
Fletcher Don 24 S-40
Fletcher John 48-42
Fletcher Ann 40-42

Flinn Mrs Mary 40-22
Flockhart Jean 38 spinster-21
Flockhart Margaret 29 spinster-21
Flockhart Jane 24 spinster-21
Flockhart Miss Catherine 21-21
Flockhart Andrew 15-21
Flohn Lewis 26-30
Flown Rebecca 24-30
Flohn David 4-30
Flohn Shane 2-30
Flohn Charles infant-30
Florence Emily C-38
Florver Margaret 30-20
Florver Richard 6-20
Florver Caroline 4-20
Flynn John 28 labourer I-30
Flynn Patrick 23 labourer I-31
Flynn James 21-41
Fogarty Jonathan 22 labourer I-24
Fogarty Lawrence 22 labourer I-31
Fogarty Michael 25 labourer I-31
Fogg John 26 farmer-16
Foletta Gotardo 25 labourer OP-13
Foley Mr-9
Foley Mrs-9
Foley Miss-9
Foley Thomas 21 labourer I-24
Foley Maurice 22 labourer I-26
Foley Philip 21 labourer-26
Foley William 24 I-28
Foley M 27 S-35
Follay Samuel 31 miner-13
Foord Mrs Emma 29-35
Foord Ellen 4-35
Forbes Augustus 17-10
Forbes Eliza B 10-34
Forbes G E-35
Forbes Mrs L-35
Forbes Edward A-35
Ford John 29 joiner-11
Ford Robert 30 miner-11
Ford William 30 miner-13
Ford Benjamin 27 labourer-27
Ford Charles-28
Ford Albert 25 labourer I-30
Ford Miss-35
Ford Joseph 31 gamekeeper S-37
Ford John 43-41
Foreman Edward 44 I-35
Foreman Lucy 44 I-35
Foreman Josephine 10 I-35
Foreman Elizabeth 8 I-35
Foreman Frances 6 I-35
Foreman Christina 4 I-35
Foreman Rachel 1 I-35
Foreman Lucy 12 I-35
Foreman Mary J 20 I-35
Foreman Sarah 18 I-35
Forembath Henry 52 miner-32
Forembath Margaret 56-32
Forester Janet 47 housekeeper S-32
Forester Margaret 25 S-32

Forester Janet 19 S-32
Forler Frank 26 shopman-43au
Forlock Miss Caroline E 22 S-31
Forrest Robert 26-28
Forster George-9
Forster H B -9
Forster John-9
Forster Mr-9
Forster Mrs-9
Forster (3 children)-9
Forster William-9
Forster Henry 24 blacksmith-11
Forster Henry 25 shoemaker-11
Forster George 20 labourer-26
Forster William adult labourer-27
Forsyth Mrs Ann-11
Forsyth James-11
Fortesque George E 25 labourer-24
Forth John 21-29
Foster Frederick-9
Foster John 38-10
Foster John 27-13
Foster William G-13
Foster John 20 miner-16
Foster John F-22
Foster Isabella-22
Foster Arthur A-22
Foster Sarah-22
Foster Mrs W H -22
Foster Henry 21 labourer-25
Foster Walter 48-28
Foster Ann 47-28
Foster Josiah 12-28
Foster Mrs-30
Foster Stephen 47 labourer-30
Foster James 19-36
Foston James-9
Foster Robert H 26 I-42
Fothergill Edward 23 labourer S-35
Fouagini G 18 farmer OP-20
Foulks E H -9
Fouracre Robert 43
Fowler Henry 25-26
Fowles Robertson 21 joiner-13
Fox John-9
Fox Richard-9
Fox Thomas A 40-11
Fox William H 27 joiner-11
Fox Frederick 21-11
Fox Mark 22 labourer OP-23
Fox Philip B-23
Fox Jonathan 56 labourer-24
Fox Heppel 50 labourer I-32
Fox Thomas A 12-32
Fox Alfred 9-32
Fox Jacob F 27 labourer-35
Fox Leona 17-35
Fox Elizabeth 36-39
Fox Henry 1-39
Fox Henry R -41
Fox William H 22-41
Foxton Thomas 46 mastermariner-13

Fraizer Robert 19 labourer I-32
Fralore Henry 25 miner-10
Frampton Daniel 38 I-34
France John-43
Franchi P OP-42
Francis Mr-9
Francis Mrs (& infant)-9
Francis Mrs Elizabeth J 35-23
Francis Adelaide 13-23
Francis Albert J 9-23
Francis Cresida A 7-23
Francis John 23 labourer-25
Francis William 20 labourer-25
Francis James 21 labourer-25
Francis Mrs Ellen 30-28
Francis Sarah 9-28
Francis William 4-28
Francis John infant-28
Francis James M 25-29
Francis Robert labourer S-31
Francis John 20-39
Francis Mary A 45-43
Francis Thomas 9-43
Frank Victor 44 labourer-26
Franklyn Mr 38 S-24
Franklyn Mrs 39 S-24
Franks Henry Levy-35
Frarley George 24 clerk I-10
Fraser George 25 labourer S-21
Fraser Alexander 22 labourer S-22
Fraser Miss Alexandrina 21 S-22
Fraser Hon Alexander-23
Fraser Mrs-23
Fraser John 25 labourer-25
Fraser Donald 24 labourer S-27
Fraser James 32-36
Fraser Peter F 20-36
Fraser John 24 S-39
Fraser William 45-43
Frater Peter R 16-35
Frederick Jonathan 33 miner-11
Frederick David 31 miner-11
Fredland Rudolph 17 labourer OP-27
Fredland Max 11 OP-27
Freland George 20 labourer-30
Freeman John-9
Freeman Joseph 28 miner-13
Freeman Caroline 26-13
Freeman Mary 6-13
Freeman Joseph 4-13
Freeman Missali 19 labourer I-24
Freeman H -28
Freeman Thomas 25-29
Freeman Louisa 23 spinster-29
Freeman Thomas 25-41
Fregown John labourer I-26
French John 31 I-35
French Mary A 30 I-35
French Susan 1 I-35
French John 26 I-37
Frengen Hans 24 OP-42
Frew Alexander 20 labourer-23

Frey Daniel 50 labourer-31
Frey R 60 spinster-31
Friedland Hermann labourer-25
Frieldlander H 19 OP-33
Friend Charlotte 50 I-42
Frinchi Guiseppi 30 lab.OP-20
Frost John 40 labourer-20
Frurrick F -32
Frurrick N -32
Fuchs W S 28 OP-42
Fuice Patrick 19 labourer I-26
Fuicher Ann E 27 housekeeper-42
Fuicher Anne 4-42
Fuicher Charles 2-42
Fuller Ellen 40 spinster-30
Fullerton Sarah 20 labourer-26
Fullerton James 25 labourer S-31
Fullingham Mary spinster-30
Fulton Hugh 24 labourer S-22
Fulton William 32 labourer S-23
Fulton James 29 S-23
Fulton Kate 18-30
Fulton Eliza 15-30
Fulton Caroline 13-30
Fulton John 20-30
Fulton James 16-30
Furey Miss Rose Ann 25 I-36
Furlonge Mrs-11
Furlonge William-11
Furner George 33 shoemaker-10
Fuvey Michael 25-41
Fyfe Henry-21
Fyson John 49 labourer S-22
Fyson George 9-22

G

Gabb Charles B 25-35
Gadd Miss J L-35
Gadd Samuel 26 labourer-35
Gadd Eliza 27-35
Gadenzi Paolo 24 OP-35
Gadini Andric 22 OP-40
Gaffney James 27 labourer I-24
Gage Robert-22
Gage Jane-22
Gage Robert 50 labourer S-32
Gairdner William S-13
Galbraith George G 24 labourer-22
Galbraith George G 28 S-37
Gales Charles F 24 labourer-25
Gallagher Edward 34 I-35
Gallagher William 16-42
Gallagher James 27 I-43
Galley Robert 47 labourer-26
Galloghy G D 26 I-10
Galloway Miss Elizabeth 27 I-32
Galloway Grace 25 I-32
Galloway Miss M S-35
Galvin John 40 labourer I-27
Galvin Mary 38 I-27
Gamble John 53 I-30
Gamble Eliza 50 I-30

Gamble Isabella 23 I-30
Gamble Ann 22 I-30
Gamble Mary 18 I-30
Gamble Thomas 55 miner-39
Gamble Thomas 28 draper S-39
Gammon John 19 labourer-20
Gantrell Henry 30 I-36
Gantrell Marianna 28 I-36
Gantrell Marian infant I-36
Gard Henry-30
Garden John 37 labourer-24
Garden Christopher 23 lab. I-31
Garden H labourer-31
Gardiner John 45 I-43
Gardiner George G 21 I-43
Gardner William-11
Gardner Martin 38 tailor S-13
Gardner Elizabeth 36 S-13
Gardner Jessie 11 S-13
Gardner George 6 S-13
Gardner Elizabeth 2 S-13
Gardner Steve 50 labourer S-30
Gardner John 38 tailor S-32
Gardner Elizabeth 31 S-32
Gardner John 9 S-32
Gardner Jessie 7 S-32
Gardner Andrew 5 S-32
Gardner James 2 S-32
Gardner Betsey infant S-32
Gardner James 36-34
Gardner William Reid 7-37
Gardner Sarah H 55-38
Gardyne Mrs Elizabeth-30
Gardyne Mary 4-30
Gardyne William 3-30
Garner Joshua 40 draper-11
Garner John K 30 labourer-24
Garner Andrew labourer-33
Garner William 28-33
Garner Arthur adult-40
Garner Mrs Blanche adult-40
Garnett Thomas H 24 ironfounder-31
Garraty Terence 32 I-29
Garraty James 29 I-29
Garside James 24 labourer-23
Garty Francis 28 labourer I-31
Garvey Palk 18 labourer-25
Gascard Charles 21-28
Gath Isaac 30 OP-42
Gaubret Mrs-34
Gaul John 36-33
Gaul Anastasia 36-33
Gaul Julia 5-33
Gaul Margaret Mary 3-33
Gaul Anna 1-33
Gaven William 27 I-40
Gayer Mrs Sarah-41
Gayer Charles 9-41
Gayer Edith 7-41
Gayer Lilly 6-41
Gayer Robert 4-41
Gayer Violet 2-41

Gaynor Thomas 28 labourer-24
Gaynor Richard 30 bricklayer-31
Geall William 27-33
Geary Thomas E 22 cordwainer-32
Gebbis 33 engineer S-10
Geddes George 20-41
Gee James 22 labourer-26
Gee James-29
Geffs Richard 22 farmer-34
Gelling Francis 36 labourer-29
Gelling John 21 miner-38
Gemmell Mr-28
Gemmell John-32
Gemmill Ms Jane Mitchell 45 S-37
Gendon Joseph-26
Genessa Master 11-34
Geoghague William 35 draper I-32
George L -9
George R W -26
Geoy Hein 22 merchant OP-16
George Margaret 26 spinster-29
Geraldo Raphael 16 OP-32
Gerdori Pietra 34 OP-35
Gerisch Joseph 50 labourer OP-24
Gerisch Louisa 30 OP-24
Gerner Mrs Theresa 45-35
Gerner August 2-35
Gerrard Charles-26
Gerrard James 25-29
Gerrard Jno F 27 labourer S-31
Gerrve T 25-34
Gershon Emil 15 labourer OP-22
Gessing Richard M 26 S-33
Gethings Henry 20 clerk I-37
Gheighton R 22 labourer-26
Gibb Miss Janet S-32
Gibbon Richard 34-24
Gibbons William 34-41
Gibbons Jane A 32-41
Gibbons William 3-41
Gibbons Rebecca J 1-41
Gibbs Henry 18 clerk-13
Gibbs M A servant-34
Gibson Mrs A-11
Gibson Joseph 22 labourer-21
Gibson William 54 labourer I-22
Gibson Harriet 44 I-22
Gibson George 20 I-22
Gibson John 18 I-22
Gibson John-23
Gibson Joshua 24 labourer I-23
Gibson Henry 37-29
Gibson Mr 52 labourer-29
Gibson William 10-29
Gibson Robert 33 clerk S-33
Gibson Mrs 40 S-33
Gibson William 17 labourer-33
Gibson G T 19 miner-40
Gibson Robert 35-43ot
Gibson Amy 32-43ot
Gibson Richard 12-43ot
Gibson William 6-43ot

Gibson Anna 3-43ot
Gibson Mary infant-43ot
Gich William John 27 farmer-42
Gifford Sarah 50-40
Gigg Robert 28 trader-40
Gikhrist John R S-41
Gilbank Miss Esther 15-23
Gilbert Edward 42 labourer S-32
Gilchrist Miss Lucy 19 S-23
Gilchrist W -9
Gilchrist Robert K 28-13
Gilders Elizabeth-42br
Gile Mr-22
Gile Miss-22
Giles John 26 labourer-25
Giles William 24 labourer-25
Giliette William 20 labourer-23
Gill Garnett 35 mariner I-10
Gill Adelaide 22 I-10
Gill James 25 I-10
Gill John 20 labourer I-20
Gill J C -22
Gill James-23
Gill Richard W 28 labourer-25
Gill George A 40 labourer-31
Gill Robert 27-33
Gill Mary Ann 26-33
Gill Thomas 20-42
Gillam Mrs Mary Ann 29-13
Gillan William 30 miner I-32
Gilleland Mary A 53-33
Gillespie Simon 27 S-32
Gillespie Sand 41 S-39
Gillilland William 28 lab.S-26
Gillin Harrier 19 spinster-16
Gillingham Louisa 26 spinster-26
Gillingham Betsy 40 seamstress-42
Gillingham Amelia 7-42
Gillingham Elizabeth Ann 5-42
Gillis Donald 37 S-43
Gillotti Domici 19 OP-35
Gilminster John 22 labourer-25
Gilmore J B 18 labourer I-22
Gilmore Mary 21 spinster I-22
Gilmore Hugh 22 I-43
Gilmour A -9
Gilmour M -9
Gilmour M junior-9
Gilmour Mary 75 spinster-27
Gingell George-9
Ginivan James 25 labourer-23
Gintomelli Vin 36 OP-35
Gintomelli Alex 33 OP-35
Giortz T C 44 merchant OP-10
Giogine Richard 31 labourer I-23
Giogine Isaac 19 I-23
Gioginne Hugh J 22 OP-36
Giovanni Pietro 26 OP-43
Gippel Joseph 21 OP-40
Gisborne W -10
Gittier Thomas J 25-41
Gittier Elizabeth 26-41

Gittins Thomas 40 labourer-22
Gittins James 15-22
Gittius Edward 21 labourer-16
Glaney Thomas 27 labourer I-22
Glanville Uddy B 21 labourer-23
Glavin Timothy 22 I-34
Glavin Daniel 23 I-34
Glasgow J G -9
Gleahill William 40 labourer I-24
Gledhill David 34-41ho
Gledhill Ann 32-41ho
Gledhill Elizabeth E 2-41ho
Gledhill Emma 14-41ho
Gleeson Nano 28 spinster I-37
(certified lunatic on arrival)
Glendenning Kate 22-34
Glendinning James 35 miner-11
Glenister William G 43-35
Glenister Maria L 45-35
Glenister Mary J 11-35
Glenister John P 9-35
Glenister Hannah 6-35
Glenister Rose E 3-35
Glenister William 15-35
Glenister Alice 13-35
Glenn Mary-34
Gleson Richard 22 farmer I-13
Glossop G -9
Glover Miss Ellen-21
Glover James 34-29
Glover H 65 widow S-30
Glover William 33-36
Glover Harriet 33-36
Glover Elizabeth 8-36
Glover William 6-36
Glover Clara 4-36
Glover Agnes 20 I-43
Goalby William 30-28
Goalby Eliza 28-28
Goalby Charles 21-28
Goddy Henry 21-29
Godfrey Thomas 20 labourer-13
Goff Thomas H 25 labourer I-22
Goff Sachariah 23-22
Golden Charles-20
Golden Michael 36 farmer I-27
Golden Edward 45-28
Goldsworthy Henry O 33-28
Goldsworthy James 29 miner-37
Golightly Thomas 40 miner-13
Goltz Gattal 23 labourer OP-24
Gonde John 78-32
Gonella Antonio 49 labourer OP-20
Gonella Saverro 42 OP-38
Good Mr-20
Good Miss-20
Good Thomas L -21
Good Jane-21
Good William 23 agri.labourer S-31
Good Jonathan M 26 labourer I-34
Good Alisha 27 I-34
Goodall Charles 21-29

Goodall Mrs-32
Goodall Mary A 15-32
Goodall Edith 12-32
Goodall H H 14-32
Goodlet Jane 31-42
Goodman Samuel 25 saddler-31
Goodman Jemima 28-31
Goodman Samuel 4-31
Goodman Minnie 3-31
Goodman Laura 1-31
Goodridge F W -9
Goodshaw W -9
Goodwin M 30 I-28
Goodwin Thomas 25-36
Gordon J -9
Gordon Samuel 36-10
Gordon Thomas 21 labourer-21
Gordon Henry 22 labourer I-22
Gordon Mary A 19-22
Gordon S D 48-24
Gordon Mrs 47-24
Gordon Eliza 22-24
Gordon Charlotte 20-24
Gordon John 18-24
Gordon Samuel 15-24
Gordon Thomas 33-24
Gordon Matilda 30-24
Gordon Richard 17 labourer I-26
Gordon Donald 29 farmer-27
Gordon Alex 25 farmer-27
Gordan Isabella 16 S-29
Gordon Michael labourer I-30sy
Gordon W 48 overseer S-38
Gordon William 34 I-39
Gore Joseph 26-35
Gorely Thomas-11
Gorman Michael 24 labourer I-27ho
Gorman Maurice 30-34
Gorman Edward 26 miner-43ot
Gorman Rosa 26-43ot
Gompert Mrs Sarah 60-33
Gornlay Solomon 20 labourer I-30
Gorton Joseph 38 sawyer-42
Gorton Thomas 34-42
Gosman Margaret 8-29
Gough Henry 24-21
Gough Mrs Margaret 40 I-22
Gough Thomas 16 I-22
Gough Charles 14 I-22
Gough Anabella 13 I-22
Gough William John 11 I-22
Gough James I-33
Gough Kate 26 spinster-41
Gouland Joseph 23 miner-31
Gouland Jane 21-31
Gould J M -9
Gourlay Thomas 26 S-36
Gourley James 32 labourer I-35
Gourley Joseph 22 I-35
Gow Robert-9
Gow Charles 35 labourer-24
Gow John 40 S-41

Gowan John 19 labourer-30
Gowling Joseph 32 labourer-24
Goyles Miss 24-24
Goyne Catherine 37 spinster-29
Goyne William 25 I-35
Goyne Frances J 22 I-35
Grace E M 30-24
Gracometti Mrs L 30 OP-20
Grady Patrick 19 labourer I-31
Graete T W 24 OP-10
Graham Alexander 31 engineer S-13
Graham Hannah 19 spinster S-13
Graham Hugh 25 labourer S-22
Graham James 27 labourer-24
Graham R R 21 labourer I-26
Graham John I-28
Graham Miss Margaret S-35
Graham Thomas-35
Graham Miss Elizabeth 26 S-36
Graham John 28 (died at sea)-40
Graham George 36-41
Graham Nathan 34 shipwright-42
Grain Peter 23 labourer-22
Grainge James 42 farmer-27
Graldie Mrs Sara-28
Graldie Sarah J 3-28
Graney Patrick 24 I-35
Graney Mary 26 I-35
Graney Thomas 3 I-35
Granger Edward 35 labourer-22
Grant A -9
Grant C -9
Grant Maxwell-11
Grant Houldby adult labourer-20
Grant Simon-23
Grant Miss Annie 23 I-24
Grant Donald 18 labourer S-27
Grant Thomas 48 I-42
Grant Mary 20-42
Grant John 23-43
Grasby George 57-29
Grattan Selina-36
Gratz Lucas 21 labourer OP-29
Gray H F -9
Gray J C -9
Gray George-11
Gray John 18 butcher S-11
Gray William 27-16
Gray Mrs Eliza-21
Gray Henry-21
Gray Catherine-21
Gray Bessie-21
Gray Alice-21
Gray Ada-21
Gray Marian-21
Gray Lelia-21
Gray Andrew 24 labourer S-22
Gray Ernest-22
Gray William 24 labourer S-22
Gray Sophia 25 S-22
Gray Elizabeth 30 spinster I-26
Gray Mary J 7 I-26

Gray James 27 lab.(died 26/1)S-26
Gray Edward 29 labourer I-27
Gray Samuel 30 labourer I-31
Gray Charles-32
Gray Mrs-32
Gray David S-33
Gray Miss-33
Gray Rachael 28 spinster S-33
Gray William 25-35
Gray Mrs Ann 24 I-36
Gray George 24 labourer S-43
Grayson John 36 labourer-27
Grayson Sarah 36-27
Grayson William 10-27
Grayson John 7-27
Grayson Clara 5-27
Grayson Annie 3-27
Grayson Mary infant-27
Grazia Antonio 41 labourer OP-26
Greare Rev S -28
Greasney Michael 35 farmer-16
Greatrex Charles-9
Greaves J L-9
Greaves George 21 labourer-31
Greely James 37-34
Green W P-9
Green William-9
Green Mrs Ann-11
Green Miss Patricia 24-21
Green W-21
Green David 50 labourer-24
Green Elizabeth 46-24
Green Robert 20-24
Green Elizabeth 17-24
Green Catherine 17-24
Green Isabella 12-24
Green Frances 10-24
Green David 7-24
Green William 4-24
Green Lindsay 2-24
Green J H 29 labourer-24
Green George 28-28
Green Louisa 30 spinster-29
Green John 26 farmer-30
Green Jeremiah 22 labourer I-31
Green H C 18-32
Green James 19-32
Green Elizabeth 7-36
Green Estella H 35 S-39
Green Anne 8 S-39
Green ? 4 S-39
Green Ralph 35-39
Green Stephen 20-41
Green Thomas 30 clerk I-41
Green A E -43
Greene Richard 56-24
Greenfell Thomas 35 labourer-27
Greenhalgh James 17 clerk-40we
Greenhalgh Ben 41-40
Greenhill Jane spinster-11
Greenhouse William 21-28
Greenlees James-41br

Greenlugh James (2nd class)-41
Greenough Kate 17-40
Greenough Mrs J 45-40
Greenwell Wm. 21 bird stuffer-13
Greenwood John 25 labourer-22
Greenwood Richard 30 labourer-23
Greenwood John 35-30
Greenwood Edward 25 labourer-32
Greenwood Normanton 17-36
Greenwood Enoch 15-36
Greenwood Sarah J 7-36
Greenwood Luke 40-36
Greenwood Mary A 39-36
Greenwood John 11-36
Greenwood Joseph 9-36
Greenwood Anne 5-36
Greenwood Luke 3-36
Greenwood Thomas infant-36
Greer George 22 labourer-25
Greer Mary-43du
Gregg Alexander 21 labourer I-22
Gregg William R 19-32
Gregg William Henry 20-32
Gregory Thomas 25 farmer-16
Gregory Thomas 24 labourer S-35
Greham Thomas S 37 labourer-30
Greham John 19-41
Greig Thomas-32
Gremason Zachariah 24-41
Gremner Jacob 19-41
Grennam Elizabeth 20 I-40
Grenville Miss G-22
Gresecke H 19 labourer OP-26
Grey William 27 farmer-16
Grey Celia 30-16
Grey Robin 24 labourer-27
Grey William 49-34
Griebel C L C 32 merchant OP-10sy
Grieve Walter 18 labourer S-22
Grieve John 40 labourer-34
Grieve Mrs 40-34
Grieve James 13-34
Grieve Margaret 11-34
Grieve David 10-34
Grieve William 7-34
Grieve Robert 4-34
Grieves William 27 labourer-21
Griffin Rupert adult-40we
Griffin Mrs adult-40we
Griffith E P W 20 labourer I-22
Griffiths Thomas-9
Griffiths W 25 labourer-10
Griffiths George 30 farmer-13
Griffiths Owen Jones 30 lab.-20
Griffiths Ann 28-20
Griffiths John 4-20
Griffiths Jane 2-20
Griffiths William 31 miner-20
Griffiths Elizabeth 32-20
Griffiths John 11-20
Griffiths Jane 9-20
Griffiths Ellen 5-20

Griffiths William 2-20
Griffiths George-21
Griffiths Charles 24 labourer-24
Griffiths Mary 23-24
Griffiths D 30-26
Griffiths Mrs 30-26
Griffiths Thomas 20-33
Griffiths Abraham 39-35
Griffiths Sarah 36-35
Griffiths John 5-35
Griffiths William 26 labourer-35
Griffiths Richard 40-41
Griffiths Thomas 40-41
Griffiths C H 24 student-43
Griful John I-36
Grigg Jacob 24 labourer S-31
Grigg Elizabeth 24-31
Grigg Jane 4-31
Grigg Hart 3-31
Grigg Mrs Letitia 36-35
Grigg James A 10-35
Grillane Thomas 25 farmer I-31
Grimbley Lily 16-27
Grimis Martin 35 labourer I-27
Grimshaw Joseph 25 artisan-38
Grindley Mrs-37sy
Grinlan Laurence 20 labourer I-31
Gripe William-30
Grisdell John-36
Grogan Andrew 24 farmer I-13
Grogan John 22 carpenter I-13
Groom H -9
Groves Frederick 25 farmer-27
Groves Frederick 26-30
Groves Charles 43 miner-38
Grubel Adam 24 OP-38
Gruchy Sorel 31 miner-11
Grundy Miss E 40-24
Grunther Nicholas 44 butcher OP-43
Guaran Daniel 28 I-41
Gubbins Alexander 18 I-36
Guerin Denis 26 constable I-32
Guerin Thomas 25 labourer I-32
Guilieri Giondomanico 27 lab.OP-13
Guinea Daniel 24 labourer S-27
Guion Ralph 30 labourer-21
Guiseppa Fevan 20 OP-33
Guiseppi Pedro 30 trader OP-40
Gulf Andrew 23 farmer S-13
Gullan William 26 labourer S-24
Gullan Louis 19 S-24
Gulle G de-9
Gullock Elijah 25 labourer S-21
Gullogher William Hy 30 lab. I-34
Gumming Mary S-31sy
Guniban John 34 tailor-31
Guniban Jane 21-31
Guniban John 1-31
Gunn Miss-21
Gunn Peter labourer S-30
Gunn William 38 labourer-32
Gunn Elizabeth 38-32

Gunner Edward 21 servant I-32
Gunning Mary 19 milliner I-11
Gunning John B 23 I-42
Gunson Mrs M B I-41
Gunter Thomas-38
Gurnet Miss-11
Gusilini Guig OP-16
Guthrie Mary 47 S-20
Guthrie June 12 S-20
Guthrie Agnes 9 S-20
Guthrie Mrs Mary 38 I-21
Guthrie Patrick 19 labourer I-31
Guthrie David A 36 S-42
Guthrie Helen 28 S-42
Guy Mrs 40-40
Gwynne Joseph 46-41
Gwynne Mrs 36-41

H

Habizio Aigro 8 OP-32
Hackay Margaret spinster-11
Hackett E 21 jeweller OP-10
Hackett A H -11
Hackett Mrs I-35
Hackett Master I-35
Hackfall Miss governess-41ly
Hactable Emily A 3-11
Haddon Frederick W 32-24
Hadley H -9
Hadley Miss A-21ad
Haigh Samuel 35 digger-21
Haigh Eliza Ann 10-21
Haigh William 33 S-43
Haigh Ann 32 S-43
Haigh Maggie 11 S-43
Haigh Unis 5 S-43
Haigh Cora 3 S-43
Haigh Florence 1 S-43
Hain William 24-35
Haining Robert 34-43du
Hainsworth John 24 I-26
Hair John H 34-43
Hair Agnes 37-43
Hair James 11-43
Hair Jessie 9-43
Hair Jane 7-43
Hair George 4-43
Hair Margaret 1-43
Halburton J H 39-27
Haldern Robert 21 labourer-24
Halfman G -9
Hall Jessie 34-10
Hall Robert 30-10
Hall Susanna 16-13
Hall Joseph 20-16
Hall James W-21
Hall Miss-21
Hall Joseph 22 labourer-22
Hall Robert 25 labourer-23
Hall Midgley 23-23
Hall Anthony 22 labourer-24
Hall James 23 labourer-30

Hall Mary 59 widow-30
Hall John 22 carpenter I-32
Hall Mrs Elizabeth 35-33
Hall James 11-33
Hall George 26 farmer-35
Hall Hamilton A 24 farmer S-35
Hall John 32-35
Hall James 23-36
Hall Jonathan-36
Hall James T I-37
Hall James 17 I-40
Hall George 36-40
Hall William 30-40
Hall Edward 23-41
Hallahan William 24 painter I-31
Hallen John 24 S-29
Halleran Edmund adult lab.I-27
Halleran Matilda adult I-27
Halley Miss Eliza 61-24
Halley Louisa 18-24
Halliam Patrick 25 I-36
Halliday Thomas 18-10sy
Halliday John 24-41
Halligan Bernard 23 labourer-25
Halligan Pat 25 labourer-25
Halloran Michael 50 labourer-25
Halloran Catherine 45-25
Halloran Alice 20-25
Halloran Timothy 18-25
Halloran John 16-25
Halloran Timothy 26 agri.lab. I-31
Hallowell Benjamin-43
Hallows Thomas 42-29
Halman William 36 labourer I-13
Halow Henry 26 labourer I-26
Halpin Edward labourer-25
Halsby Charles 59 agri.lab.-31sy
Halsinger George 59 OP-36
Halton Thomas 20-36
Halton James 21 engineer-40
Haluf Hannah 19 spinster I-27
Hame John-27
Hamel J -9
Hamill John 28-41
Hamilton J 30 tobacconist S-10
Hamilton John 23 farmer S-13
Hamilton Robert H 21 lab. I-21
Hamilton Robert-21
Hamilton Mrs-21
Hamilton Dundas-21
Hamilton James-21
Hamilton Gilbert-21
Hamilton Robert-21
Hamilton Alexander 28 lab.S-22
Hamilton Mary 25 S-22
Hamilton Robert 23 labourer S-22
Hamilton Miss Agnes 24 S-24
Hamilton Andrew 20 labourer S-24
Hamilton James 20 labourer-25
Hamilton W G 36 labourer-25
Hamilton Frederick labourer-26sy
Hamilton John 19 I-32

Hamilton Mrs S 25 S-34
Hamilton Mr S-35
Hamilton Mrs S-35
Hamilton William A 22-36
Hamilton Thomas jun 20-41ly
Hamilton Andrew 28 I-42
Hamilton James 27-42
Hamilton Ann Jane 18-42
Hamilton Jane 12-43
Hamilton Alexander 18-43
Hammery Jonathan 25 labourer-25
Hammond Michael 19-34
Hammond Robert William-37
Hammond Charles 17-42
Hammond Richard 38-43
Hammond Elizabeth 37-43
Hampson James 20-43
Hamworth John 25 mason-16
Hanaron Thomas 28 labourer-26
Hancock Samson 25 farmer-11
Handley James 30-36
Hanham James-9
Hanham George-9
Hanham Mrs-9
Hanichan Patrick 25 labourer I-32
Hanigan Patrick 55-34
Hanly Pat 30 labourer I-21
Hannah Adam 24 labourer-22
Hannah Ann 25 spinster-34
Hannican Pat 26 I-40
Hannigan Thomas 35 labourer-16
Hansell Jacob 19 labourer OP-30
Hansen O W OP-38
Hansford Walter J 34 labourer-26
Hansford Mrs 36-26
Hanson John 29 labourer-20
Hanson Charles 29 labourer I-23
Hanson John 34 OP-32
Hanson Adolph 29 OP-32
Hanson Sir R D -35
Hanson John 25-42
Hantorg Nills H 30 labourer OP-30
Harbinson David 18 labourer I-23
Harbridge William 30-43du
Harbridge Kate 30-43
Hardcastle Mrs-22
Hardcastle Miss-22
Hardcastle Andrea 25 OP-40
Hardell Thomas 30 grocer-32
Hardell Selina 25-32
Hardell T S 2.1/2-32
Harderson H 19 I-40
Harderson John 18 workman I-40
Hardey John 39 miner-16
Hardie James 22 labourer-27
Hardie Walter R clergyman-39
Hardie Mrs-39
Hardie Edith 6-39
Hardie Gertrude 4-39
Hardiman Martin 27 I-36
Harding John-9
Harding Richard 20 agri.lab.-31

Hardle W Carl 21 OP-29
Hardle Catherine 28 OP-29
Hardman William 30 miner-13
Hardman William 29 I-43
Hardsides Mary spinster-11
Hardwick James-9
Hardwick W-9
Hardwick Arthur 19-16sy
Hardy N G-11
Hardy James 31 servant-31
Hardy Flora 28-31
Hardy Flora 4-31
Hardy Eulalia 1(died 8.1.1868)-31
Hardy B -36ad
Hardy Mrs-36ad
Hardy George-36ad
Hargreaves Bessy 50-10
Hargreaves Elizabeth 10-10
Hargreaves Henry 35 labourer-10
Hargreaves Miss Isa 28-21
Hargreaves William 23 labourer-24
Hargreaves John 26 labourer-27
Hargreaves Mary 26-27
Hargreaves Mary Ann 3-27
Hargreaves Thomas 1-27
Harkiners Mary 20 spinster-29
Harland George 60 labourer-24
Harle Jonathan 27 grocer-11
Harley John 20 labourer-26
Hanna Robert 22 labourer I-30
Harman Max 42 OP-33
Harmanham Andrew 24 servant I-40
Harmer Michael 17 I-34
Harmer Samuel 34-34
Harmer Jane 27-34
Harmer Mary E 9-34
Hammersly Mrs-9
Harndorf Jonathan 25 lab.-25
Harnett Thomas 22 labourer I-32
Harper Joseph 27-13
Harper Joseph 27-13
Harper Emma 25-13
Harper William 4-13
Harper Alfred 2.1/2-13
Harper Ellen 1-13
Harper George 46-22
Harper William 27-36
Harrald Edward 24-23
Harrald Daniel 33-33
Harrald Ann 30-33
Harrald Margaret 6-33
Harrald Mary A 3-33
Harrant James 21 engineer-10
Harries Henry 22 OP-23
Harrington William 34 labourer-22
Harrington William S 41 lab. I-26
Harrington I P 41 I-26
Harrington Wm 47 bricklayer-36
Harrington John 17-41
Harrington Rudolphus 19-41
Harrington Edward 21-41
Harrington William 16-41

Harris William-9
Harris John-11
Harris Thomas 26 miner-11
Harris Michael 29 miner-13
Harris Mrs 24-16
Harris Hugh 26-16
Harris James 48 miner-16
Harris Jonathan 26 labourer-16
Harris John 28 miner-16
Harris James 33 labourer-21
Harris John 29 labourer-22
Harris Catherine 18 spinster-22
Harris Elizabeth 16 spinster-25
Harris Simon 22 labourer-26
Harris Mrs B 33-29
Harris Percy 12-29
Harris Walter 6-29
Harris John 23-29
Harris Joseph 21 labourer-30
Harris Miss E J-35
Harris R T 23 baker-35
Harris Matthew 34-36
Harris Phillip 21-36
Harris John 29 miner-37
Harris James 21-37
Harris James 52 carpenter S-38
Harris Elizabeth 47 S-38
Harris David 19 stableman-40
Harris Essex Rees farmer-43ad
Harris Jane-43ad
Harris John A 7-43ad
Harris George R 3-43ad
Harris Minnie infant-43ad
Harrison James 55 tailor-13
Harrison Maria 50-13
Harrison John 27 labourer-22
Harrison Joshua 29-27
Harrison Henry W 30-29
Harrison Sarah 28-29
Harrison John R 17 fitter-32
Harrison George-36
Harrison James 29-39
Harrison Anne 28-39
Harrison Eva M 2-39
Harrison William 26 miner-39
Harrison F W 17-43
Harrison Harriet 10-43ly
Harrison Agnes 8-43ly
Harrison George 7-43ly
Harry J -9
Harry William 27 labourer-24
Harry William 20 miner-37
Harstenos H 27 OP-10
Hart Henrich 18 labourer S-20
Hart James 25 labourer-20
Hart Margaret 26-20
Hart Mary A 6-20
Hart John 32 labourer S-22
Hart James 23 labourer-23
Hart S H 21 labourer-23
Hart Michael 29-33
Hart George 32-34

Hart Sarah 37-34
Hart Sarah E 9-34
Hart Henry G 7-34
Hart Thomas F 5-34
Hart Charlotte L 3-34
Hart James R 1-34
Hart Henry 29-34
Hart Samuel-41
Harte Jon 40 labourer-26
Hartier Nathaniel 25 labourer-35
Hartle T 28 OP-41
Hartley H -9
Hartley John-9
Hartley William-9
Hartley John-11
Hartley John 28 farmer-13
Hartley John E 20 labourer-30
Hartley William 36 draper-39
Hartley George 36-42
Hartley Martha 34-42
Hartley Ernest 13-42
Hartley Frederick 11-42
Hartley Ada 9-42
Hartley Lizzie 7-42
Hartley William 3-42
Hartley George infant-42
Hartley Henry H 21-42
Hartley William Henry 19-42
Hartman Theodore OP-37
Hartman Auguste OP-37
Hartman Adelaide 5 OP-37
Hartmann Carl OP-42
Hartney Patrick 21 labourer I-27
Harton A S 38 labourer-40
Hartrick Henry 33 labourer OP-33
Hartwell Leonard 25-41
Hartwell Frances 23-41
Hartwell Harry 1.1/2-41
Harvey Richard 27 miner-13
Harvey Richard 28 farmer-20
Harvey James 72 labourer S-32
Harvey Janet 68 S-32
Harvey Janet 36 S-32
Harvey Jane 30 S-32
Harvey Isabella 22 S-32
Harvey Mary 29 spinster-34
Harvey William 22-34
Harvey Edmund I-36
Harvey Crosbie W I-39
Harvey Thomas 19 clerk-39
Harvey Rev Ld Charles(2nd cl.)-41
Harvie William-11
Harvie William 28 labourer-22
Harwood Elizabeth 36 spinster-13
Harwood Gerald 19-43
Haskett Ann 35 spinster-27
Haslam James 22-28
Hassell Ann 27 S-36sy
Hassett Pat 30 labourer I-23
Hassett Miss Bridget 21-23
Hastings Ellen 24 servant I-32
Hastle Thomas J 24 clerk S-41

Hathaway Charles 36(died 18/3)-13
Hathaway Thomas 36(died 27/3)-13
Hathcote George 22 labourer-24
Hathcote Mary 23-24
Hatton George 45 labourer-30
Hatton A -31
Hatton Francis 28-38
Haughton Stephen 23-26
Haughton Mrs 21-26
Hausen Mrs Marie 25 I-32
Haustey Felix 33 OP-37
Haw Thomas 28 labourer-25
Hawdon Mrs I-23
Hawdon Mrs M-23
Hawdon Miss E-23
Hawdon Miss A-23
Hawe William 24 labourer I-31
Hawe Robert 48-35
Hawe Eliza 47-35
Hawe Annie 6-35
Hawe Mary J 20-35
Hawe Elizabeth 17-35
Hawke J -9
Hawke Mr-29
Hawke Mrs-29
Hawkey Henry 21-42
Hawkins Jeffraison 45 clerk-13
Hawkins Henry H 23-26
Hawkins John 19-33
Hawksworth Mrs Mary 28-21
Hawley R -9
Hawls Henry 20-41
Haworth James 40-38
Haworth Charles 19 weaver-38
Hawson John 29 labourer-31
Hawthorne ? 29-13
Hay Ann 26-16
Hay Charles 3-16
Hay Abel 1-16
Hay George 22 labourer-21
Hay Robert 24 labourer S-22
Hay James 22 S-31
Hay M A 37 dressmaker S-40
Hay Alex 19 student S-40
Hay William E 1-40
Hay Mrs Mary Ann 29-40
Haydon William 35 labourer-23
Hayes Emma 21-13
Hayes Frederick 4-13
Hayes Honora 21 spinster I-22
Hayes Patrick 25 labourer I-27
Hayes Matthew 18 labourer-27
Hayes George 50 labourer I-31
Hayes Edward 48-34
Hayes Thomas 22-34
Hayes John 29-35
Hayes Jane 27-35
Hayes Walter J 5-35
Hayes Aaron H 4-35
Hayes Mary A 2-35
Hayes John 25 labourer-39
Hayes Ann 45-42

Hayes Teresa 11-42
Hayman Marcus 34 labourer-22
Hayward George-9
Haywood Mr 29 labourer-23
Hazell William 27 miner-13
Headland Mrs Mary Ann 40-40
Headon Mrs Hannah 30-37
Heald Benjamin 22 labourer-35
Healeey Catherine-39
Healeey Catherine 11 39
Healeey Mary A 9-39
Healeey William G 5-39
Healy Cornelius 20 labourer-25
Healy James 27 labourer-26
Healy Martha 18-26
Heard Alfred 30 labourer-27
Hearle James 25 miner-11
Hearle James E 36-36
Hearle Louisa E 36-36
Hearle Emma E 10-36
Hearle Harriet E 4-36
Hearn Morris 26 labourer-13
Hearn Jessie 30 butcher-16
Hearn Elizabeth 29-16
Hearn Thomas 4-16
Hearn Mary 2-16
Hearn Edward C 1-16
Hearne Thomas-21
Hearne Mrs 35 servant-41
Heath Mrs G 35-33
Heath George H 7-33
Heath Robert 26-42
Heatherton George 42 miner-39
Heatherton Francis 41-39
Heatherton William 16-39
Heatherton Elizabeth 13-39
Heatherton Jane A 9-39
Heatherton Mary 4-39
Heatherton Joshua J 1-39
Heaton Mrs Mary A 25-24
Heaton Jane A infant-24
Heaton Richard 28 labourer-24
Heaton Joseph 37 labourer I-33
Heaton Sarah 37 I-33
Heaton Betsy Ann 1 I-33
Hebb Joseph 33-35
Hebb Agnes 28-35
Hebb Frederick 5-35
Hebb Mary A 2-35
Hecht John 41 OP-33
Heck August 24 OP-42
Hedley Miss Jane 32-24
Heernery Elizabeth 31 widow-37
Heernery William Clement 2-37
Heffeman John 27 labourer I-21
Heffenstein Gustav 17 miner OP-21
Heffenstein Miss Julia 19 OP-21
Heffeman William 25 I-38
Hegan Pat 28 labourer I-34
Hegarty Jonathan 30 labourer-24
Hegarty Mary 24-24
Hegarty Honora infant-24

Hegarty William infant-24
Hegarty James 44 I-36
Hegarty Eliza 30 I-36
Hegburn Edward 30 labourer-24
Hehir John 26 I-33
Heife Ellen 29 spinster S-34
Heil N spinster-37
Heinks John S 27/17? I-27
Heising F 26 labourer OP-22
Heisterson Helen-33
Heisterson Fanny-33
Heldebranat Peter 11 OP-16
Heldenbrand Jonathan 36 OP-28
Helffenstein Mrs Margaret 38 OP-23
Helffenstein Gustav 19 OP-23
Helffenstein Henry 17 OP-23
Helflus Mr-26
Helflus Mrs-26
Heller Hayden-36
Helmborg Erick 40 labourer OP-27
Helps James 38 gardener-37
Helsall William 30 labourer-29
Hembry James 21-34
Hembry Ambrose K 28-34
Hemming A S adult spinster-10
Hemming B 19-10
Hemmons Louisa 31-33
Henderson H -9
Henderson John-11
Henderson Sarah-11
Henderson Mason 18 compositor-11
Henderson Olive spinster-11
Henderson Mary-11
Henderson Robert W-11
Henderson E Septimus-11
Henderson Francis 38 labourer-16
Henderson Mary 34-20
Henderson Elizabeth 2-20
Henderson George 30 labourer S-21
Henderson Alexander 19 S-21
Henderson John 14 S-21
Henderson James 30 labourer-22
Henderson Elizabeth 33 servant-24
Henderson Miss Jane 29 S-24
Henderson Mrs Mary 30 I-24
Henderson John 24 labourer-25
Henderson John 21 labourer-26
Henderson Robert 20 I-28
Henderson Thomas 22 I-28
Henderson Miss Margaret 26 S-32
Henderson Mrs S-32
Henderson Edward 20 labourer-34
Henderson Miss Ann-35
Henderson Miss Elizabeth 30-35
Henderson Gordon 51-35
Henderson Mary 49-35
Henderson John 16-35
Henderson Robert 14-35
Henderson George miner-37
Henderson Ann 25-381a
Henderson William 25 mechanic-40
Henderson Mrs 26-40

Hendrick Pat 27 labourer I-23
Hendrick Sarah 25 I-23
Henessey William 35 tailor I-32
Henessey Bridget 30 I-32
Henessey John 9 I-32
Henessey Mary 7 I-32
Henessey Catherine 5 I-32
Hennesey Patrick 25 farmer I-16
Hennesey James 32 I-16
Hennessy Mary 24 spinster I-26
Hennessy James 30 I-35
Hennet Alice 20 spinster S-16
Henry Mary 21 spinster-22
Henry Mary 22 I-26
Henry Rodman 29 labourer-28
Henry R R -35
Henry Charles 38 artisan 37
Henry Maria 23-37
Henry John 32 irondresser S-39
Henry James B 23 I-40
Henry Selma 20 I-43
Henshaw John 17 labourer-16
Henson Thomas 44-41
Henson Emma 36-41
Henssler John C OP-35
Henston Richard 20 labourer-27
Hepburn Patrick 24 I-31
Hepburn Jane 28 I-31
Hepburn Thomas 21 labourer I-31
Hepburn Robert 19-43
Herbage William-9
Herbert M 25 engineer I-10
Herbert Thomas 30 labourer-24
Herbert Matthew 38-41
Herbert Isabella 37-41
Herbert David 34 S-42ot
Herbert Jane 42 S-42ot
Herbert Robert 20 S-42ot
Herbert Thomas 18 S-42ot
Herbert Maggie 17 S-42ot
Herbert Mary 14 S-42ot
Herbert Jane 10 S-42ot
Herbert Agnes 8 S-42ot
Henry Mary 21 spinster-22
Hergfeldt Adolph 19 trader OP-40
Herman Nathaniel 22 OP-36
Hermann Morris OP-42
Hern Matthew 22-32
Heron O -9
Heron W 24 I-10
Herron Edward 30-35
Herron Martha 30-35
Hertel Louisa 29 spinster-22
Hervey Rev Lord C A-41br
Hervey Garrett 40-41
Hervey Bridget 35-41
Hervey Bridget 9-41
Hervey Nicholas 7-41
Hervey Kate 5-41
Heselton Edward 39 S-33
Hesford Earnest 24-42
Hesford Edwin 22-42

Hesketh James 23 labourer S-35
Hesketh Joshua 21-36
Hesler Frederick J 30 lab.S-33
Hesse Mrs Catherine 40-28
Hesse Marie 11-28
Hesse Louisa 9-28
Hesse Ida 7-28
Hester James-35
Hester Mrs C-35
Hester Rosa-35
Hester Lucy-35
Hester Jefferson-35
Hester Mildred-35
Hester Sydney-35
Hestwell John F 48 labourer I-26
Hetherington Robert 25 lab.-21
Hetherington John 20-36
Heuschuren Jonathan 27 lab.OP-24
Hevine Charles 18 labourer I-26sy
Hevitson John 26 labourer-25
Hewett George 32 cooper-16
Hewett Alfred 36 brewersman-40
Hewitt Margaret 36 I-39
Hewit Johanna 38 I-39
Hewitt Margaret 40 spinster I-40
Hewitt Thomas 35 engineer-42we
Hewlings Samuel-21
Hewlitt John 40-29
Hewson Thomas 24 labourer-21
Hewson Richard 30 labourer-24
Hey Mary 30-41
Heyes Mrs Mary 50-32
Heyes James 38 miner-39
Heywood Thomas 30-24
Hichinbotham W-29
Hickerley William 27 lab. I-26
Hickey Dennis 20 farmer-16
Hickey Margaret 28 spinster I-20
Hickey Patrick adult labourer I-27
Hickey Catherine adult I-27
Hickey John 24 I-32
Hickey Bridget 35 servant I-42
Hickman Elias 17 clerk-37
Hickman Thomas B 25-42
Hicks Robert 21 I-10
Hicks Thomas 34-32
Hicks Daniel 20 coach builder-37
Hicks William 30-42
Hicks Bessie 26-42
Hidman William 32-32sy
Higetrave Joel 18 OP-43
Higg Mrs Ann J 33 S-30
Higg Ann J 15 S-30
Higg James C 10 S-30
Higg Mary M 7 S-30
Higg Eliza J 5 S-30
Higgie Miss Margaret 26-24
Higgin Philip 33 miner-11
Higginbotham H K -10
Higgins Joseph-9
Higgins Mrs-9
Higgins Pat 23 labourer I-21

Higney E 52-32
Higson Daniel 20-34
Hilero Robert George 23 lab.S-24
Hilero Elizabeth 25 S-24
Hill John-9
Hill Eliza 23-11
Hill John 34 compositor I-13
Hill Mary 30 I-13
Hill Thomas 2 I-13
Hill Patrick 26 policeman I-16
Hill James 25 labourer-22
Hill Joseph 19-22
Hill Robert 24 labourer-22
Hill John 27 labourer-27
Hill Robert 33 labourer-27
Hill John-29
Hill Joseph 20 labourer I-31
Hill William 37 farmer-31
Hill Eleanor 39-31
Hill William G 13-31
Hill Edward 9-31
Hill Frances 3-31
Hill Henry 68-36
Hill Stephen 45-36
Hill Chris C 23 cattledealer-37
Hill Abner 34-41
Hill Horatio 31-43
Hill Julia 31-43
Hillerman Ms Margaretha 22 OP-30
Hillier Stephen Y 44-36
Hilton John 26 labourer-32
Hilton Edward 52 timekeeper-42sy
Hilton William baker-42sy
Hilton Mary Ann 48-42sy
Hinderman G 48 OP-41
Hinderman Mrs 48 OP-41
Hinderman William 18 OP-41
Hindle Robert 34 I-35
Hindle William 34 labourer I-35
Hindle John 14 I-35
Hindley Jno 39 labourer-23
Hindley Mary 42-23
Hindley Jno 8-23
Hindmarch William 27 miner-27
Hindmarsh William 31 miner-37
Hindmarsh Margaret 27-37
Hindmarsh Sarah 3-37
Hindmarsh Thomas 1-37
Hinds John J 29-13
Hines Ann 31-11
Hingeton Thomas 22 S-32
Hinne Henry 19 farmer-16
Hinson Mr-9
Hinson Mrs (& infant)-9
Hinvert C 22 farmer S-39
Hirst William 27-43
Histone James 31-28
Hitchen John H 46 miner-39
Hitchox William-11
Hitchox Anne-11
Hitchox Henry-11
Hitchox Virtuous-11

Hitchox Elizabeth-11
Hitchox infant-11
Hobday Harriet 10-29
Hoben Eliza 25 dressmaker-37
Hobley W -9
Hobson Sara J 23 spinster-29
Hobson Robert J 20 clerk-35
Hockart Eug 22 OP-10sy
Hocking Richard 32 miner-11
Hocking William 23 miner-13
Hocking C 43 spinster S-31
Hocking Albertus 30 S-32
Hocking N H -33
Hocking Phillip 23-39
Hodden Miss Ann E 19 I-24
Hodding Mary 38 widow-13
Hodding Mary Agnes 14-13
Hodding Henry 12-13
Hodding Kate 11-13
Hodge Ann 36 spinster-28
Hodge Owen 8 I-29
Hodgells Joseph H-9
Hodgells Thomas-9
Hodgetts Mr-9
Hodgetts Mrs-9
Hodgins Eliza 24 spinster-25
Hodgins Ellen 22 spinster-25
Hodgkiss Frank 15 labourer-25
Hodgson Mrs-9
Hodgson William-9
Hodgson Maria spinster-11
Hodgson James 18 labourer-20
Hodgson J E 34-24
Hodgson Ellen 36-24
Hodgson Anthony labourer I-26
Hodgson John E-29
Hodgson Mrs Elizabeth 50-35
Hodgson John-36
Hodgson Thomas 27-36
Hodgson Jane 24-36
Hodgson Mary 21 spinster-38
Hodgson F W 43-39
Hodgson William 41
Hodgson Maria-41
Hodgson Jane 26-42
Hodgson John 22 builder-42
Hogan Mathias 21 labourer I-27
Hogan Thomas 25 labourer S-30
Hogan John 25 farm lab I-31
Hogan John 30 labourer I-32
Hogan Michael 16-35
Hogan Michael 19 I-36
Hogarth Mrs E-9
Hogarth Thomas-9
Hogarth William-9
Hogarth T -22
Hogarth Thomas 20 labourer S-23
Hogarth William 49 miner-35
Hogarth Bohan I-41
Hogg D -9
Hogg Samuel 18 labourer I-21
Hogg R spinster S-31

Hogg Robert 28-33
Hogg Adam 28 labourer-34
Hogg Andrew 27-34
Holah William 24 miner-13
Holan Kate spinster I-37
Holden Isaac 23 miner-27
Holden John B 28 labourer-24
Holden James C 21-24
Holden Mr-34
Holden John 35-41
Holder Michael 43 I-36
Holder Mrs 28 I-36
Holdsworth Wilfred 30 stonemason-16
Holdsworth William 34 labourer-24
Holdsworth Hannah 35-24
Holdsworth James 7-24
Holdsworth William J 3-24
Holdsworth Joseph 2-24
Holdsworth Mary infant-24
Holdsworth Miss Jessie 20 I-35
Holines George 38 shoemaker-31
Holines Elizabeth 37-31
Holines Mary 11-31
Holines Harry 8-31
Holines Catherine 5-31
Holines Amy 2-31
Holland Ann 24 servant-34
Holland Frank 30 farmer-39
Holland Ann-39
Hollander Lewis 32-32
Hollander Hannah 32-32
Hollander John 6-32
Hollander Golda 5-32
Hollander Eva 4-32
Hollander Laura 3-32
Hollander Rachel infant-32
Hollander George R 30 labourer-34
Hollander Jacob 36-35
Hollander Annie 31-35
Hollander Janet 10-35
Hollander Dora 7-35
Hollander Bella 5-35
Hollander Juliet 2-35
Hollander Lewis 1-35
Hollander Flora 1-35
Hollander Abraham 12-35
Hollard Harry 26-40
Hollings William 30 labourer-20
Hollingworth John 33 labourer-33
Holloway Mr-13
Holloway Georgiana-13
Holloway Henry W-13
Holloway James 23 labourer-20
Holloway Benjamin-36
Holman John 46 miner-13
Holman Mary A spinster-34
Holme James-41
Holmes C E -9
Holmes James 21 labourer-25sy
Holmes George H 25-29sy
Holmes Margaret I-32
Holmes M 52-34

Holmes Ann 50-34
Holmes John 24 bricklayer-43ot
Holt G D -9
Holt William 40 labourer-11
Holt Thomas 24 labourer-20
Holt Ann 20-20
Holt (infant)-20
Holt William 58-28
Holt Jane 54-28
Holt Margaret 20-28
Holt William 18-28
Holt Margaret 2-28
Holt Martha 22-39
Holt J G 33 traveller-42
Holt Eliza 24-42
Holtz Isidor J 23 labourer-28
Home J -9
Honey Thirza P 26 spinster-16sy
Honig Ernestine 36 OP-29
Honrege Richard 46 I-41
Hood Adam 21 labourer-25
Hood Mary 18 spinster-25
Hookway Georgina-9
Hoole William 25 labourer-21
Hooper John labourer-26
Hooper Jane 18 spinster-27
Hooper Grace 32-33
Hooper Frederick 11-33
Hooper Richard 10-33
Hooper Hagar 7-33
Hooper Thomas 13-33
Hoopman Heinrich 21 lab. OP-27
Hoopman Miss Henriette 14 OP-27
Hope D J -9
Hope Mrs Elizabeth 26-16
Hope John 5 S-35
Hope Christina 62 S-35
Hope Charles-40
Hopkin James 25 labourer-23
Hopkins T B 27 farmer-10
Hopkins W H 20 brushmaker-10
Hopkins John-22
Hopkins Mr 29-24
Hopkins Mrs 29-24
Hopkins Morgan 15 labourer S-24
Hopkinson Samuel 30 labourer-27
Hore Joseph 30 I-35
Horgan Eliza 27 spinster-25
Horle S D 23-10
Horlock C J 19 draper-34
Horlock Henry 27-36
Horlock Sarah 29-36
Horn Mr-42
Horne James 23 baker-27
Horner Robert 16 labourer I-21
Hornigi Richard 46 OP-41
Horsefall Frances 40 spinster-34
Horsfall James-9ca
Horster A merchant-39
Horswill William Henry30 lab.S-31
Horton William 35 farmer-13
Horvell Noah 22 farmer-20

Horwood George-9
Hosken George 19 miner-13sy
Hoskin Richard 20 miner-16
Hoskin John 20 I-35
Hosking George junior-9
Hosking George senior-9
Hosking W 28 miner-10
Hosking W 45 engineer-10sy
Hosking James 41 miner-11
Hosking John 21 labourer-23
Hosking Mrs Jane 41-26
Hosking Rebecca 53-27
Hosking Mary Ann 21-27
Hosking Emma R 19-27
Hosking Elizabeth W 17-27
Hosking Jane Ann 14-27
Hosking James John 12-27
Hosking Richard 20 labourer-30
Hosking G T 29 I-32
Hosking William 33 farmer-39
Hosking Ellen 20-39
Hoskings William 55 miner-11
Hoskings John 20-11
Hoskings James 21 labourer-22
Hoskings Thomas 21 labourer-22
Hossack A G 40 labourer S-30
Hosser John S C 23 farmer-21
Hosworthy Stephen 40-36
Hotty Giovanni 10 OP-36
Hough Thomas 21 labourer-23
Hough Sydney 48 merchant-40
Houlton Henry 30-35
Hounsley Robert 23 labourer-20
Hourden James-22
House Samuel-23
House Mrs-23
House H M -23
House A M -23
Housley Mrs Dinah 35-23
Housley Mary J 8-23
Houston John-36
Howard Mary spinster S-31
Howard Bridget 21 spinster-37
Howard Robert 46 engineer-38
Howard Isabella 45-38
Howard William 21 stoker-38
Howard Elizabeth E 15-38
Howard Theodore 13-38
Howard Isabella 10-38
Howard Thomas 7-38
Howard Robert 5-38
Howard John 3-38
Howden Thomas 22 grocer-41
Howdon Cyril G-23
Howe George 35-29
Howell John-9
Howell Sophia 41-13
Howell Walter C 19-29
Howell Edward 28 I-32
Howell William 29 labourer-38
Howils Melissa 20-27
Howiton Louis 27 labourer S-32

Howlett Robert 40-29
Howlett Mrs 35-29
Hoyan Miss Eliza 28-24
Hoyans Joseph 21 farmer I-10
Hoyans Edmund 18 I-10
Hoyle John 36 workman-38
Huber G 30 workman I-40
Huddart James 14 labourer-20
Hudson J -9
Hudson B adult-10
Hudson Thomas 19 chemist-16
Hudson Maria-21
Hudspeth Joseph 24 miner-13
Hugh Mrs Gwenllian 34 S-21
Hugh Jenkin 14 S-21
Hugh Edward 12 S-21
Hugh Robert 9 S-21
Hugh Rees 6 S-21
Hugh Thomas 4 S-21
Hughes Frederick K 30 miner-13
Hughes Sarah-9
Hughes H 28 labourer-10
Hughes George 21 grocer-16
Hughes John 30 labourer-20
Hughes Margaret 35 labourer-20
Hughes Eleanor 11-20
Hughes John 9-20
Hughes June 7-20
Hughes Sarah 5-20
Hughes Jane 19 spinster-22
Hughes Patrick 25 labourer I-24
Hughes Thomas 31 labourer-24
Hughes David 24-24
Hughes Francis-26
Hughes I Hyle-26
Hughes Adam-26
Hughes Edward 35 merchant-27
Hughes Isaac 55 labourer-27
Hughes William 42 labourer-29
Hughes Edwina 39-29
Hughes William 5-29
Hughes Ellen 2-29
Hughes Emma infant-29
Hughes Mary 24 spinster-30
Hughes David 36 labourer I-31
Hughes Margaret 30 I-31
Hughes William Edward 3 I-31
Hughes William 32 labourer S-31
Hughes Jane-33
Hughes Jane 23 spinster-33
Hughes James 21 medical student-34
Hughes W A 54 labourer-35
Hughes Catherine 52-35
Hughes Ellen 23 servant-38
Hughes Thomas Isodore 23-41
Hughes William 36-41
Hughes Hannah 28-41
Hughes Patrick 14-41
Hughes Annie 11-41
Hughes William 8-41
Hughes Charles 5-41
Hughes Nathaniel 3-41

Hughes Alfred 23–42
Hughes George P 40–42
Hughes Charles P 13–42
Hughes Thomas miner–42
Hughes Thomas 45–43
Hughes Elizabeth 44–43
Hughes Lucy 22–43
Hughes Mary E 17–43
Hughes George J infant–43
Hull Joshua 26–23
Hulme William 32–28
Hume David 48 miner–13
Hume Robert 24 miner–13
Humpage E –9
Humphreys Mrs–9
Humphreys Thomas–9
Humphreys John 35 labourer–20
Humphreys Ann 34–20
Humphries Thomas 25 labourer–23
Humphries Ann 22 spinster–23
Humphries Deborah 20–23
Humphreys Edward 28 S–24
Humphreys Mrs Margaret 45–24
Humphreys Frederick 7–24
Humphreys William E 23 clerk S–27
Hunard Tim 25 labourer I–40
Hunt C J –9
Hunt Fitzmaurice 27 labourer I–20
Hunt William 28 labourer–26
Hunt William Vere labourer I–31
Hunt William 17 farmer–34
Hunt William 30 labourer–34
Hunt John William 29–41
Hunter James–11
Hunter Benjamin 39 tradesman–13
Hunter Margaret 35–13
Hunter George 11–13
Hunter Margaret 8–13
Hunter William 43 labourer–22
Hunter H S labourer S–30
Hunter William 40 labourer S–30
Hunter Ellen 30 S–30
Hunter Francis 5 S–30
Hunter Patrick 3 S–30
Hunter John infant S–30
Hunter William 25 labourer–31
Hunter Arthur M 46 S–32
Hunter Joseph B 25 labourer S–32
Hunter Mr 16 labourer I–40
Hunter Robert 17–40
Hunter William 36–43
Hurley Maria 21 spinster I–40
Hurley James 22 farmer I–40
Hurren Joseph 37 labourer–28
Hurst J 20 spinster–11
Hurst William–22
Hurst Charles–31
Hurst Mrs–31
Hurst Mary Ann 6–31
Hurst William Henry 24–34
Hurst Charles 32 printer I–35
Hurst Thomas 30 draper–40

Hurst Thomas 28–41
Husband I F 7 I–26
Husband Mary 55–37
Hussey Robert–22
Hussey Edward 30 stonemason–32
Hussey Ellen 30–32
Hussey Celia 13–32
Hussey Catherine E 9–32
Hussey Mary A 5–32
Hussey Margaret 2–32
Hussey Richard E infant–32
Husson Bridget 21 I–42
Huston William 18–41
Hutchings James–9
Hutchings James 21 labourer–20
Hutchins A 22 spinster–27
Hutchins Euphenia 56 spinster–27
Hutchinson T 17–10
Hutchinson Joseph 11–27
Hutchinson John G 22 labourer–33
Hutchinson David 31–35
Hutchinson Elizabeth 30–35
Hutchinson Marguerite 3–35
Hutchinson David 1–35
Hutchison Benjamin 19 labourer–35
Hutchison Hannah 16–35
Huthnance John 35 miner–13
Huttner Marcus 19 I–29
Hutton William 43 labourer–13
Hutton John 24 joiner–20
Hyde Timothy 25 farmer I–39
Hyde Denis 35–41
Hyde Ellen 30–41
Hyde John 13–41
Hyde James 9–41
Hyde Michael 2–41
Hyelop Robert 24 blacksmith S–31
Hyman Mrs E 24–33
Hyman Hannah 1 (died 6/4)–33
Hyman Joseph 31–33
Hyman Solomon 4–33
Hynes Michael 23 labourer–25
Hynes Peter 19 labourer I–30

I

Ibbotson T J 21–42ot
Ibin John 21 farmer–38
Ibin Robert 19–38
Ibsen Albert 20 OP–36
Iddison Roger–21
Impey Charles 19–41
Inge G –9
Ingham Thomas 22 labourer–32
Inghang William 26–43
Inglis Rev J–23
Inglis Mrs Jessie–23
Inverity David 55 shoemaker S–37
Inverity Jane 49 S–37
Inverity James 29 S–37
Inverity David 23 S–37
Inverity Elizabeth 16 S–37
Inverity William 14 S–37

Inverity Mary Ann 11 S–37
Inverity Sarah 8 S–37
Iounas Albert 22 merchant OP–16
Ireland Barton–23
Iron W J 21 farmer I–40
Irvine William 20 labourer I–22
Irvine Samuel 19 labourer–25
Irvine Richard 24 labourer I–31
Irvine Patrick I–36
Irvine Fanny–42
Irving George W 34–25
Irving Mrs Ellen 30–30
Irving James J 6–30
Irving Margaret 34 spinster–30
Irving W B clergyman–37
Irving Thomas–43du
Irwin Miles 28 labourer–22
Irwin James 16 I–32
Isaac Solomon 40–35
Isaac Sarah 34–35
Isaacs I 50 watchmaker–10sy
Isaacs Miss Sarah 27 I–24
Isaacs John 48–42
Isaacs Sarah 51–42
Isaacs Elizabeth 22–42
Isele Charles 17 clerk OP–41br
Ivey James 20 carpenter–11

J

Jack Richard 41 miner–13
Jack Thomas 34 miner–13
Jack Samuel 19 miner–13
Jack William 12 miner–13
Jack Samuel 26 labourer–23
Jack Andrew 31 labourer S–24
Jack Archibald H 30–27
Jack Margaret–36
Jacka John 23–42
Jackson Mrs Elizabeth 24–13
Jackson James D 25 miller I–13
Jackson William 24 miller I–13
Jackson Abraham 45 labourer I–20
Jackson Miss Elizabeth 30–24
Jackson George 25 labourer–24sy
Jackson John 29–24
Jackson William 38–24
Jackson James 26 labourer–27
Jackson Lucy 23–27
Jackson Frank infant–27
Jackson Robert 20 labourer–27
Jackson Joseph 29–28
Jackson Thomas 40 labourer–30
Jackson Thomas 20 stonemason–31
Jackson Henry 17–36
Jackson Eliza 35 spinster–38
Jackson Joseph 21 clerk–40
Jackson William 51–40
Jackson George 37 farmer–41
Jackson Samuel 56–42
Jackson Ellen 50–42
Jackson Thomas 21–42
Jacob Miss 18 spinster–22

Jacoboolm Julius 20 clerk OP–42
Jacobs Samuel 31 clerk–13
Jacobs A W 20 labourer OP–24
Jacobsen Mathias 27–36
Jacobson Jacob E 20 labourer–25
Jafessen Heinrich 37 lab. OP–22
Jafessen Belli 26 OP–22
Jago John H 17 labourer I–20
James H –9
James Daniel 21 smith–10
James R 24 accountant–10
James Louisa 24–10
James Edmund 25 engine driver–11
James Mary 23–11
James Elizabeth spinster–11
James M Jane spinster–11
James Mrs Lydia 35–23
James Martha 7–23
James John 28–23
James Mary 28–23
James Martha 9–23
James David 5–23
James Jonathan 21 labourer S–24
James Elizabeth 21 S–24
James Simondo S 16 labourer–27
James William 28–28
James John 40 labourer S–31
James Margaret 38 S–31
James Samuel 13 S–31
James Bessy 11 S–31
James John 6 S–31
James Charles 3 S–31
James infant S–31
James Robert 24 I–35
James Alfred J 24 accountant–37
James Charles 21 surveyor–37
James Henry S 55 brayier–39
James Ann A 52–39
James Arthur G 18–39
James John 16–39
James Thomas 38 seaman–39
James Margaret 38–39
James William adult–40
James Mrs adult–40
Jameson Mrs Margaret 47 S–21
Jameson D R I–36
Jameson Charles 19 S–39
Jamieson John 25 S–11
Jamieson Nathaniel–11
Jamieson Sarah–11
Jamieson Leslie 21 labourer S–21
Jamieson John 15 labourer S–27
Jamieson Miss Elizabeth 30 S–29
Jamieson Francis 33 labourer S–30
Jamieson Annie 24 S–30
Jamieson Francis 3 S–30
Jamisen Thomas 22 labourer–24
Jamisen Henry 28–24
Janneron Franz OP–39
Janneron Helene OP–39
Janing Chatrina 17 servant OP–38
Jardine Thomas–9

Jardine John 35 labourer–26
Jardine Jane 34–26
Jardine John 5–26
Jarman Anne 30 spinster–34
Jarrett Sean 32 OP–35
Jarsey William 34 labourer–32
Jarsey Elizabeth 40–32
Jecham Hector 29 labourer OP–26
Jeffares Albert 22 labourer S–36
Jefferson Sarah 34 I–20
Jefferson Elizabeth 11 I–20
Jefferson Robert 9 I–20
Jefferson Ann 6 I–20
Jefferson Mrs Elizabeth 33–23
Jefferson Anne 10–23
Jefferson Harry 6–23
Jeffery Mr junior–9
Jeffery Mr senior–9
Jeffrey N 31–10sy
Jeffrey R 18–10sy
Jeffrey Lavinia–11
Jeffrey infant–11
Jeffrey William 49 mine agent–11
Jeffrey Bessey 9–16
Jeffrey John H 31 miner S–27
Jeffrey Mrs Nanny 60–41
Jelper Margaret 32 spinster S–34
Jelper Margaret 18–34
Jenkin Alfred S–43
Jenkin Mrs S–43
Jenkins E –9
Jenkins John–9
Jenkins Joseph–9
Jenkins Mary–9
Jenkins John labourer I–21
Jenkins Elizabeth I–21
Jenkins Mrs Margaret 38–23
Jenkins William 13 (died 7/2)–23
Jenkins Ann 8–23
Jenkins Mary 6–23
Jenkins George 23 labourer–25
Jenkins Morgan 21–28
Jenkins Rees 26–28
Jenkins Mary 24–28
Jenkins Robert 2–28
Jenkins William D 25–29
Jenkins David 27–33
Jenkins George 21 draper–37
Jenkins William 21 miner–38
Jenner Frederick–21
Jennings Benjamin 36 miner–11
Jennings Mrs J 35–35
Jennings Eliza 9–35
Jensen Jorgen 39 OP–41
Jentalm Rev H –27
Jep Richard 23–35
Jerret William 55–12sy
Jerret Miss Charlotte 25–23sy
Jerret Mary 18–23sy
Jervis James 53 farmer–13
Jervis Ann 51–13
Jervis Caroline 24–13

Jervis Elizabeth 15–13
Jervis William 14–13
Jervis Lucretia 12–13
Jervis John C 42–27
Jervis Miss 24–27
Jervis Frederick P 8–27
Jervis Anthony 20 I–32
Jessop Samuel 28–41ho
Jeune J –9
Jewell Joseph 31–10sy
Jiggiman Adolph–41
Jobe Thomas 27 miner–11
Johill Briget 17 spinster–16
John Casey 22 I–42
Johns Joseph 34 labourer–21
Johns Henry 19–32
Johns Thomas 32–33
Johns Phillip–42
Johns Phillip jun–42
Johnson D –9
Johnson Andrew 23 OP–10
Johnson C J 25 merchant–10sy
Johnson George 32 smith–10
Johnson Ann 32–10
Johnson Albert–10
Johnson S 36–10
Johnson W 25–10
Johnson Antony 23 miner–11
Johnson Elizabeth 20–11
Johnson James–11
Johnson Mrs–11
Johnson John 43 labourer–13
Johnson Mary 38–13
Johnson Thomas 10–13
Johnson Mary 6–13
Johnson Sarah 4–13
Johnson James E–16
Johnson Mrs–16
Johnson William 20 labourer–23
Johnson Frederick 19–28
Johnson George 37–28
Johnson Mark 25 labourer–28
Johnson Mrs 46–33
Johnson Mrs E G–34
Johnson M 32–34
Johnson James 3–34
Johnson James 23–35
Johnson Betsy 22–35
Johnson Margaret infant–35
Johnson Samuel 52–36
Johnson Eliza 52–36
Johnson Annie 26–36
Johnson Charlotte 21–36
Johnson Richard 20–36
Johnson Samuel 13–36
Johnson Joseph 44 chemist–40
Johnson William Henry 30–42
Johnston John–9
Johnston Mr 20 farmer–16
Johnston John 19 labourer I–21
Johnston John L 21 labourer I–21
Johnston Samuel 23 labourer I–21

Johnston William 55 farmer–21
Johnston Isabella 50–21
Johnston Henry 15–21
Johnston Mary Ann 12–21
Johnston Samuel 23 labourer I–22
Johnston Sarah 38 spinster–22
Johnston Isabella 22 spinster–33
Johnston Kate 20–33
Johnston Samuel 20–33
Johnston Jacob 26–35
Johnstone Daniel 35 labourer I–20
Johnstone Mary 25–20
Johnstone Anne I–20
Johnstone James 24 labourer–33
Johnstone Thomas A 34–33
Johnstone J 28 farmer I–37
Johnstone Samuel 19 servant I–37
Johnstone Arthur 19 S–38
Johnstone George 24 S–38
Johnstone Daniel 42 S–43
Johnthribhurst Albert adult–40
Jones James–9
Jones Robert–9
Jones Robert–9
Jones Robert–9
Jones John 23 sawyer–10sy
Jones George 41 carpenter–11
Jones Morgan 25 labourer–11
Jones Daniel 37 land agent–13
Jones John 19 farmer–13
Jones Richard 27 farmer–13
Jones William 28 miner–13
Jones William 35 farmer–13
Jones Catherine 34–13
Jones Miss 20–20
Jones Mrs Janet 28–21
Jones Morgan 9–21
Jones Mary Ann 6–21
Jones Catherine 4–21
Jones Miss Mary 24–21
Jones Edwin 17 labourer–22
Jones Miss Sarah 29–22
Jones Edward 53 labourer–23
Jones Tamat 53–23
Jones Sarah 24–23
Jones Frances 18–23
Jones Mary 13–23
Jones Thomas 12–23
Jones Mr–23
Jones David 24 labourer S–24
Jones Jane 22 S–24
Jones David 43–24
Jones Henry 32 labourer S–24
Jones May 38 S–24
Jones Jane 20 servant–24
Jones Edmond 22 labourer–25
Jones Henry 20 labourer–25
Jones Alfred H 18 labourer–25
Jones John 20 labourer–26
Jones Martha Anne 25 spinster–27
Jones Catherine 47–28
Jones Thomas 23–28

Jones Elizabeth 20–28
Jones David 18–28
Jones Margaret 13–28
Jones John 8–28
Jones Margaret 30 servant–28
Jones Patrick 20 I–28
Jones Robert 30–28
Jones Marian 34–28
Jones Mary 8–28
Jones Thomas 4–28
Jones David 21–29
Jones Evan 54–29
Jones Titus 41–29
Jones Margaret 15 spinster–29
Jones Ellen 31 spinster–29
Jones Edward 18 I–32
Jones Henry J 25 labourer–32
Jones John 18 labourer–32
Jones Benjamin 16–32
Jones Rachel 20 I–32
Jones Richard 29 labourer S–32
Jones E spinster–33
Jones Evan 40–33
Jones D 35–33
Jones James 28–33
Jones Mrs Mary 36–33
Jones Harriet 1–33
Jones Eliza 9–33
Jones Mary 42 spinster–33
Jones W J 45 labourer–33
Jones William 33–33
Jones Isaac 20–34
Jones John 47–34
Jones Sarah 50–34
Jones Sarah 9–34
Jones David 7–34
Jones Elizabeth 6–34
Jones Thomas 13–34
Jones Robert 36–34
Jones Marian 28–34
Jones George L 45 S–35
Jones Ann 40 S–35
Jones William 23–35
Jones Richard 48 I–36
Jones Fanny 40 I–36
Jones Fanny 13 I–36
Jones John Henry 11 I–36
Jones Richard 15 I–36
Jones Robert 26–36
Jones Rowland 32–36
Jones Ellen 32–36
Jones Jane J 4–36
Jones George R 2–36
Jones Edwin M infant–36
Jones Thomas 30 miner–37
Jones David 20–37
Jones William 44 stationer–37
Jones Llewellyn 40 miner–38
Jones Mary 56–39sy
Jones W A 22 I–40
Jones William 34–41
Jones William 18–41

Jones David 28–42
Jones Jane 32–42
Jones Arthur 11–42
Jones James E 10–42
Jones Zacaias 7–42
Jones Florence 5–42
Jones Edith infant–42
Jones Hugh miner–42
Jones Elizabeth 51–43
Jones Robert 19 carver–43
Jope Samuel 18–27
Jope Henry 14–27
Jordan Sarah 49 widow–13
Jordan Robert 31–13
Jordan Archibald J 22 labourer–32
Jordan Michael 27 labourer I–42sy
Jordan Catherine 26–42
Jordenson Harry 28 OP–36
Joseph J –9
Joseph Henry 26 miner–13
Joseph John 30 labourer–21
Joseph Margaret 27–21
Joseph Joseph 6–21
Joseph Leah 18–21
Joseph Mrs Amelia 27–35
Joseph Sophia 4–35
Joseph Miss E 25–35
Joshua John 26–28
Joske Paul–30
Joske Mrs–30
Joske A 6 OP–32
Joske Margaret 3 OP–32
Joung Fenwick 37 labourer S–31
Jowett Benjamin 34 labourer–20
Jowett John 7–20
Joy Maurice 22 labourer I–23
Joyce John 26 labourer I–31
Judge James 33 labourer–30
Judson Samuel 28copperworker–10sy
Judson Sarah 24–10sy
Jugpen Thomas L 18 labourer I–26
Junion James 18 labourer I–31
Jupori Gesto 14 OP–38
Jury James 25 labourer–24
Juryman John 22–13sy
Justins T A 26–43

K

K– Michael 22 S–34
Kadori Giovanni OP–38
Kane Elizabeth 33–11
Kane Elizabeth 7–11
Kane John 3–11
Kane Margaret 4–11
Kane John 20 labourer I–27
Kane Robert–42
Karton Thomas 27 miner–11
Kasker Samuel 26 I–35
Kasston Christian 23 OP–23
Katefield Theodore 31 lab. OP–30
Kavanagh Rev Michael–23
Kavanagh Daniel 30 I–34

Kavanagh Margaret 29 I-34
Kavanagh Mary 5 I-34
Kavanagh Hannah 4 I-34
Kavanagh Catherine 3 I-34
Kavanagh Arthur 1 I-34
Kavanagh Mrs 27 I-43
Kay Mary 35-16
Kay Elizabeth 17-16
Kay Jane 11-16
Kay Mary 8-16
Kay Robert Scott 6-16
Kay Rev D -23
Kay Mrs-23
Kay John 26 labourer-25
Kay John 25 labourer-30
Kean Kate 23 spinster I-27
Keane Michael 30 labourer-25
Keane Margaret 30-25
Keane James 26 labourer I-27
Keane Christian 23 labourer I-27
Keane Christopher 28-41
Keanes James 22 I-42
Kearney Edward 42 labourer-26
Kearney Mary Ann 22 spinster-26
Kearney William 5-26
Kearney William 46 labourer I-26
Kearns Hugh 42 I-33
Kearns Ellen 37 I-33
Kearns Henry 13 I-33
Kearns Ellen 6 I-33
Kearns Patrick 17 I-33
Kearton C -9
Keating Michael 33 labourer I-21
Keddle Mr 20-26
Keefe Thomas 32 clerk-11
Keefe M 12 I-38
Keegan Catherine-10
Keenan Bridget 19 I-43
Keene Daniel 22 farmer I-16
Keene Adelaide 26 I-38
Keene James 42-41
Keene Elizabeth 36-41
Keep Mrs-28
Keep Frederick 7-28
Keep Ernest 5-28
Keep Margaret 5-28
Keep infant-28
Keet Michael H labourer-25
Keeton Barnard 32-34
Keifer Catherine 20 OP-41
Keig Charles T 24 mechanic-42
Keighley John 22 joiner-13
Keighley John 30 miner-37
Keily Thomas 40 farmer I-37
Keily Johanna 45 I-37
Keily Charles 17 I-37
Keily Mary 14 I-37
Keily Thomas 6 I-37
Kell Robert 15-35
Keller Patrick 32 labourer I-30
Kelly E 25 I-10
Kelly John 30 labourer S-13

Kelly Alexander 26 labourer S-13
Kelly Patrick 27 labourer-13
Kelly Thomas 49 miner-13sy
Kelly Margaret 52-13
Kelly John S 20 miner-13
Kelly Daniel 17 labourer-16
Kelly Francis 21 labourer-23
Kelly Pat 28 labourer I-24
Kelly Ellen 25 I-24
Kelly Pat infant I-24
Kelly Alexander 29 labourer I-26
Kelly James 32 labourer I-26
Kelly Miss M 20-26
Kelly Robert 63 labourer-26
Kelly William 21 labourer I-26
Kelly Rev M -27
Kelly Jonathan 19 I-28
Kelly Martin 20 labourer I-30
Kelly Matthew 16 draper I-32
Kelly Robert Hy 30 S-33
Kelly Margaret 20 S-33
Kelly George 50-34
Kelly M -34
Kelly John 21 I-34
Kelly John 10 I-35
Kelly John 30 labourer-35
Kelly Gertrude 30-35
Kelly Phillip 19 I-35
Kelly Patrick 24-36
Kelly Ann 23-36
Kelly James infant-36
Kelly Sarah 11 I-36
Kelly Thomas 9 I-36
Kelly Julia 8 I-36
Kelly William 26-36
Kelly Mrs Bridget 20 I-37
Kelly James 30 I-37
Kelly Rosa 41 spinster-38
Kelly Thomas 20-40
Kelly Caesar 16-40
Kelly Patrick 26-41
Kelly Robert 17-41
Kelly James 29 I-42
Kemp John 38 labourer I-31
Kendall James 35-10
Kendall Hanna 25-10
Kendall Wm 21 machinist-10me
Keneally Thomas 25-41
Kennaly John 20 I-32
Kennedy James-9
Kennedy Thomas 37 miner-11
Kennedy James 25 labourer I-13
Kennedy Edmund 23 labourer I-13
Kennedy Mrs B 25-20
Kennedy Patrick 4-20
Kennedy Ellen 24 spinster-20
Kennedy William 21 labourer-24
Kennedy Jeremiah 23 lab.-25
Kennedy William 22 labourer-27
Kennedy Alex 46 labourer S-29
Kennedy Francis 28 baker I-32
Kennedy Sarah 35 spinster-32

Kennedy Angus 32-36
Kennedy Catherine 33 (d.17/10)-36
(died of gastric fever)
Kennedy Flora A 6-36
Kennedy Malcolm 4-36
Kennedy Peter 1-36
Kennedy David I-39
Kennedy James 40 miner-39
Kennedy Robert 19-41
Kenningley James 28-35
Kenningley Mary A 26-35
Kenningley Elizabeth 5-35
Kennish William 30-38
Kenny Michael 19 I-32
Kent Thomas 20 labourer-34
Kenwick William B 19-38
Kenworthy Robert 26-42
Kenworthy Elizabeth 22-42
Kenyon Miss Mary 25-21
Keohan Michael 20 labourer I-16
Keohan Thomas 27 farmer I-38
Kerman Ann 35 spinster-20
Kermeen George 30 labourer-27
Kermode Nathaniel A 21-41
Kerns Ellen 23 spinster I-40
Kerr Eliza 40 spinster-25
Kerr Thomas 22 labourer I-26
Kerr John 55 labourer S-27
Kerr Isabella 25-42
Kerr James 4-42
Kerrigan Rodger 17 labourer I-24
Kerrigan Ellen 30-43
Kershaw James 39-43
Kerwan John 26 labourer-26
Kess Karl 24 OP-43
Kessack Agnold 17-38
Kesterson William-21
Kewish Mrs Jane 35-36
Kewish Catherine J 3-36
Khull M 22 spinster-34
Kick W -34
Kick Mrs-34
Kick William 9-34
Kick John 7-34
Kidd Alex 39-29
Kidd Alex 11-29
Kidd Jane 20 spinster-29
Kidd John 39 engineer-41
Kidd Sarah 37-41
Kidney William-11
Kiely Mrs Catherine 50 I-21
Kiely Catherine 11 I-21
Kiely Joanna 9 I-21
Kiernan Philip 20 labourer-13
Kierney Michael 20 I-36
Kilgore William 30 I-36
Killen Robert 22 I-35
Killey Miss Isabella A 19 S-35
Kilpatrick John 50 labourer S-21
Kilpatrick Ellen 52 S-21
Kilpatrick William John 16 S-21
Kilpatrick Jane 20 spinster I-22

Kilpatrick George 55-42
Kilpatrick Jane 50-42
Kilpatrick Cassie 20-42
Kilpatrick Thomas 35-42
Kilpatrick Esther 36-42
Kilpatrick Thomas J 11-42
Kilpatrick William James 10-42
Kilpatrick Eliza Jane 8-42
Kilpatrick George 6-42
Kilpatrick Mathew infant-42
Kilroy Martin 25 labourer I-26
Kilyenger George 50 labourer I-26
Kinahane Joseph B 21-10
Kinaston Henry 42 draper-39
Kincaird Robert 25 policeman I-16
Kinder Wm. Dastyard 24 farmer-11
Kindred Jonathan 38 labourer-24
Kindred Sarah 37-24
Kindred Nicholas 29-24
King William H 21 draper-16
King Jonathan 21 labourer I-24
King Minnie 30 servant-28
King Hannah 28 spinster-30
King Benjamin 19-40
King Nicholas 57-42
Kingscote W -9
Kingston James 66 tailor-32
Kinicky William 26 miner-34
Kinna Bernard M 20 labourer-16
Kinniff Phillip 23 labourer-35
Kinnovan Michael labourer-23
Kinsella James 46 labourer-24
Kinsella Catherine 43-24
Kinsella Margaret 17-24
Kinsella Mary 19-24
Kinsella Elizabeth 14-24
Kinsella Ann 11-24
Kinsella James 10-24
Kinsella James 8-24
Kinsch J C W -34
Kinsman Joshua 25 mason-11
Kinsman William 20-11
Kinvig Richard 32-42
Kirby Ann 20 spinster I-22
Kirby Bridget 19 spinster I-22
Kirby Daniel 28 labourer I-24
Kirk Ebenezer 25 S-24
Kirk James 19 labourer I-27
Kirk John 35 merchant S-37
Kirk Janet 25 S-37
Kirkbridge William 33 labourer-31
Kirkham G A 20-42
Kirkland John 35-41
Kirkness James 19 labourer-27
Kirsh George adult OP-40
Kirwan John-9
Kissack James 17 labourer-26
Kitchin R -9
Kitching Guy 22-34
Kite Clara E 15 spinster-34
Kite Alice 14-34
Kite Charlotte E 16-34

Kite John 20-34
Kite John 45-34
Kite Maria 44-34
Kite Samuel 11-34
Kite Walter 9-34
Kitt Thomas Henry 25 labourer-32
Kitto Mrs Kate-37
Kitto Frederick 10-37
Kitto Helen 8-37
Kitto Ernest V 1-37
Klingender Edward 15 OP-36
Knapp Henry 29-34
Knapp C A 25-37
Kneebone Henry 28 miner-11
Kneebone Joshua 36 miner-11
Kneebone John 32-11
Kneebone Thomas 36-11
Kneebone Mary Ann 36-11
Kneebone Elizabeth 28-11
Kneebone Mary 7-11
Kneebone William 33 miner-11
Kneebone William 13-11
Knight Walter-9
Knight Mrs-22
Knight A H 38-24
Knight Mrs 39-24
Knight Charles 22 draper I-35
Knight Elizabeth 28-40sy
Knight David 37 traveller-42
Knott James 40 labourer-23
Knott James Robert 22-36
Knott Philip 34-41
Knott Mary 27-41
Knott Henry 8-41
Knott Albert 5-41
Knott Elizabeth 2-41
Knowles John-29
Knowles S Copley 26 spinner-37
Knox Andrew 20-29
Knox Robert 16-34
Knox William 20-34
Knox John 18-41
Knuckey Thomas 27 miner-13
Knuckey Nicholas 30 miner-13
Knuckey Oliver 26 miner-13
Knuckey Nicholas 11-13
Koch William 20 OP-38
Koen John 25 I-33
Kohl Peter 45 labourer OP-29
Kolen Aaron 23 OP-43
Kolteman P M 30 labourer OP-30
Korzelinski J -9
Koster Henry 22 farmer OP-13
Kosterlitz Lewis 27 lab. OP-24
Kowalski Marcus 18 clerk OP-38
Kracke Anton OP-42
Kravbetter Sebastian 46 OP-38sy
Kroez Johannes 23 labourer OP-31
Krolm Henrich 19 labourer OP-26
Kronfeld Rosalie OP-38
Kuoto Reinholt 36 labourer OP-30
Kurtry Andrew-39

L

Labb Jonathan 25-24
Labner Thomas 24 coaler-10
Lacey William 30 I-28
Lacey John 28 I-31
Lack John 50 labourer-23
Lack Mary 50-23
Laddams P -9
Lagard Ernest 34 labourer-30
Laidland Mrs E 46-22
Laidland Edwin 18-22
Laidland Hannah I 13-22
Laidland Mary E 11-22
Laidland Louisa E 9-22
Lain William 21 miner-11
Laird John 34 boilermaker S-31
Laird Catherine 35 S-31
Laird Charles 9 S-31
Laird John 7 S-31
Laird Abraham 5 S-31
Laird Andrew 3 S-31
Laird Margaret 1 S-31
Laird Mary 14 S-31
Laird E K -39
Laity Mrs Margaret 43-28
Laity William 16-28
Laity Edwin 12-28
Laity William 4-28
Lajar Miss Caroline 27-24
Lake Francis 23 clerk-16
Lake Thomas 67-16
Lake Susan 60-16
Lake Richard 33 musician-16
Lake Emma 34-16
Lake William 42 surgeon-16
Lake Charles 28 labourer-23
Lamachia Andrew 37 OP-32
Lamachia Dominico 5 OP-32
Lamachia Pasquel 10 OP-32
Laman Frederick 21 labourer I-20
Lamb William 21 engineer-21
Lamb Ellen 50 widow-21
Lamb Owen 24 labourer-26
Lamb Alexander 21-41
Lambert John-22
Lambert Mr-27
Lambert William 40 labourer-31
Lambert Mrs Anne 24-33
Lambert Bridget A 1-33
Lambton James 28 carrier-11
Lambton Margaret 60-11
Lamont George 39 labourer I-24
Lamplugh G R 23 labourer-21
Lanacchii A 46 OP-40
Lanacchii Prospero 11 OP-40
Lanacchii Pacquil 10 OP-40
Lanacchii Saverio 9 OP-40
Lanacchii Dominic 8 OP-40
Lancashire Edwin 25-36
Lancaster Joseph 29 machinist-13
Lancaster Henry 38 labourer-24

Lancaster Alfred 21–24
Lance Joseph 53 miner–13
Lance John H 20–36
Lance Charles Edward–40
Lancout John 32 engineer S–40
Lancout Mrs 30 S–40
Landor William 40 farmer S–38
Landregan William 21 labourer–27
Landy Michael 22 labourer I–31
Lane Miss–9
Lane Mr–9
Lane Mrs–9
Lane Thomas–11
Lane John 35 labourer–27
Lane Ann Sellars 21 spinster–27
Lane Hannah 10–27
Lane Joseph 39 labourer–27
Lane Joshua 19–labourer–27
Lane Samuel 42–34
Lane Harriet 44–34
Lanelle Thomas 33 I–35
Lang Thomas R–28
Lang Mrs–28
Lang I R –28
Lang T T –28
Lang Margaret–28
Lang Mary infant–28
Langdon George–22
Langford John 22 I–28
Langford Lizzie 22–28
Langhead William 34 I–40
Langley Charles 36 horsedealer–10
Langley Mary 30 spinster I–20
Langley Bridget 28 matron–25
Langston Frances T 17–37
Langton Mrs W 33–39
Langton William 11–39
Langton Edith 9–39
Lanigan John 25 I–32
Lanigan Thomas 24 I–32
Lantry Ann spinster–25
Lantry Ellen spinster–25
Lanyon William 19 miner–13
Lanyon Susanna 23–13
Lanyon William infant–13
Lapontle Bridget 40 spinster–30
Lapping Albert E 16 labourer I–30
L'Arbalestier J–9
Lara Mary 19 I–28
Laracy Ellen–42
Lardi Poalo 28 OP–28
Larkin Thomas 22 farmer–16
Larkin Alexander 42–34
Larkin James 25–41
Larkin Mary 38 I–42
Larkin Edward 13 I–42
Larmel Alex 21–29
Larritt M A spinster–32
Larselo Borrend 38 OP–40
Larsen J K 27 spinster OP–41
Larson Peter labourer–25
Lassham Albert 22 S–37

Lassham Mrs 22 S–37
Latimer John R 19–41
Laufranchi Luigi 22 OP–28
Laugherty James 23 labourer–32
Laughton James 23 labourer–27
Launder John 22 labourer I–20
Laurie Alfred 17 labourer I–32
Lavender Charles 33 labourer I–31
lavender Julia I–31
Lavers Benjamin 24–16
Law Peter–11
Law June–11
Law James–11
Law Robert–11
Law Joseph 32 labourer S–22
Law Joseph W 36 S–31
Lawes Jane 22 labourer I–31
Lawler James 28 labourer I–35
Lawless J H –9
Lawless C T 50–30
Lawless Mrs 30–30
Lawless Emily Ann infant–30
Lawless John 21–34
Lawless C F 58 I–40
Lawless Mrs H B 35 I–40
Lawless Emily A 6 I–40
Lawley Thomas 23–34
Lawlor James 24 labourer I–23
Lawn James 5 labourer–23
Lawn George 19–23
Lawn Thomas 21–23
Lawray Richard 40–38
Lawray Phillis 25–38
Lawrence Charles–21
Lawrence William–21
Lawrence Mary–21
Lawrence Joseph 47 gardener–31
Lawrence Elizabeth 47–31
Lawrence Joseph 26 S–34
Lawrence Joseph 26 S–34
Lawrence Jane 26 S–34
Lawrence Lovelady J 1 S–34
Lawrence Thomas 60–36
Lawrence A H –42
Lawrence James 50–43
Lawrence Mrs 45–43
Lawrence Maggie 20–43
Lawson M spinster–11
Lawson Robert I–33
(suicide by drowning 3/3)
Lawson Henry 38 butcher–34sy
Lawson Mary 30–34
Lawton John 24 I–37
Lawton Edward 27 mechanic–42
Laycock Peter 22 plumber S–43
Le Maitre F J –9
Leach Cornelius labourer–25
Leachenberg Julia 40–40
Leachenberg Kate 6–40
Leah Alice 40–28
Leah John 6–28
Leah Robert 4–28

Leah James 35–36
Leak William 32–36
Leak Selina 26–36
Leake William 36 joiner–10
Lealey Joseph 22 I–30
Lealy Michael 25 I–35
Leard N B 27 I–10sy
Learoyd Thomas 23 chemist–13
Learoyd Mr–21
Leary Pat 24 labourer I–24
Leary G S 25 warehouseman–37
Leary Stephen 30 I–38
Leathern William J 18–41
Leaver Robert 51 labourer–25
Leche James T 30 labourer S–31
Leder James 26–43
Ledsaff Mr 37 groom–16
Ledson Charles 24–34
Ledwidge John–9
Lee Joseph–9
Lee Richard–9
Lee H 40 porter–10
Lee Matthew 23 farmer I–13
Lee Eliza 42–20
Lee James 11–20
Lee Maria 8–20
Lee Celia 6–20
Lee Hugh 3–20
Lee Charles 22 labourer–21
Lee John 27 labourer–22
Lee Isaac 28 OP–28
Lee H M –29
Lee Peter 34 labourer–30
Lee Elizabeth spinster–37
Lee George 45–37
Lee Esther 38–37
Lee William 24 merchant–41br
Lee John 21–41
Lee William 24–41 (2nd class)
Leech Burton 30–26
Leech John 27 labourer I–31
Leeds Alexander T 21 grocer I–11
Lees Joseph 30 butcher–10
Lees Thomas 36 merchant–13
Lees Fanny 30–13
Lees George 42 butcher–16
Lees John 31 mechanic–40
Lees Mary 30–40
Lees Emma 11–40
Lees Ada 5–40
Lees Anna 1–40
Leesmith J 40–41
Leesmith Mrs M E 28–41
Leet William 24 labourer I–24
Leet Anna Bella 24 I–24
Legard T –9
Legge Charles 19 labourer–27
Legge Alice Ann 18–41ly
Leggs Mrs Joanna 27–21
Leggs Thomas 9–21
Leggs Anna 4–21
Leich George William–31

Leichenstein Bernard 32–43
Leichenstein Mrs G–43
Leichenstein Rachel 12–43
Leichenstein Annie 8–43
Leichenstein Albert 4–43
Leichenstein Bertha 3–43
Leichenstein David 2–43
Leighton D –9
Leill Charles 17–41 (2nd class)
Leith H S J –9
Leith W H –9
Leith James 19–27
Leity William 28 miner–11
Lemande B 20 spinster–27
Lemon Martin 21 I–28
Lennon J –9
Lennon Richard 20 labourer I–22
Lennon Mrs Mary A 40–35
Lennon Selina 5–35
Lennon Harry 1–35
Lennox John 36 labourer S–27
Lennox Jane 36 S–27
Leny John George 24 lab. OP–26
Leonard John 26 labourer–23
Leonard John 19 labourer–25
Leonard Joseph 18 labourer–25
Leonard Nicholas 22 labourer–25
Leonard Pat 22 labourer I–27
Leonoe Isabella 50 spinster–26
Leslie James 19 labourer–25
Leslie Ellen 23 spinster–27
Leslie Ellen adult spinster S–27
Leslie Mrs–28
Leslie William 14–28
Leslie Alexander 12–28
Leslie John 10–28
Leslie Francis 3–28
Leslie W G 22 I–39
Lester Hugh 32 carpenter–39
Lester Sarah 32–39
Leurmoun Henry–34
Levey Herbert B 21 labourer–35
Levick James–20
Levick Herbert–20
Levinson Mark 17 labourer I–24
Levinson Bertha 50 OP–39
Levinson Eva 17 OP–39
Levinson Naliam 15 OP–39
Leviston Daniel 21 labourer–33
Levit Samuel OP–39
Levy B –9
Levy J S –9
Levy Laurence–11
Levy Louis–23
Levy Mrs–23
Levy M –27
Levy Mr–30
Levy Miss Elizabeth 22–32
Lewens George–26
Lewis Henry–9
Lewis J 25 shoemaker–10
Lewis Andrew 13–11

Lewis Louisa spinster–11
Lewis Thomas 37 mason–11
Lewis John R 23 labourer–21
Lewis Thomas 20–21
Lewis Mrs Jane 31–24
Lewis William 24 labourer–24
Lewis E 23 spinster–28
Lewis James 38 miner I–32
Lewis Annie 32 I–32
Lewis Agnes 10 I–32
Lewis William 30–32
Lewis Miss Ann 30–35
Lewis John–36
Lewis Catherine 22 spinster–37
Leycestester G W –35
Leyland John 38 labourer–22
Leyland Jane 34–22
Leyland George 13–22
Leyland James Henry 8–22
Leyland Ellen 1–22
Leyland Alice 3–22
Libbald R G –10
Lickle A 2 OP–10
Liddell Mrs Jane 23–13
Liddell James 22 S–39
Liddicott Richard–29
Liddle John 25 miner–11
Liddle Christopher 24 labourer–22
Liddle Albert E 20 labourer S–23
Liddle Joshua 21 labourer–24
Liddle William 32 miner S–31
Lightfoot Thomas–9
Lightfoot Robert 55–35
Lightfoot Thomas 51–35
Limbrick Joseph 39 S–35
Linder Stephen 23 labourer–36
Lindred Lucy–22
Linnell John 53 labourer–27
Linnell June 53–27
Lintoch Sarah M 23 S–42
Lisle Robert 41 labourer S–22
Lisle Mary 45 S–22
Lister Thomas B–23
Litcher Charlie 44 labourer–24
Little H –9
Little John 23–10
Little William 19–10
Little William 21 I–35
Littleford Samuel 18 lab.–25
Littlejohn D –9
Littlejohn Edward 15–29
Litten A R 20 OP–33
Livall Mrs 60–22
Livers Claus 25 labourer OP–27
Livesey Benjamin–11
Livingstone William 25–41
Llewellyn James–9
Lloyd George 27 labourer–20
Lloyd Samuel 19 labourer–20
Lloyd B S –21
Lloyd Joseph 41 labourer–24
Lloyd Mary 42–24

Lloyd Martha 19–24
Lloyd Charles William 34–29
Lloyd Rachel 22–29
Lloyd infant–29
Lloyd Joseph 23 blacksmith–31
Lloyd James 50–34
Lloyd J H 24–34
Lloyd S spinster–34
Lloyd Margaret 25–39
Lloyd John A–43
Lloyd Mary C 17–43
Loade Mary–16
Loane Mary 13 spinster I–28
Lobley Ralph S 20 labourer–23
Lock W G –35
Locke Alexander 24–36
Locke Margaret 20–36
Locke Arthur 19–43
Lockyer Thomas 26–24
Loddrington Robert 19–10sy
Loe James 22–35
Loft George 25 mason–38
Logan Mrs E 62 S–22
Logan Margaret 40 spinster–22
Logan R 40 S–24
Logan Miss Elizabeth 30 S–29sy
Lomas William 25 labourer–22
Londen James 42–27
Londen Janet 33–27
London John 43 labourer–27
London Jane 47–27
London Jane 16–27
London Thomas 21–42
Long Thomas 21 farmer–13
Long Benjamin 34 labourer–21
Long John 28 labourer–26
Long Etty 29–26
Long Martha 8–26
Long William 6–26
Long Robert 2–26
Long John infant–26
Long Thomas 26 labourer–27
Long Robert 20 machinist–40br
Long Letitia 20–40
Long Patrick–42
Longhrey Jonathan 27 I–28
Longhrey James 22 I–28
Longmore Miss–31
Longstaff John 31–21
Longstaff Ann 26–21
Longstaff Mary 35 cook–41la
Lonsdale Thomas 30 labourer–21
Lonsdale John 25–21
Lopdell John 25 artisan I–38
Lore D 30–26
Lorentzen Tuergen 22 lab. OP–26
Lorimer Mr–21
Lorimer Mrs–21
Lorimer T B–21
Lorimer infant–21
Lorrison Bessie 19–42
Loughmann Michael 23–41

Loundes R –9
Love Mr 32–31
Love Mrs 27–31
Love Miss 5–31
Love Rosanna–32
Love E Mary 9–32
Love D C –36
Love Robert 22 farmer I–38
Low A C 21 surveyor–38
Low Thomas C S–42ot
Low Alexander 42 engineer S–43
Lowan Jonathan 36 labourer I–24
Lowden Mrs Mary 25–22
Lowden John 5–22
Lowden John 24–41
Lowden Robert 30–42
Lowdon Mrs Mary 30–22
Lowdon Wilhelmina 7–22
Lowe Robert 42 labourer I–20
Lowe Margaret 19 spinster S–27
Lowe Catherine 20 spinster S–27
Lowe William 28–34
Lowe James 36 joiner S–37
Lowe J 21 spinster–41ge
Lowers Alexander–16
Lowry John 19–42du
Lowthian William labourer I–23
Lowthian Mary A I–23
Lozer Thomas 20 labourer I–24
Lozer William 14 I–24
Lucas Edward 18 labourer–22
Lucas Mrs Martha 29–23
Lucas George J 8–23
Lucas Melinda 6–23
Lucas Mrs Fanny 29–30
Lucas Fanny L 9–30
Lucas Kate V 5–30
Lucas Mary G infant–30
Lucas William 27–34
Lucien G M 28 OP–16
Lucien Mrs Rosa 35 OP–16
Lucinda Joseph 16–36
Lucy C E 45 spinster–33
Lucy Edwin R 16 clerk–37
Luffman Ann S 55–33
Luignani Guiseppi 63 lab. OP–20
Lumsden James 23 labourer–24
Luney James 26 labourer I–31
Lunney Andrew adult farmer I–40
Lusands Martha 54 matron–25
Lusands George 12–25
Lush Robert C(died 13.4.1870)I–35
Luscombe Mrs Alix 50–41
Luton Mrs Louisa 28–35
Luton Anna Maria 4–35
Lyan Mary 29 spinster–22
Lydas Mrs–11
Lydas Annie–11
Lydas Edward–11
Lydas Rose–11
Lydiard John–23
Lydiard Louisa–23

Lydiard Anne E–23
Lydiard Mary–23
Lydiard Charles–23
Lydiard George–23
Lyle Samuel 20 labourer–21
Lynch Esther 16 spinster–22
Lynch William 24 labourer I–22
Lynch Miss Eliza 20 I–24
Lynch Michael 20 labourer I–24
Lynch I 31 miner–27
Lynch Thomas 29 labourer I–27
Lynch Ann 22 spinster I–28
Lynch Thomas labourer I–28
Lynch Thomas 27 I–29
Lynch Richard 21 I–35
Lynch Mrs Margaret 40–41
Lynch Michael 28 S–43
Lynn Matthew 25 labourer–22
Lynn William H 30–41
Lyon John L 34–38
Lyon Elizabeth P 31–38
Lyon Margaret 9–38
Lyon Patrick D 2–38
Lyon Bertram F 1–38
Lyons Luke 47 labourer I–22
Lyons William 31 labourer–26
Lyons John 29–26
Lyons Michael 25 I–41
Lyster Arthur 23 S–21
Lyster William 35 farmer I–37

M

McAdam Thomas 25 farmer I–13
McAllister Rose 18 I–42
McAnley John 30 S–41
McAntin Hugh 20 labourer I–26
McArthur Robert 14 S–31
McAtear Miss Rose 19 S–23
McAtonaney James 29 farmer I–16
McAtonaney Eliza 25 I–16
McAuliffe John 20 labourer I–26
McAuliffe Dennis 28 labourer I–28
McBain Joseph 25 S–10
McBain Jessie 26 S–10
McBain Peter 27 labourer–25
McBay Jonathan 24 labourer I–24
McBean L –27
McBean William–27
McBechine David 47stonecutter S–37
McBirney Samuel 23 labourer I–23
McBride Wadden 25 S–24
McBride Edward 43 I–35
McBride John 25–39
McBride Samuel S–39
McBride Mrs S–39
McBride Daniel 30 labourer I–40
McCaffey William 20 labourer I–31
McCallum Geddes 26–41
McCancey Alexander 25 farmer–16
McCandlish Emma 26 spinster S–33
McCandy Thomas 50 labourer I–22
McCandy John 20 I–22

McCandy Matilda 18 I–22
McCandy Isabella 15 I–22
McCandy Catherine 11 I–22
McCann Arthur J 20 I–29
McCann Kate 16 I–29
McCann James 22–34
McCaren Charles 25 labourer I–31
McCarter Miss Fanny–23
McCarter Edith–23
McCarthy Joshua 30 labourer I–22
McCarthy Timothy 24 labourer I–23
McCarthy Timothy 25 labourer I–27
McCarthy Daniel 20 labourer–27
McCarthy Patrick 26 I–36
McCartney D 34 merchant S–10
McCartney John 23 labourer I–27
McCartney Thomas 21 I–28
McCartney William H 29 I–29
McCartney Mrs A 24 I–29
McCartney Laura A infant I–29
McCarty Patrick 28 labourer I–31
McCasker Miss Margaret 30 S–27
McCathy Ann 19 spinster I–31
McCauseland Oliver labourer S–21
McCauseland Mary S–21
McCausland James 32 I–36
McChange Michael 37 clerk I–13
McClaush William 40–27
McClaush William 17–27
McClay Jonathan M 40 lab. I–24
McClean Edward–9
McClean J –9
McClean James 26 labourer I–27
McClean Thomas 25 labourer S–31
McClean George 25–33
McClelland H 23 grocer I–10
McClleland John 22 labourer I–22
McClelland Miss 18 S–26
McClelland Maria 16 S–26
McClelland Benjamin 25 I–41
McClement I G 43 I–42
McClure Miss Mary 30–32
McClure Samuel 23 farmer I–32
McClure Sarah 18 I–32
McClure Thomas 16 gardener I–32
McClure William 50 I–32
McClure Rachel 50 I–32
McClure William J 21–41
McCole Catherine–23
McColough James 29 labourer I–26
McComb George 20–41
McCombe Louisa 22 spinster S–31
McCombe Francis 4 S–31
McCombe Eda infant S–31
McConnell B –9
McConnell Mary 18 S–10
McConnell Louisa (died at sea)–11
McConnell William–11
McConnell James 21–42
McConnell John 19–42
McConnell Hugh 16–42
McConnell William 10–42

McConnell William 54 S-42
McConnell Letitia 56 S-42
McConnell Elizabeth 26 S-42
McConnell Mrs Thos. 24 S-42
McConnell Mrs Rosanna 25 S-42
McConnell Margaret Jane 3 S-42
McConnell Harriet Letitia inf S-42
McConnell William 30-42
McConochie Mr-9
McConochie Mrs (& infant)-9
McCormack John 18 labourer-27
McCormack Catherine 20 I-33
McCormack John 25 I-33
McCormack Henry 20 labourer I-36
McCormack James 35-42
McCormick James T W adult-10
McCormick William 27 lab. S-20
McCormick Mary 24-20
McCormick John I-29
McCormick Robert 35-43
McCormick Mary 16-43
McCornish Hugh 29 farmer S-13
McCornish James 33 farmer S-13
McCosey John 35 I-31
McCoster Michael 22 I-33
McCowery Teresa 11 S-23
McCoy H -9
McCoy Edward 26 farmer I-40
McCrea Julia I-24
McCrea Margaret 60 widow S-24
McCrea Duncan 36 S-24
McCrea Julia 36 S-24
McCrea Margaret 9 S-24
McCrea Christopher 7 S-24
McCrea Donald 5 S-24
McCrea Mary A 3 S-24
McCubbin Alexander 43 lab. S-35
McCubbin Elizabeth 36-S-35
McCubbin Catherine 11 S-35
McCubbin William 9 S-35
McCubbin Elizabeth 7 S-35
McCubbin Mary 5 S-35
McCubbin Alex 3 S-35
McCubbin Agnes 13 S-35
McCue James 45 labourer I-31
McCue Mary 44 I-31
McCue Jane 15 I-31
McCue Elizabeth 13 I-31
McCue Alexander 18 I-31
McCuishar Mary 30-11
McCulla James 23 I-28
McCulla William 23 I-33
McCullen Robert 60 labourer-25
McCullen Sarah 50-25
McCullen Eliza 18-25
McCullen Margaret 15-25
McCullin Robert 23 labourer-25
McCullock James 27 labourer S-24
McCullock Andrew 45 S-29
McCullock Elizabeth 45 S-29
McCullock Elizabeth R 23 S-29
McCullock Emily B 18 S-29

McCullock Ada 16 S-29
McCullock Ernest A 14 S-29
McCullock Herbert R 12 S-29
McCullock Percy V 6 S-29
McCullock Christopher 46 S-36
McCullock Mary 42 S-36
McCullock John S-39
McCullock C M 21-40
McCutcheon D 20 labourer-27
McDemitt Hugh 17 I-40ho
McDermat Denis 35 labourer-27
McDermott John-10
McDermott Mrs W-10
McDermott infant-10
McDermott T 19 accountant I-10
McDermott John 24 labourer-28
McDermott Mary 24 spinster-28
McDermott Michael 21 lab. I-31
McDermott Bernard 37 lab. I-38
McDonagh Robert 11-25
McDonald Wm 42 mariner-10
McDonald James 22 labourer S-21
McDonald G C 32 labourer-26
McDonald John labourer-26
McDonald Daniel 18 S-28
McDonald William B 30 S-28
McDonald William 22 I-28ho
McDonald William 48 lab. S-31
McDonald J H 22 labourer S-32
McDonald Malcolm 57 S-33
McDonald Joseph 26 upholsterer I-38
McDonald William 26 farmer S-39
McDonald Kate 28 I-40
McDonald Margaret 24 S-43
McDonnell C R S-28
McDonnell Mrs A S-28
McDonnell John 25 I-29
McDonnell James 22 servant I-37
McDonnell Jane 21 I-37
McDonough John 22 labourer I-24
McDonough John 40 I-29sy
McDonough James 19 labourer I-32
McDougal John 23 S-33ad
McDougall Alexander 21saddlerI-31
McDougall John 29-34
McDougall John 33 S-36
McDougall Jane 35 S-36
McDougall Ellen 7 S-36
McDougall Mrs Mary 25 S-40
McDowall Samuel-23
McDowall S-33
McDowall Robert 22 I-43
McDowell A 21 spinster-28
McDowell James 30 seedsman S-38
McDowell James 22 miner I-39
McDowill David 28-43
McDowill Isabella 21-43
McDowill Elizabeth infant-43
McDuff James 35 labourer-13
McDuff John-13
McDuff Sarah-13
McElhatton Robert 25 lab.-20sy

McElhatton James 20-20sy
McElphine William 24 lab. I-22
McElvogne John 55-42
McElvogne Martha 44-42
McErlean John 25 farmer I-16
McEvan Charles 30 labourer S-27
McEvegue John 42 I-33
McEvegue M 42-I-33
McEwan Margaret 48 I-29
McFarland John 28-33
McFarlane Thomas 50 labourer S-20
McFarlane Miss Eliza 24 I-23
McFarlane George 33 S-24
McFarlane Henry W 22 labourer-27
McFarlane Mary 50 spinster S-27
McFarlane Miss Catherine 31 S-27
McFarlane Miss Christinia 22 S-27
McGarity John 22 shoemaker I-32
McGarry M 19 labourer I-24
McGee William I-26
McGeorge Samuel 22 clerk I-35
McGerch Grace 26 spinster S-34
McGerriss John 23 clerk I-32
McGill C 21-42
McGillicuddy M 21 I-29
McGilvray Jane 60 painter S-42
McGlone James 18-41
McGlynn John 30-41
McGovan Jonathan 22 labourer I-24
McGowan James 24 labourer I-32
McGrath Denis 24 labourer I-16
McGrath Patrick 26 labourer I-22
McGrath James 20 I-28
McGrath Charles 21-34
McGrath John 25 I-36
McGrath James 18 labourer I-40
McGreale Patrick 25 I-28
McGregor Robert 23 labourer S-36
McGrelland Bernard S-36
McGribbon Edward 21-41
McGrill Lachlan 58 S-36
McGrisk Patrick 60 labourer I-22
McGuigan James 17 labourer-I-21
McGuinness Joshua 25 accounts I-43
McGurgan Eleanor 24 I-41
McGurgan Mary 22 I-41
McHaraka Michael 22 labourer I-28
McHarry James 20 I-36
McHarte William 30 I-33ad
McHenry Pat 20 labourer I-26
McHenry Alice 27 spinster-40
McHugh Patrick 24 labourer-25
McIlroy Hugh 17 labourer I-22
McIlroy Jonathan 16 labourer I-22
McIlwain Ann 22 spinster S-31
McIlwain Andrew infant S-31
McInerney Pat 28 labourer I-32
McInnis Donald 17 S-36
McInroy William 53 labourer S-32
McInstay John 29 I-35
McIntosh John 30 labourer-26
McIntosh Findley 40 S-35

McIntosh Margaret 25 S-40sy
McIntyre Thomas 20 labourer I-26
McIntyre James 23 labourer S-30
McIntyre John S-42
McIntyre Elizabeth S-42
McIver David 14 labourer I-31
McIver William 13 I-31
McIver Margaret 65 I-32
McJames John 28 labourer-25
McKavanagh Lizzie 16 I-42
McKay D -9
McKay A 19-10
McKay Miss 25-10
McKay George 35 carpenter-11
McKay George 21 labourer S-21
McKay Thomas 23 labourer S-24
McKay James H 44 labourer S-30
McKay John L 30 S-33
McKee Frederick B 22 lab. I-21
McKean Mrs (& infant)-9
McKean William-9
McKean James-9
McKean Sarah 32 servant I-31
McKearn David 20 agri.lab. I-31
McKeefry William 20 labourer I-16
McKeerve William 24 labourer I-30
McKeerve Maria 28 I-30
McKellar Archibald 54 lab. S-31
McKellar Thomas 14-31
McKellar Thomas 46 sheepfarmer-31
McKellar Mrs 43-31
McKellar Rachel 10-31
McKellar Campbell 8-31
McKellar Catherine 7-31
McKellar Ernest 5-31
McKellar Grange 3-31
McKellar Miss Agnes 25 S-32
McKelvie James 38 labourer S-34
McKenna S -9
McKenna James 50-34
McKenna Mary 50-34
McKenna Anne 14-34
McKenna Francis I-35
McKenna John 24 I-35
McKenna Patrick 22 I-35
McKenna Lawrence 36-42
McKenzie J -9
McKenzie Donald 26 mason S-11
McKenzie Joseph 26-13
McKenzie James 24 farmer-16
McKenzie Hugh 30-16
McKenzie Alexander-21
McKenzie Mrs-21
McKenzie Alexander-21
McKenzie Miss Christina 20-21
McKenzie John 27 labourer S-23
McKenzie John 22 labourer S-26
McKenzie Andrew 40 labourer S-27
McKenzie Donald 45 labourer-30
McKenzie Rev H 34 labourer I-31
McKenzie Helen 36 I-31
McKenzie James infant I-31

McKenzie Maud 29-34
McKenzie Alexander 66-36
McKenzie Joseph 14-36
McKenzie William 56 S-36
McKenzie Isabella 54 S-36
McKenzie John 35 S-36
McKenzie Catherine 32 S-36
McKenzie Margaret 10 S-36
McKenzie Catherine 7 S-36
McKenzie William 5 S-36
McKenzie Thomas 3 S-36
McKenzie John 1 S-36
McKenzie Isabella 21 S-36
McKenzie Robert 16 S-36
McKenzie George 13 S-36
McKenziy Rev M I-28
McKeone Daniel 18 I-40
McKeown Robert 23 S-34
McKeown John J 27 S-39
McKerion John adult labourer-27
McKichmice Elizabeth 20 S-31ad
McKichmice male(born 9.1.1868)S-31
McKie H B 21 accountant-39
McKigney William 24-41
McKillop John 25 labourer-26
McKillop Elizabeth 24 spinster-26
McKing Mary 18 spinster I-34
McKinlay Henry 43 I-23
McKinlay Alex 25 labourer-35
McKinley John 20-41
McKinley S 24 spinster-41
McKinnon Alexander 30-34
McKnight Miss Charlotte 17-24
McKnight Michael 26 labourer I-32
McKnight Thomas 28 miner I-39
McKoun Hugh 47 I-34
McKoun Ann Jane 42 I-34
McKowley John 22-41
McLachlan A -9
McLalhlan Hugh 24 labourer S-21
McLandilan John 34 labourer-25
McLaren Robinson 40 lab. S-30
McLarry Thomas 26 I-36
McLarry Ann 24 I-36
McLaughlin Mrs 23-26
McLaughlin James 21 lab. I-27
McLay Archibald-11
McLay John-11
McLay Archibald-11
McLaymont John 43-43
McLean Jachlin 25 farmer S-20
McLean Jessie 20 spinster-20
McLean Miss 21-34
Mclean A L 17-34
McLean Daniel 19 farmer-37
McLean William John 22 I-41
McLean Alexander 22-43sy
McLear Alex 27 S-29
McLear Lauchlan 20-29
McLear Robert 22 S-39
McLelean Ann Jane 21 I-42
McLellan William 27-36

McLellan Winifred 28-36
McLellan Michael 6-36
McLellan Margaret 3-36
McLenahan John 30 farmer S-16
McLenahan Bessie 23 S-16
McLenahan John 1 S-16
McLennan John 20 ploughman S-31
McLennan Mary 23 I-43ho
McLennan Jessie 25 I-43
McLennon J -9
McLeod Robert 22 carpenter S-13
McLeod Eveline 10-21
McLeod William 25 labourer-27
McLeod Duncan 29 S-33
McLeod Kate 29 S-33
McLintock William 30-35
McLintock Mary 28-35
McLogan Sarah 36 S-43
McLorinan Charles-9
McLoughlin Peter 27-41
McLoughlin Eliza 27-41
McLoughlin Lawrence 6-41
McLoughlin Eliza 4-41
McLoughlin Mary 1-41
McLoven Mr 32 mason-16
McMahon John 25 labourer-22
McMahon Denis 23 labourer I-24
McMahon John 23 labourer I-27
McMahon John 25 labourer I-27
McMahon Margaret 21 I-27
McMahon Joseph 54 labourer-31
McMahon Susanna 17 servant I-32
McMahon Michael 50-34
McMahon Thomas 16-34
McMartin Ellen 50 spinster S-26sy
McMartin George 16 S-26sy
McMartin James 11 S-26sy
McMartin Jane 11 S-26sy
McMasters Hugh 30 labourer S-30
McMeekan James 19 S-24
McMeekin James 24 labourer I-24
McMelhuish Martha 50 I-32
McMetham Hugh-23
McMetham Mrs-23
McMichael William 24 farmer-16
McMiking Gilbert 18-43
McMillan Jessie 20 spinster S-28
McMillan Mary 26 spinster I-34
McMillan Thomas 25 artisan S-38
McMillen Pat 29 carpenter I-32
McMillen Ellen 27 I-32
McMillen Ellen 12 I-32
McMillen Eliza 9 I-32
McMillen Edward 6 I-32
McMillen Patrick 4 I-32
McMullan John 30 labourer S-26
McMullan Margaret 27 S-26
McMullan Henry 9 S-26
McMullan James 3 S-26
McMullan Mary 29-42
McMullan Madeline 19-42
McMullen John 19 labourer-13

McMullen Mrs J F S-40
McMullen A H 21 S-40
McMullen Mary E 18 S-40
McMullen James G 16 S-40
McMullen G R 14 S-40
McMullen C A 8 S-40
McMullen A V 12 S-40
McMullen A F 10 S-40
McMurray Alexander 38-43
McMurray Christina 35-43
McMurray Anne 15-43
McMurray Alexander 13-43
McNair John-9
McNally Hugh 40 labourer-21
McNally Mary 38 S-21
McNally Charles 20 labourer I-30
McNally Peter 25 I-33
McNamara E -9
McNamara Jonathan I 22 lab. I-24
McNamara Pat labourer I-26ad
McNamara Patt 25 labourer I-31
McNamara John 22 tailor I-32
McNamara James 24 I-33
McNamara John 26-41
McNamera Catherine 50 I-42
McNaught David 34 labourer S-23
McNaught Miss Elizabeth 27 S-23
McNaught James 45 labourer-23
McNaughton George 40 lab. S-23
McNean Lachlan I-31
McNean Eliza I-31
McNeil James 35 stoker-31
McNeil Christina 32-31
McNeil James 10-31
McNeil Caroline-33
McNeil John 25-42
McNeill Adam 18 I-11
McNeill Andrew 25-38
McNichol Mr-9
McNichol Mrs-9
McNichol infant-9
McNicol Grace 51 S-33
McNicol Margaret 19 S-33
McNicol John 17 S-33
McNicoll John 17 I-33
McNight Pat 23 labourer I-21
McNolan Rev-28
McPhail Neil 26 labourer S-20
McPhee John 59 S-34
McPhee Dougal 19 S-34
McPhee Donald 17 S-34
McPhee Mary 20 S-34
McPherson James 28 labourer-24
McPherson Miss-27
McPherson Daniel 41 S-36
McPhikinore Phillis 40-35
McQuade Patrick 24 labourer I-13
McQuade Mrs-23
McQuaid Joseph 24 grocer I-40sy
McQuirbrind Robert 23 I-33
McRae Alexander 24 labourer S-22
McRae John 30 labourer S-24

McRae John 20 S-36
McRay Adam 23 labourer-22
McRea Miss Margaret 24 S-24
McRenna Charles 33 moulder S-40
McRimmon Donald 38 labourer S-22
McRimmon Ann 24 S-22
McSorley William 26 labourer-27
McSweeney John 22 labourer I-27
McSweeney Owen 24 blacksmith I-32
McTaggett Hugh 27 bottlemaker S-32
McTaggett Eliza 26 S-32
McTaggett Helen 4 S-32
McTaggett John 2 S-32
McTaggett Hugh 1 S-32
McTalagi Mrs I-28
McTalagi Ada I-28
McTavish A D -9
McVeagh David 28 labourer I-35
McVeigh Charles 40 farmer I-16
McVey Hugh I-41
McWilliam R -9
Mab Lewis K 17 labourer OP-23
Mab Solomon 18 OP-23
Macauley Colin 20 labourer-30
Macauley James 29-34
Macauley Thomas 19-36
Maccally John 50-42
Macdonald Colin 22 labourer-25
Macdonald Charles 21 S-33
Macdowell E 26 land surveyor-39
Macfarlane Alan-21
Macfarlane Mrs Margaret-21
Macfarlane Jane-21
Macfarlane Wilhelmina-21
Macfarlane Agnes M A-21
Macfarlane Caroline-21
Macgregor Charles C 26 lab. S-23
Macgregor Walter 21 lab. S-31
Macher John-23
Macher Mrs-23
Machlin E -9
Machlin H -9
Macilveen Joseph 28 farmer S-16
Macintyne Frances 37 S-39
Mack Miss-21
Mack Miss Jane-21
Mackay Peter 37 labourer S-23
Mackay Ann 34 S-23
Mackay Matthew 10 S-23
Mackay Catherine 8 S-23
Mackay Peter 3 S-23
Mackay Mary A 1 S-23
Mackay(female born 15.2.1863)S-23
Mackay Miss A 39-26
Mackay James J-36
Mackay Edmond 19 farmer I-41
Mackenzie Alexander 38 S-36
Mackenzie J W -38
Mackenzie Mrs-38
Mackenzie A 36 saddler S-40
Mackenzie Mary 32-42
Mackenzie Peter 8-42

Mackenzie John 7-42
Mackenzie Lucy 4-42
Mackenzie Janet 2-42
Mackenzie Alexander 21 S-43
Mackenzie Donald 25-43
Mackey Mrs I-41
Mackie Alex 78-27
Mackie John 30 weaver-34
Mackie Anthony 23 solicitor S-37
Mackie Helen 24 spinster S-37
Mackie William 32 coachporter S-40
Mackinnon L 42 S-24
Mackinnon Mrs 40 S-24
Mackinnon L C -35
Mackinnon C 30-39
Maclegan T S 35 accountant S-37
Macmillan Robert 26 lab. S-33
Macnamara Jane 20 spinster I-22
Macorlaster Miss Margaret S-33
Macpherson Mr S-31
Madden Charles 33 labourer-23
Madden Margaret 22-23
Madden Eleanor 1.1/2-23
Madden William 23 labourer I-30
Maddison Edward 35 labourer-24
Maddox Richard 19 labourer-16
Madegan Pat 18 labourer I-40
Madely Mary 16-26
Madigan Thomas 20 labourer I-21
Madigan John 28 labourer-27
Maglaughlin James 34 I-42sy
Magram Miss Ellen 40-35
Magrane Patrick 40 I-20
Magrane Thomas 11 I-20
Magrie G 18 labourer OP-27
Maher Richard 31 labourer I-23
Maher Mary 20 I-31
Maher William 58 labourer I-31
Maher Bridget 50 I-31
Mahers Honora 35 spinster-25
Mahon Patrick M 22 labourer I-22
Mahoney Cornelius 40 I-26
Mahoney Ellen 30 I-26
Mahoney Florence 5 I-26
Mahoney Johanna 3 I-26
Mahoney Mary infant I-26
Mahood Edward 28 labourer-25
Maidment Thomas 28-26
Maigher Thomas 31-41
Maigher Mary 35-41
Maigher Michael 7-41
Maigher William 6-41
Maigher Tim infant-41
Mailer James W 19-33
Mailes David 32-13
Main Archibald 24 labourer S-22
Main George 16 OP-40
Main Joachim 25 OP-40
Main Rudolph 21 OP-40
Main Nicholas 19 OP-40
Maine Nicholas 40-30
Maine Miss-39

Maines Charles 18–41
Makin Henry 32 I–34
Makin Christopher 28–42
Malcaly James 23 I–11
Malcaly Johanna 13 I–11
Malcolm James 19–34
Malcolm Nicol 32–36
Malcolmson James 40 labourer–31
Mallock I W 34–24
Mallam B W –21
Mallett Mr–23
Mallon Ms Margaret 25(d.3/2) S–23
Malone Edward 30 labourer I–21
Malone John 21 labourer I–22
Malone Roger 23 I–36
Maloney John 21 labourer I–32
Maloney Rev P H –34
Maloney Michael 22–41
Malony James 22 I–28
Malpass William 38 stewart–42
Malpass Letitia 28–42
Malpass Henry William 5–42
Mancock Josiah 24 farmer I–31
Mandelick J –9
Mandelick M –9
Mann Miss Matilda 29–24
Manne John 30 labourer I–32
Manning George 34 labourer–23
Manning Thomas 25 labourer–25
Manning James 33 I–35
Mansell George–9
Mansfield Miss Margaret 20 I–27
Mansford T –9
Manson William 61–29
Manson Thomas 14–29
Mantiunt Emma 27 spinster–20
Mantle Victor 16 OP–43
Mappleman Joseph 25–32
Maquire Bernard 30 labourer I–21
Maquire Mrs 25 I–21
Maquire infant I–21
Maquire Michael 23 labourer–23
Maquire J F 40–24
Maquire Mrs 38–24
Maquire child 4–24
Maquire S adult labourer I–27
Maquire Francis 27 I–28
Maquire Thomas 32 labourer–30
Mara John H –20
Marantelli Lorenzo 24 OP–43
Marchioni Batt OP–38
Marden Janet 23 spinster–30
Marden Edward 23 labourer–31
Mardon William–23
Mare Edward 42–41
Mare Bridget 36–41
Margolion Fanny 23 OP–43au
Margrett William 41–43
Marie Jacques 17 OP–35
Markesey John 24 labourer–22
Marks Thomas–9
Marks A 26 dealer–10sy

Marks Thomas 22 miner–13
Marks Soloman 20 labourer–16
Marks Henry 34 labourer–23
Marks Mary 31–23
Marks Eva 5–23
Marks Jacob 3–23
Marks Emma 1–23
Marks Jacob 40–26
Marks Matthew 50–26
Marks Elkane 19 labourer–28
Marks Solomon 18–28
Marks Thomas 31–29
Marks Edward L 36–33
Marks Abraham 17–35
Marks Amelia 29–36
Marks Morris 10–36
Marks Clara 9–36
Marks Rebecca 5–36
Marks Leah 3–36
Marks Jeanette 1–36
Marks Henshall 17 miner OP–39
Marlow William 21 sailor I–13
Marnell William 26 miner–27
Marnell Ellen 26–27
Marooney Michael 30–42
Marper S –34
Marr John 22 I–43
Marral William–41
Marriott George H 16–30
Marsden Miss L 35–23
Marsden Ann 26 sp.governess–41br
Marsden Elizabeth A 36 " –41br
Marsden Eliza A 36–41 (2nd class)
Marsden Henrietta M 26–41 (2nd cl)
Marshall Thomas 20–10
Marshall Robert–11
Marshall William 28 miner–16
Marshall Thomas 26 labourer–24
Marshall Mrs Elizabeth 30–26
Marshall Agnes 10–26
Marshall Jesse 8–26
Marshall William 3–26
Marshall David infant–26
Marshall David 40 labourer–30
Marshall J J –32
Marshall Mrs–32
Marshall Florence 9–32
Marshall Maude 6–32
Marshall Violet 4–32
Marshall Ann 32–42
Marshall William 8–42
Marslen F 24 I–43
Marston John–9
Martin C R –9
Martin George–9
Martin J –9
Martin N –9
Martin T –9
Martin Thomas 36 miner–13
Martin Ellen 17 spinster–16
Martin William 22 labourer–21
Martin Robert–22

Martin Jane–22
Martin James 26–25
Martin Mary 31–25
Martin Edward 24 labourer I–26
Martin Peter 20 I–26
Martin Joseph–26
Martin Samuel 30 labourer–26
Martin James 24 labourer I–27
Martin John 18 labourer I–27
Martin John 30 labourer–27
Martin Barbara 30–27
Martin David 26 labourer–27
Martin Alfred 20 labourer–28
Martin James 32–30
Martin Mrs–30
Martin Miss Jessie S–32
Martin Mr labourer–34
Martin John 27 I–36
Martin Teresa 25 I–36
Martin Elizabeth 2 I–36
Martin Carl 28 OP–38
Martin William 55 farmer I–39
Martin Robert 40–42
Martin J P Lang 27–43
Martin Martha 32–43
Martin Sexton 30–43
Martindale Joseph 31–36
Martintrowe John 23–41
Martinwell Mrs (& infant)–9
Martlock William–21
Martley Miss I–31
Marton Heraim 32 OP–24
Marzay Thomas 30 labourer–23
Masana Palk 46 labourer OP–30
Mascioni Domeneco 24 OP–40
Masd Gea 24 OP–35
Mashuter Robert 31–36
Mason Peter 18 miner–13
Mason George Henry jr 24 lab.–21
Mason Miss Maria 45–23
Mason William 60–24
Mason Garni 38–26
Massey George P W 38 merchant–16
Massey Celia Sophia 31–16
Masters William H–41
Masunier C 27–10
Mates T R 33 labourer–23
Mates Thomas 21 steward–35
Mathenson Godfrey 31–29
Matherson Michael 25–35
Matheson John 24 miner–20
Matheson Sackville 27 farmer–21
Matheson Isabella–23
Matheson Alouise 21 spinster–40
Mathews Mrs–9
Mathews – spinster–25
Mathews Joseph 22 labourer–25
Mathews Ralph 20–25
Mathews Barnard–9
Mathie Claud 34–34
Mathieson Mrs Jenie 34–35
Mathieson John 10 S–35

Mathieson William 6 S-35
Mathieson David 45 S-36
Mathieson Duncan 28 farmer S-42
Mathieson Jessie 28 S-42
Matthew Henry 23 I-38
Matthews John I 17 labourer-20
Matthews Mrs M 33-22
Matthews Thomas 11-22
Matthews Peter 9-22
Matthews Margaret 7-22
Matthews Patrick 5-22
Matthews William 4-22
Matthews Peter 36 labourer-23
Matthews William 19 labourer-23
Matthews William-27
Matthews Wilfred-27
Matthews William 28 labourer-27
Matthews Isaac 24 labourer-27
Matthews Mary 15 spinster-27
Matthews W -31
Matthews Samuel 26-33
Matthews August 31 labourer-35
Matthews Maria 40-35
Matthews Alex F S-35
Matthews Henry 18 S-35
Matthews Nathaniel 24 labourer-36
Matthews William 22-36
Matthewson Thomas 27 butcher-10
Mattison William 29 labourer S-35
Mattrass Miss Elizabeth 34-21
Maunderson George 48 labourer-26
Maunderson Jane 47-26
Maunderson George 21-26
Maunderson Ann 18-26
Maunderson Elizabeth 15-26
Maunderson Jane 11-26
Mauvery Hermann OP-38
Maxted I M -31
Maxwell Hugh 22-10
Maxwell Robinson 22 clerk-13
Maxwell F -27
Maxwell Richard labourer I-32
Maxwell William 9-34
Maxwell Wilfred C-35
Maxwell Mrs Margaret 36-36
May John 27 labourer OP-23
May William 22 labourer-32
May Miss Eliza 21 S-35
May John C 21 clerk-42
Mayall Joseph 23 labourer-22
Mayer Major Fred I-35
Mayer Jane I-35
Mayfield Charles 45-42
Mayhew Eliza 26 milliner-10
Mayland Booth 35-29
Mayne Mrs Clara 17-20
Mayne Sarah 11-20
Mayne Selina 10-20
Mayne Richard 40 labourer-20
Mayne Sophia 36-20
Mayplas Eda 15-42
Mayzochi Speran 28 OP-40

Mayzorina Petro 26 OP-40
Mayzorina Catherin 60 OP-40
Mazzalletta Fernando 33porter OP-38
Mazzalletta Felice 33 OP-38
Meade Thomas 35-43
Meadows John 25 labourer-21
Meagher Miss Ellen 19-25
Meagner Michael 25 I-11
Mealing Henry J 24-41
Meaney Michael 22 labourer I-24
Mechan Mrs Ann 50-39
Mechan Francis 17 I-43
Meddon Mrs Ann 42 S-35
Meddon Elizabeth 20 S-35
Meddon Harriet 17 S-35
Meddon Emily 14 S-35
Meddon Thomas 12 S-35
Meddon Francis 9 S-35
Meddon Anne 7 S-35
Meddon Agnes 5 S-35
Medici Joseph 32-34
Medici Hannah 26-34
Medici Michael 7-34
Medici Mary J 3-34
Medici Joseph 1-34
Medlin James 21 labourer-25
Medlyn Joseph 21 miner-10
Medlyn Matthew 18 labourer-26
Mee Richard 28-29
Meehan Charles 28 labourer I-26
Meehan John 26 I-26
Meehan Thomas 40 I-35
Meehan Mary 41 I-35
Meehan Ellen 9 I-35
Meehan Thomas 6 I-35
Meehan Catherine 15 I-35
Meehan Ann 12 I-35
Meehan Patrick 17 I-35
Mehany Robert 19 miner I-37
Mehany Alexander 17 I-37
Mehany Margaret 24 spinster I-37
Mehany Jane Orr 1 I-37
Mehany Thomas 22 farmer I-37
Mehany William 27 I-37
Mehary John 30-41
Mehary Margaret 25-41
Mehary Samuel 3-41
Mehary James 1-41
Meharry James 32-34
Meikle William-33
Meikle Anne-33
Mein D George adult(d.at sea) S-40
Mein Mrs adult S-40
Mein Beatrice 10 S-40
Mein Augusta 8 S-40
Mein Anne 6 S-40
Meincke Mrs 26 OP-40
Meincke (infant) OP-40
Melbourne Thomas 27 labourer-24
Melbourne Samuel 37 labourer-30
Melbourne Margaret 32-30
Melbourne John R 11-30

Melbourne Samuel 3-30
Melbourne Ralph inf (died)-30
(died 23/5 of bronchitis)
Melbura John 30 miner-11
Melican Patrick 22 labourer I-31
Mellen H J 40 labourer-26
Melling James 31 engineer S-35
Melling Mary 33 S-35
Melling Thomas 21 collier-39
Mellor Mrs-16
Mellor William 27 labourer-22
Mellor Mr-23
Mellor Mrs-23
Mellor James 36-33
Melody William 19-33
Melt Joseph 20 labourer OP-30
Melville Miss Charlotte 21 I-24
Melville Agnes 21 spinster-30ad
Melvin John 24 labourer S-22
Mendelsohn Louisa 23 OP-23
Mendlesolm M 18 I-29
Menzes Nicholas 26 farmer OP-30
Menzies Joseph 53 teamerchant-10sy
Menzies Euphemia 44-10sy
Menzies John 21-10sy
Menzies Margaret 17-10sy
Menzies Janet 16-10sy
Menzies Elizabeth 15.1/2-10sy
Menzies William 12-10sy
Menzies Mary 10-10sy
Menzies Agnes 7-10sy
Menzies Andrew 6-10sy
Menzies Emily 4-10sy
Menzies Amelia 4-10sy
Menzies Mary-42
Menzies Jane 19-42
Menzies Ellen 16-42
Menzies Samuel 13-42
Menzies Robert 11-42
Menzies Daniel 9-42
Menzies William 6-42
Menzies Thomas 3-42
Mercier Charles-9
Merrine George 35 miner-13
Merrine Ellen 35-13
Merrine George infant-13
Merriman Herbert 20-35
Merriman Mary A 20-35
Merriman William 71-35
Merry J -9
Merry George-9
Merser John 18 servant S-11
Mes(de)Giovanni 34 labourer OP-26
Mescall Jonathan 21 labourer-24
Mescall Daniel 22-43
Messenger George 29 labourer-22
Messner Frederick labourer OP-23
Metcalf Joseph 22-34
Metcalf Elizabeth 22-34
Metcalf William 1-34
Methen John 27 labourer S-34
Meuyoki Pietro 20 OP-26

Meyer Heinrich 18 labourer OP-22
Meyer Joseph 19-34
Meyer Abraham 14 OP-39
Meyer Solomon 11 OP-39
Micer Jonathan 42 S-24
Michael (St) Antonio I-36
Michel John 32 labourer-25
Michel Annie 23-25
Michell Edward 34-28
Michelson Oscar 23 lab. OP-30
Middleton Joseph 51-10
Middleton Mrs 33-10
Middleton Harriet 14-10
Middleton John 30-27
Middleton John 50-27
Middleton Emma 43-27
Middleton Ann 15-27
Middleton James 22-34
Middleton John 45 labourer-34
Middleton William 50-35
Middleton James-36
Midgley Josh 63 labourer-20
Midgley Tim 21 I-36
Midgley Thomas 19 I-36
Midkiff Anthony 24-41
Midkiff Samuel 18-41
Miels Thomas 25 labourer I-38
Milburn John 20-36
Mildram W P 35 labourer-25
Mill Thomas 20 labourer-26
Mill Robert 22-26
Mill William H 21-34
Millar W G -9
Millar Thomas 23 I-16
Millar Richard 26 labourer-22
Millar Margaret 35 S-43
Millar Margaret 12 S-43
Millar George 8 S-43
Millar Elizabeth 6 S-43
Millar Cecilia 4 S-43
Millburn Harriet 37-16
Millburn Mary Ann 10-16
Miller George-9
Miller James 28 miner-11
Miller Alexander 30 miner-16
Miller Margaret 32-16
Miller Henry 18-21
Miller James 35 labourer-25
Miller Sabilla 29-25
Miller Mary 10-25
Miller Jane 9-25
Miller Elizabeth 7-25
Miller Robert 2-25
Miller William 4-25
Miller Charlotte 2-25
Miller James infant-25
Miller James 31 labourer I-26
Miller R W-26
Miller Roda-26
Miller Robert infant-26
Miller Ada infant-26
Miller James 27 labourer S-31

Miller Jane 26 S-31
Miller Robert 9 S-31
Miller James 6 S-31
Miller William 4 S-31
Miller Clementine infant S-31
Miller James 22 labourer S-32
Miller John 20 S-32
Miller Thomas 20 I-32
Miller Bart 32 S-35
Miller Miss Ceceli OP-35
Miller F Bowyer-37
Miller Alice-37
Miller A S 8-37
Miller Charles-38
Miller John B 38 artisan-38
Miller David 32 S-42
Miller Gibson 21-42
Milliken Alexander 18 lab.-21
Milliken Joshua 20-21
Milliken Alexander 28 miner I-39
Milliken Chilly 20 I-39
Mills A -9
Mills Henry 22 miner-13
Mills William H 36-13
Mills James H 10-13
Mills Thomas 32-33
Mills Mrs H 32-34
Mills Henry 29-38
Millward John 26 labourer-26
Milmay Hugh-27
Milne Jessie 22 spinster S-26
Milne John 40-27
Milner Jonathan Joseph 22 lab.-28
Milnes Thomas 40 labourer-26
Miner James 31 labourer-33
Miner Matthew 19 labourer S-33
Minogne Mary 40 spinster I-28
Minogue Michael 16 I-28
Mirchall John 26 farmer S-16
Misson F -9
Mitchelhill Peter 52 S-40
Mitchelhill Mrs 49 S-40
Mitchelhill C E 23 S-40
Mitchelhill Margaret F 21 S-40
Mitchelhill Jessie B 19 S-40
Mitchelhill Rachel B 17 S-40
Mitchelhill Elizabeth H 16 S-40
Mitchelhill John 14 S-40
Mitchelhill William H 12 S-40
Mitchelhill David C 10 S-40
Mitchelhill Samuel C 8 S-40
Mitchelhill Louisa H 7 S-40
Mitchell M -9
Mitchell William-9
Mitchell Jonathan 42 miner-10
Mitchell James 31 miner-11
Mitchell John-11
Mitchell William James 22 lab.-11
Mitchell Henry 22 miner-13
Mitchell John 28 miner-13
Mitchell Thomas 42 labourer-20
Mitchell Thomas 11-20

Mitchell Nathan 34 farmer-21
Mitchell Richard S 33 labourer-21
Mitchell Dorothy 27-21
Mitchell James 11-21
Mitchell Thomas 8-21
Mitchell Miss Bridget 17 I-23
Mitchell Arthur 26 labourer-24
Mitchell Mrs Janet 22-24
Mitchell Robert 36 labourer-24
Mitchell Elizabeth 19-24
Mitchell Ann 17-24
Mitchell Samuel 32 labourer-24
Mitchell Ann 29-24
Mitchell Jonathan 22-24
Mitchell Miss Jane 18-24
Mitchell Robert 28 labourer-26
Mitchell Charlotte 28-26
Mitchell Mary I 4-26
Mitchell Elizabeth 3-26
Mitchell James 18 labourer-27
Mitchell John W 19 labourer I-27
Mitchell William J 21 gardener-31
Mitchell Mark 20-33
Mitchell Miss Geo-35
Mitchell Thomas-36
Mitchell Joshua I-39
Mitchell Lilias C 29 S-39
Mitten Thomas 36 miner-13
Mixner James-9
Mobren Christopher-36
Modino Carlo 34 labourer OP-23
Moffatt Alexander 30 lab. I-26
Mogie William 15 I-43
Moliere P G 26 OP-29
Molinari Garzia 45 OP-41
Molinari Luigi A 15 OP-41
Molinari Enrico B 13 OP-41
Moline Mrs-30
Moline Charles-30
Moloy Daniel 35 labourer I-27
Molloy James 39 labourer-22
Molloy James 17 I-33
Moloney William 34 labourer I-11
Moloney Edmund 31 I-11
Moloney Eliza 13-26
Moloney Catherine 44 widow-26
Moloney Patrick 17 I-28
Molony Denis 27 labourer I-21
Molyneaux William Henry 33-34
Molyneaux Elizabeth 21-34
Molyneux John 23 labourer I-22
Molyneux Arthur 23 labourer I-27
Monahan Pat 16 labourer I-24
Monashe Miss 20-27
Money John 64 I-36
Monison A 20 I-10sy
Monons John 22 accountant I-10
Monroe George 28-41
Monroe Elizabeth 25-42br
Montague Jane 17 S-33
Montgomery - spinster-25
Montgomery Walter-30

Montgomery George 47 miner I-39
Moody Charles-9
Moody R C-9
Moody William 30 miner-13
Moon Daniel 40 labourer-22
Moon J H 38-39
Mooney John 18 I-11
Mooney Thomas 23 I-11
Mooney James 30 blacksmith-13
Mooney Andrew 35 labourer-26
Mooney Margaret 32-26
Mooney Daniel 7-26
Mooney Agnes 5-26
Mooney Margaret infant-26
Mooney Henry 22 I-34
Moor John E R 29 labourer-22
Moor Catherine 34 spinster-22
Moore Henry-9
Moore W -9
Moore Philip 17-10
Moore M -11
Moore Hamilton 30 labourer-22
Moore W G 38-24
Moore Elizabeth 37-24
Moore Thomas labourer-25
Moore Catherine-26
Moore Martin 44 labourer-26
Moore Ann 45-26
Moore Philip 11-26
Moore Jane 35 spinster-29
Moore Thomas B 17 labourer-31ho
Moore Arthur 30-33
Moore John 21 I-33
Moore Joseph 32-33ad
Moore Edward 26-34
Moore Robert 18-34
Moore Robert John 22-35
Moore William T labourer I-35
Moore Thomas 24 I-36
Moore Alexander 23 farmer S-37
Moore Letitia I-39
Moore Jane 23 I-40
Moore Joseph-40
Moore Julia-40
Moore Percy 22 farmer I-40
Moore William 38 tradesman-40
Moore John 43-41
Moore William-41
Moorhead Miss Susanna-36
Moran Darby 28 labourer I-23
Moran Miss Eliza 32 I-23
Moran Robert 22 I-28
Moran Charles 21 Sydney-31
Moran Hugh 20-36
Moran Miss Mary I-36
Moran Kate 20-42
Morecroft N -9
Morel Mons-22
Moreland James 32 miner-13
Moretti A OP-42
Morewood Thomas 42 sawyer-40
Morewood Jane 40-40

Morewood E E 11-40
Morewood A J 9-40
Morewood J I 7-40
Morewood M E 3-40
Morgan M-9
Morgan Edward 40 tailor S-11
Morgan Thomas 26 labourer I-21
Morgan Herbert 30 labourer-22
Morgan James 22 labourer I-23
Morgan Patrick 23 I-23
Morgan John 45 labourer-23
Morgan Daniel 30 labourer-25
Morgan Jane 29-25
Morgan Edward 4-25
Morgan Gwellean infant-25
Morgan John 44 labourer-26
Morgan Sarah 30-26
Morgan Mary 3-26
Morgan Morgan S 33 S-28
Morgan Robert 26-28
Morgan Jane 25-28
Morgan Robert L 22 labourer-30
Morgan Pat 26 I-32
Morgan Benjamin 25-33
Morgan Charles 36-33
Morgan Miss Maria 26-35
Morgan Honora 25 spinster I-37
Morgan Mary 25 spinster I-37
Morgan John 40 miner-37
Morgan William B 50-42
Morgan Annie 42-42
Morgan Mary Jane 11-42
Morgan George Henry 10-42
Morgan William C 9-42
Morgan Annie E 7-42
Morgan J Daniel 5-42
Morgan Thomas S C 3-42
Morgan Charles R infant-42
Morgant Austachio 20 farmer OP-20
Morley John-10
Morney Jno 25 accountant I-10
Moroney James 20 labourer I-27
Moroney Samuel 26 labourer I-32
Morpeth Edward 26 labourer S-31
Morphet John Henry 26 S-36
Morral John 26 labourer S-31
Morral Joseph 24 S-31
Morran Charles 11-39
Morris John 25-10
Morris Frederick H 17 grocer-16
Morris Mrs Grace 36-24
Morris Ellen 16-24
Morris Eliza 14-24
Morris Anne 10-24
Morris Thomas 8-24
Morris Grace 6-24
Morris Mrs H 24-26
Morris Master 4-26
Morris Thomas 30 labourer-26
Morris Sarah 30-26
Morris Bernard infant-26
Morris Moses 23-28

Morris Kate 24-28
Morris Esther 2-28
Morris Ann infant-28
Morris John D 33-29
Morris Patt 23 I-29
Morris Susan 41 spinster-29
Morris N E -32
Morris Mrs-32
Morris Miss-32
Morris Frederick-35
Morris William 19 blacksmith-37
Morris Mrs Rachel 63-39
Morris Griffith 36-42
Morrisay Margaret-10
Morrisay Ann 25-20
Morrisay Ann I-20
Morrison J -9
Morrison James 19 I-28
Morrison John 24 S-31
Morrison Robert H M S-31
Morrison James 24 S-32ad
Morrison James L -34
Morrison Elizabeth 25 servant S-37
Morrison Anne 17 S-37
Morrison Jessie 15 S-37
Morrison John 32 mason S-37
Morrison Catherine 31 S-37
Morrison John 9 S-37
Morrison George 7 S-37
Morrison William 5 S-37
Morrison Peter 3 S-37
Morrison Catherine 1 S-37
Morrissey Jonathan labourer-25
Morrissey Mary 25-36
Morrisy Lawrence 23 farmer-13
Morrow Richard 35 miner-11
Morrow John 31 labourer-26
Morrow J Y -34
Morrow John A 19 plumber-38sy
Morrow Mrs E 27-39
Morse Miss Rose 19-36
Mort Alfred M 48-36
Mort Annie E 38-36
Mort Frank 5-36
Mort Hydro 1-36
Mortimer Jno 37 labourer-23
Mortimer Mary 38-23
Mortimer Susanna 16-23
Mortimer Mary 10-23
Mortimer Louisa 2.1/2-23
Mortimer William 1-23
Mortlock Thomas-9
Mortlock William 34-24
Morton Margaret 50-10
Morton John 29 farmer-13
Morton Martha 29-13
Morton John 3-13
Morton Jane 62 matron-25
Morton Jane 29 spinster-25
Morton Joseph 34-41
Mosgrave Mrs Anne 60 I-39
Mosgrave Helene 5 I-39

Moskins Mrs Jane-20
Moskins Emma-20
Moskins Jane-20
Moss Robert 21 clerk S-13
Moss Bernard 29 labourer OP-24
Moss Mrs J 30 OP-24
Moss Kate 19 spinster-29
Moss Lazarius 33-35
Moss Helena 30-35
Moss John 16-42
Moss Bernard 13-42
Mossovini Giovanni 18 lab. OP-23
Motson Charles-22
Motson Mrs-22
Motson Eda-22
Motson Fanny-22
Motson Lilly-22
Motson Mina-22
Motson Alfred-22
Motterhead William 24-43
Mouat John-9
Mould William 21-36
Mounsey Fletcher 27 labourer-27
Mounsey Margaret 24-27
Mounsey William 34 labourer-27
Mounsey John 63 labourer-27
Mounsey Sarah 61-27
Mounsey Joseph 21 labourer S-27
Mounsey Joseph 43-33
Mounsey John 20-33
Mounsey Joseph 18-33
Mounsey Samuel 15-33
Mounsey Edwin 13-33
Mounsey George H 10-33
Mounsey Margaret E 4-33
Mountford Henry labourer-30
Mountford John-41
Mousah Max 17 labourer OP-21
Mowat James 34-35
Mowat James 30-36
Mowat Mrs 30 I-36
Mowat Eli infant I-36
Moylass Bridget 22 spinster-25
Muddiman W M I-34
Muddyman Henry 28 labourer-34
Muddyman Miss M 26-34
Muddyman Robert L 12 labourer-34
Mudie William-21
Mugeven Michael 20 I-28
Muhall Thomas 21 labourer-25
Muhall Kate 19 spinster-25
Muhally Thomas labourer-25
Muir Archibald 35 draper S-16
Muir James 39 labourer S-24
Muir Agnes 34 S-24
Muir Christopher 11 S-24
Muir James 10 S-24
Muir Andrew 9 S-24
Muir Robert 7 S-24
Muir Elizabeth 5 S-24
Muir Marian 4 S-24
Muir William 2 S-24

Muir Isabella infant S-24
Muir Matthew 45 labourer S-31
Muir Janet 36-31
Muir Andrew 8-31
Muir Agnes 6-31
Muir Annie S 4-31
Muir Mary J 1-31
Muir Willie infant-31
Muir Elizabeth 17-31
Muir John 21 S-38
Muir James 32-40
Muir Elizabeth 30-40
Muir Elizabeth 4-40
Muir James 1-40
Muirhead William 32 miner-40
Mulcahy Cornelius 42 I-36
Mulfahy Richard 34 farm lab I-31
Mulhan Lott 27 labourer I-20
Mulgin Mrs M P I-41
Mulholland James 18 labourer S-33
Mulholland Ann J I-39
Mullany Hannah servant-30
Mullen Samuel-9
Mullen John 28 I-28
Mullen Thomas M 18-41
Muller Adam 25 labour-25
Muller August 28 labourer OP-30
Muller Marie 24 spinster OP-30
Muller Rosine 23 OP-30
Muller Sophie 19 OP-30
Muller George-42ad
Mulligan Patrick 22-41
Mullin Bernard I 27-16
Mullin John 28 labourer-22
Mullin Ann 24-22
Mulqueen Michael 21 labourer I-21
Mulqueen Thomas 25 I-21
Mulvey Matthew 20 farm lab I-31
Mumford Miss A 19-24
Muncaster Edward 24 farm lab S-31
Munce Joseph 35 labourer I-23
Munce Eliza 30 I-23
Munce Joseph 8 I-23
Munce Jane 6 I-23
Munce John 4 I-23
Munce Joseph 35 labourer I-23
Munce Margaret 28 I-23
Munce Sarah 9 I-23
Munce Joseph W 5 I-23
Munce - 1 I-23
Munday James 18 porter-32
Mungovan Miss Anne 20 I-21
Mungovan Miss Mary 18 I-21
Mumney Patrick 25 labourer-20
Munro Neil R 9-34
Munroe John 36 S-28
Munse John 21 labourer-22
Munse Hugh 25 labourer-23
Munse - infant-23
Muntz William 23 miner-21
Mullin Bernard I 27-16
Murcer John 28 farm lab-31

Murchie Mrs-11
Murchie infant-11
Murchie James-11
Murk John 45-40
Murlagh Matthew 20 I-16
Murnance David 24-28
Murphy D-9
Murphy Moses 29 clerk I-11
Murphy James 24 bookmaker I-13
Murphy Teresa 25 spinster I-13
Murphy Catharine 20 spinster I-13
Murphy John 36 labourer I-13
Murphy Michael 35 labourer I-13
Murphy Catharine 10 I-13
Murphy Josephine 30-20
Murphy Mary 8-20
Murphy Catherine 6-20
Murphy Margaret 1-20
Murphy Margaret 20 spinster I-20
Murphy Edward 30 labourer I-22
Murphy I L 21 labourer I-22
Murphy Michael 27 labourer I-22
Murphy Jane 25 I-22
Murphy Mary Jane 1 I-22
Murphy Rev J-22
Murphy John 30 labourer I-23
Murphy Michael 30 labourer I-23
Murphy James 21 labourer-25sy
Murphy Jonathan 22 labourer-25
Murphy Patrick labourer-25sy
Murphy William 21 labourer-25
Murphy Edward 17 labourer S-26
Murphy Eugene 16 S-26
Murphy Margaret 14 S-26
Murphy Mary 30 spinster I-26
Murphy Johanna 24 spinster I-26
Murphy Daniel 20 I-26
Murphy Daniel J 22 labourer I-27
Murphy Thomas 27 labourer I-27
Murphy Eliza 27 spinster I-27
Murphy Rev D I-28
Murphy John 21 labourer I-29
Murphy Edmund 26 labourer I-30
Murphy John 20 I-30
Murphy John 30 farm lab I-31
Murphy Mary 27 I-31
Murphy Hannah 2 I-31
Murphy Margaret 18 servant I-31
Murphy Moses 25 I-31
Murphy Catherine 35 I-31
Murphy Owen 25 labourer I-31
Murphy Thomas 13 I-31
Murphy Barnard 10 I-32
Murphy Patrick 19 I-32
Murphy William I-33
Murphy Luke 30-36
Murphy Dennis labourer I-37
Murphy John 30 farmer I-37
Murphy William 22 I-37
Murphy John 32 miner I-39
Murphy James 20-41
Murphy Michael 17-41

Murphy Daniel 22 I-42
Murphy Dennis 22 I-42
Murphy Margaret 23 I-42
Murphy Jane-42
Murphy Rebecca 18-42
Murphy Edward 14-42
Murphy John 7-42
Murphy Patrick 30 I-42
Murrance John 21 labourer-25
Murray James 26 storekeeper-13
Murray Jane 23 farmer I-13
Murray John 25 bookeeper-16
Murray Thomas 22 labourer I-16
Murray Anthony 48 labourer S-21
Murray Mrs H 47 S-21
Murray Sarah 11 S-21
Murray Miss Catherine 24 S-21
Murray Jno 26 labourer-23
Murray William 21 labourer S-23
Murray James 27 labourer I-24
Murray James 28 labourer-24
Murray Jonathan 36 labourer-24
Murray Mary A 40-24
Murray William 2-24
Murray Jonathan 22 labourer-24
Murray Thomas 19 labourer-24
Murray James 16 labourer-25
Murray Robert 25 labourer-25sy
Murray Susanna 22-25sy
Murray Jane 2-25sy
Murray Robertina infant-25sy
Murray Agnes 23 servant-26
Murray William 23 S-26ad
Murray Patrick 32 miner I-27
Murray James 40-28
Murray Janet L spinster-30
Murray James 18 labourer-34
Murray William 28-34
Murray Robert 25 labourer I-37
Murray Mary Ann 22 I-37
Murray James W -38
Murray Mrs-38
Murray Mrs Mary-38
Murray Henrietta 5-38
Murray Denis 29 farmer I-39
Murray Ellen 26 I-39
Murray John 40-41
Murray Joseph 26 I-42
Murray Walter 34 S-42
Murray W G -43
Murray Mrs-43
Murrell William 38 labourer-32
Murrell Honora 35-32
Murrell John 9-32
Murrell William 4-32
Murrell Elizabeth 1-32
Murtagh John 38 labourer-42
Murtagh Julia 38-42
Murtagh Bernard 7-42
Murtagh Catherine 7-42
Murtagh Alexander 5-42
Murtagh John W 3-42

Murtagh August T 1-42
Musschialla Louis 40 lab. OP-30
Musschialla Hannah 41 OP-30
Musschialla Peter 8 OP-30
Musschialla Louis 6 OP-30
Mycroft Isaac 34 mason-13
Myer Henry H 34 labourer-23
Myer Amelia 30-23
Myer Louis 32 labourer-23
Myer Olivia 25-23
Myers Simon labourer S-31
Mylan John 24 I-33
Mylchreen Alfred C 15-32
Myles Alfred 18 labourer-25
Myrnning Jane servant-28

N

Nabb Abraham 42 I-36
Nabb Ann 34 I-36
Nabile O -22
Naddell James 35 labourer S-35
Naddell Helen 25 S-35
Naddell Helen 1 S-35
Nagle Edwin 20 labourer I-32
Naher Cornelius 23 I-32
Naigle Theado 24 labourer OP-30
Nail Bridget 20 I-31
Nail Winifred 17 I-31
Nail William 20 blacksmith I-31
Nail William 50 blacksmith I-31
Nail Bridget 50 I-31
Nail Sarah 15 I-31
Naish Mary A 39-34
Nalder W Frank 21 labourer I-31
Nally Patrick 23-41
Nally Eliza 28-41
Nanly Daniel 24 farmer I-31
Napier Mrs Mary-26
Napier J merchant-39
Narallo Falinzo 44 labourer OP-32
Narallo Dominzo 14 OP-32
Nasella Catherina OP-36
Nasella Catherina 7 OP-36
Nash James-29
Nasmith Joseph 20-37
Nathen Aaron 22 miner-31
Natherill James 60 S-43
Natherill Ann 60 S-43
Natherill Minnie 8 S-43
Natman Mrs Janet 44-34
Natman Elizabeth 9-34
Natman Jemima 7-34
Natman William 3-34
Natteras William 22 labourer-23
Nayle Eleanor 26 nurse-42
Nayler Mr B S-27
Nayler Mrs-27
Naylor Eleazer 23 labourer-24
Naylor James 36 labourer-25
Naylor James 35 labourer I-31
Naylor Elizabeth 30 spinster-34
Naylor Margaret 28 spinster-34

Naylor Simon 28-42
Neace Hans 19 OP-38
Needing George L 52 OP-41
Neenan Timothy 30 labourer I-32
Neeson Joseph 24 labourer I-24
Neeson Andrew 25-27
Negan Patrick 28 workman I-38
Neil Amos 24 farmer I-16
Neil George 37 farmer-16
Neil Patrick 18 labourer I-30
Neil Patrick 19 I-35
Neill William 20 labourer-24
Neill Luke 35-41
Neill Bridget 30-41
Neill Mary A 8-41
Neill Bridget 4-41
Neill Catherine 2-41
Neill (baby born)-41
Neilon Miss Isabella 16 S-23
Neilson David 27 labourer S-39
Neilson Andrew 42-42
Neland George 30 miner-13
Nellthorpe Mrs Caroline 28-21
Nelson Mr 41-16
Nelson Mrs 21-16
Nelson James 27 labourer-22
Nelson Robert J 27 labourer I-23
Nelson Titus 30 labourer-26
Nelson John 43 labourer-31
Nelson David 57-39
Neness Edmund 34 labourer-23
Neness Elizabeth 30-23
Neness Miss Sarah 40-23
Nepinall Mr-11
Nepinall Mrs-11
Nepoen Luis OP-36
Nepren William L 19 baker-37
Ners Jimmy 9-26
Nesbitt Noble 29 labourer-27
Nesbitt Edward 6-27
Nesbitt Mrs June 20 I-35
Nesbitt William James 1 I-35
Ness Thomas-39
Ness Hannah-39
Nestod John 22-37
Netherington Thomas 28 lab. S-24
Nettleship Miss Ann 26-24
Nettleton Hannah 30-16
Nettleton Mary Ellen 1-16
Neuse William 40-43
Neville Mrs Elizabeth 24-16
Neville James 1 (died)-16
(died 11/12 of pneumonia)
Neville Robert 22 farmer I-16
Neville Walter 35-36
New Frederick A 23 clerk-40
Newall Richard 23 needlemaker-10sy
Newall Sarah 23-10sy
Newall Miss S-31
Newall infant S-31
Newbold Robert 31 farmer-11
Newbury Emma-32

Newcombe Essex 26 joiner-20
Newcombe William 33 labourer-23
Newcombe John S 32-labourer-27
Newell H -9
Newey William 34 I-36
Newey Annie 37 I-36
Newlands James 28 labourer S-23
Newley John 35-10sy
Newman John 19 miner-13sy
Newman John 40 farmer-13
Newman Ellen 38-13
Newman Agnes 7-13
Newman Henry 34-13
Newman Margaret 22-13
Newman Rudolph 19 OP-28
Newman Mrs J-43
Newsham D C adult OP-40
Newsome Squire 34-33
Newton F A 17 builder-16
Newton Thomas 41 cornmiller-16
Newton Alice 42-16
Newton Samuel F 16-16
Newton Richard H-21
Newton Chris-23
Newton Maria-23
Newton Jane-23
Newton Edith-23
Newton Chris-23
Newton Sydney-23
Newton Andrew 18-28
Newton Henry R-31
Newton Thomas 33-39
Newton Harriet 33-39
Newton Alice 5-39
Newton Florence 1-39
Newton Thomas 40 builder-39
Newton Elwena E 33-39
Newton Alice E 10-39
Newton Herbert W 8-39
Newton Francis T 5-39
Newton Clara J 3-39
Neylan Bridget 28 spinster I-29
Nibbett Jonathan 24 labourer-24
Nichol James 22 S-32
Nichol Mrs S-32
Nichol Alexander S-32
Nicholas Charles H 11-21
Nicholas John 28 labourer-21
Nicholas Nicholas 21 labourer-21
Nicholas Job 39 labourer-31
Nicholas Eliza 38-31
Nicholas Eliza Jane 6-31
Nicholas Grace 3-31
Nicholas Edward 2-31
Nicholes James 25 labourer-27
Nicholes John 19 labourer-27
Nicholls H -9
Nicholls Thomas S-11
Nicholls Mrs Harriet 28 I-23
Nicholls Sophia 6-23
Nicholls Miss-29
Nicholls Miss Elizabeth 52-32

Nicholson Thomas H 39 farmer-13
Nicholson Mrs L 41-26
Nicholson Ann 11-26
Nicholson John C 9-26
Nicholson Wilhelmina 8-26
Nicholson W 34 labourer-27
Nicholson Clara 27-27
Nicholson Malcolm 2-27
Nicholson Helen 39 spinster S-31
Nicholson Mark-32
Nicholson John-32
Nicholson Barbara servant S-35
Nicholson S B 21-36
Nicholson John 45 grocer I-37
Nicholson Catherine 42 I-37
Nicholson Sarah 20 I-37
Nick Peter 27 labourer-23
Nick Eliza 27-23
Nicol Mr 21 farmer S-16
Nicol Thomas-16
Nicola Paulina 16 OP-42
Nicolas Hannah 42-10
Nicolas Thomas 13-10
Nicolas William 9-10
Nicolas G H 5-10
Nicolas Eliza 3-10
Nielaus Jean 22 OP-38
Nielaus Jean 21 OP-38
Niff Thomas 24 trader-40au
Niggerman Bernard 24 clerk OP-13
Nightingale J -9
Nilsen H J OP-38
Nilson William 22 farmer-27
Nine Edward 35 miner-11
Nine William 33-11
Nisbett Jonathan 24 labourer-24
Nissen Johanna 20 OP-40
Nixon H -9
Nixon Albert 56 bricklayer-11
Nixon George 22 cooper-11
Nixon A 13-41
Nixon Robert 40-41
Noall William-9
Nobb William 27 miner-13
Noble Miss Ann 32-24
Noble John A 31 labourer-26
Noble James 26 labourer-30
Noblet George-9
Nock William 22 labourer OP-27
Noel Matthew 20 labourer-22
Nolan David 38 labourer I-23
Nolan Joseph 24 labourer I-24
Nolan Martin 21 I-27
Nolan Archibald 19 labourer I-30
Nolan Thomas 15 farm labourer I-31
Nolan Patrick 22 I-32
Nolan John 20 I-32
Nolan Nicholas 20 I-35
Nolan Mrs Ellen 34-36
Nolan John 5-36
Noonan James 17 I-28
Noonan Bridget 14 I-31

Noonan Simon 12 I-31
Noonan Thomas 25 labourer I-31
Noonan Ellen 20 I-31
Noonan Pat 45 I-31
Noonan Bridget 45 I-31
Norcott Samuel 21-41
Norindar Eliza 34-42
Norman Jonathan 45 joiner-10
Norman W 24 builder-10
Norman Mr-11
Norman R N 21 labourer I-31
Norman Henry 22-41
Normington Mrs Rebecca 47-23
Normington Louisa 11-23
Normoyle John 50 I-33
Norris William-9
Norris Donald 30-34
Norris Patrick 9-34
Norris Daniel 7-34
North H I 20 labourer-26
North Jesse 27-41
Nortley Robert 20 miner-13
Nortley Stephen 17 miner-13
Norton Jane 25-34
Novas Michael 20 labourer-33
Nowell J W-11
Nozier Samuel 23 OP-42
Nueman Benjamin 25 I-29
Nugent John 20 I-35
Nugent John 24 I-36
Nugent Ronald R 16-41
Nulty Thomas 28 labourer-25
Nulty Barnard 27 weaver I-32
Nunan Matthew 21 I-28
Nunan Maurice 14 I-28
Nutt Matilda 20 spinster-27
Nutt Mary Ann 18 spinster-27
Nuttal John 28-29
Nuttal Mary 28-29
Nuttal Harriet 2-29
Nuttal Betsey infant-29
Nutting I B -43
Nutting Miss-43

O

O'Boyle Charles 57 labourer I-23
O'Boyle Anne 52 I-23
O'Boyle Mary 24 I-23
O'Boyle Anne 22 I-23
O'Boyle Owen 20 I-23
O'Boyle Charles 17 I-23
O'Brien Michael 25 I-24
O'Brien Miss Elizabeth 20 I-28
O'Brien Pat 26-28
O'Brien Mrs E I-29
O'Brien Patrick 21 labourer I-31
O'Brien Thomas 22 I-32
O'Brien John 32 I-34
O'Brien Cornelius 24 I-41
O'Brien John 20 I-41
O'Brien Julia-42
O'Brien Thomas 30 I-43

O'Callaghan R W 20-33
O'Callaghan Jeremiah 26 lab. I-42
O'Callaghan Ellen 25 I-42
O'Connell Daniel 25 farmer-16sy
O'Connell James 24 I-41
O'Connoll Nicholas 40 I-42
O'Connor Pat 26 labourer-25
O'Connor Jonathan 22 I-28
O'Connor Mary 50 housekeeper I-31
O'Connor Daniel 32 labourer I-32
O'Connor Thomas 21 I-32
O'Connor O I-39
O'Connor Charles 19-42
O'Connor William 17 I-43
O'Corvan Miss Margaret-22sy
O'Dea Kyran J 21 labourer I-22
O'Donnell Nicholas 24 lab.-25
O'Donnell Cornelius 25 lab. I-27
O'Donnell Anastana I-30
O'Donnell Mary I-30
O'Donnell Francis 26 shoemaker I-31
O'Donoghue David 20 labourer I-31
O'Donoghue Patrick 58 I-35
O'Donoghue Bridget 54 I-35
O'Donoghue Patrick 28 I-35
O'Dwyer Edward 37 labourer I-26
O'Grady Martin I-42
O'Grady Bridget I-42
O'Grady Mary Jane 4 I-42
O'Grady William Joseph 1 I-42
O'Hagan Charles 25 I-43
O'Hanlon John 21-36
O'Hara Patrick-9
O'Hara Louisa 20 spinster I-28
O'Hara Helena 18 spinster I-28
O'Hara Mary 16 spinster I-28
O'Hara Olivia 14 spinster I-28
O'Hara Henry 11 I-28
O'Hara William 9 I-28
O'Hara Henrietta 15 I-28
O'Hara Mr 46 labourer I-28
O'Hara Mrs 34 I-28
O'Hara Miss 17 I-28
O'Hara Arthur 12 I-28
O'Hara Katherine 8 I-28
O'Hara William 5 I-28
O'Hegan Pat 35 labourer I-24
O'Hegan Catherine 26 I-24
O'Hegan Peter 5 I-24
O'Hegan Mary A 2 I-24
O'Kane Patrick 22 I-36
O'Keane Daniel 20 labourer I-21
O'Keane Daniel J 24 labourer I-33
O'Keane Maurice 22 I-33
O'Keefe John 26 I-16
O'Keefe Michael labourer I-33
O'Keefe Thomas 23-40
O'Keefe William 19 I-42
O'Keefe D S 22 I-42
O'Keilly Thomas 30 S-35
O'Laughlin Patrick 22 I-28
O'Leary Bridget 19 spinster I-13

O'Leary Jeremiah 25 I-36
O'Loughlin John 19 labourer I-28
O'Mahoney Peter 27 labourer-25
O'Mallie John 26 I-36
O'Mara John 22 farm labourer I-31
O'Mara Daniel 55 farmer I-42
O'Mara Mary 45 I-42
O'Mara Mary 22 I-42
O'Mara John 26 I-42
O'Mara Patrick 24 I-42
O'Mara Daniel 20 I-42
O'Meara Patrick 21 labourer I-31
O'Meara Tim 19 I-31
O'Neill Mrs Alice 24-16
O'Neill Charles John 2-16
O'Neill Miss Elizabeth 21 I-34
O'Shannasy John 34 I-24
O'Shaughnessy Martin 40 lab. I-27
O'Shaughnessy Johana 37 I-27
O'Shaughnessy Bridget 11 I-27
O'Shaughnessy Johan 48 I-43
O'Shaunasy Denis 26 labourer I-27
O'Shaunassy Hon J I-30
O'Shaunassy Mrs I-30
O'Shaunessy James 59 I-28
O'Shaunessy Mrs 42 I-28
O'Shea James 30 I-35
O'Shea Mary 25 I-40
O'Shea Tim 21 farmer I-40
O'Sullivan John 21 farmer I-16
O'Sullivan Francis 37 lab. I-24
O'Sullivan Ann 26 I-24
O'Sullivan Mary 6 I-24
O'Sullivan Miss Johanna 30 I-26
O'Sullivan Patrick 30 lab. I-26
O'Sullivan Annie 21 spinster I-27
O'Sullivan Owen 21 I-28
O'Sullivan Jeremiah 45 farmer I-35
O'Sullivan Mary 45 I-35
O'Sullivan Patrick 22 I-42
O'Toole Martin 22 labourer I-22
Oakes George E 23 labourer-33sy
Oates John labourer-34
Oates Samuel 28-35
Oberben Frederick miner OP-39
Oberben August OP-39
Odell Thomas 27 labourer-26
Odey Henry 22 labourer-22
Odger Edwin-29
Odger Elizabeth-29
Odger infant-29
Ogden Miss Sarah Maria 21-25
Ogden Joseph 24 labourer I-26
Ogilvie John 56 mechanic-40
Ogilvie Ann 56-40
Ogilvy W H -9
Ohlsen Laurence 29 OP-29
Oldfield Fanny 23 spinster-29
Oldfield John Henry 32-29
Oldknorr Frank 18-21
Olgiate A 23 OP-26
Olise Julius miner OP-39

Olive E C -22
Olive Henry 21 labourer-24
Oliver Daniel-11
Oliver William 21-29
Oliver Mr-31
Oliver Mrs-31
Oliver Charles 35-33
Oliver David grocer-41
Ollis Mrs A -11
Ollis Francis-11
Ollis Elizabeth-11
Ollis Louisa-11
Openshaw Mr-20
Opil Richard 32 miner-11
Opil William 28 miner-11
Opitig Miss Eunica 16 OP-35
Oram G 19 butcher-10
Orange Richard C 43-42
Orgill Henry 23 labourer-21
Orgill William 19-21
Orgill Henry 21-34
Ormandy James 28 engineer-38
Orme Edward C -11
Ormerod J -9
Ormerod George 18-32
Ormiston Robert 22 farmer S-13
Orr Archibald 27 miner S-13
Orr Jessie 23 S-13
Orr infant S-13
Orr Archibald 46 labourer S-22
Orr William-22
Orums George 35 labourer-21
Orums Jessie 28-21
Orums William 6-21
Orums Martha 4-21
Orums Jessie 2-21
Orums George 1-21
Orven John-22
Osborn Job 27 labourer S-21
Osborne Mrs Mary 40-16
Osborne William Thomas 14-16
Osborne Hannibal 10-16
Osborne Alfred 8-16
Osborne Mary Elizabeth 6-16
Osborne John 4-16
Osborne George-20
Osborne William 18 labourer-23
Osborne Eliza 30 spinster-28
Osborne James 20 I-28
Osborne Mrs J 35-29
Osborne Arabella 13-29
Osborne Ernest A 11-29
Osborne Bessie 8-29
Osborne Richard E P 6-20
Osborne Herbert F 5-29
Osborne Percy C 3-29
Osborne William Henry 15-29
Osborne H H -37
Osborne Mrs-37
Osborne A -37
Osborne Mrs Sarah-37
Osborough James 21 labourer-23

Osmond Philip 30 carpenter–11
Ossie James 20 labourer–35
Oswin Richard–9
Ott Catherine 25 spinster I–27
Otter Peter 17 labourer S–32
Ottwell Elizabeth 22–43
Ousley Ross A 24 spinster–34sy
Outhred H D 26 butcher–10
Outhwaite Robert–23
Owen R–9
Owen Alexander 24 farmer S–13
Owen Joshua 35–29
Owen Ellen 25–29
Owen Mary E 8–29
Owen John William 4–29
Owen Margaret infant–29
Owen Ewens 30 labourer–32
Owen Thomas 28–32
Owen Lewis 21–32
Owen John S 21–32
Owen Francis 27 I–33
Owen Henry H 14 labourer–34
Owen William 19 saddler–34
Owen Robert farmer S–37
Owen John 24 farmer–38
Owens John 34 labourer–27
Owens Sarah 29–27
Owens Robert 40–36
Owens William J 30 farmer–39
Oxley Richard 40 labourer–26
Oxley Ann Jane 35–26
Oxley James 11–26
Oxley Esther 10–26
Oxley George 8–26
Oxley Jane 6–26
Oxley Rachel 3–26
Oxley Matilda infant–26
Oxley William 14–26

P

Packer Noli 23–36
Padman Thomas 48–24
Page John–11
Page William–31
Page (2 Misses)–31
Page George 38–34
Page Janet 42–34
Page David 10–34
Page Janet 6–34
Page Alexander 4–34
Page George 1–34
Page Elizabeth 12–34
Paget Craven 22 joiner–13
Paice George 27–11
Painer W 37 S–10
Painter Alfred 22 miner–13
Painter Susan 22 spinster S–31
Pairgraves John 25–28
Paisley John 17–41
Paitchard Samuel 34 gardener–37
Paller Emily 47 S–35
Pallett W G –9

Palmer William 38 merchant–16
Palmer R R 20–33
Palmer William 47–35
Palmer Mary A 49–35
Palmer Elizabeth 21–35
Palmer Rebecca 17–35
Palmer George 33–42
Palmer Mary Ann 32–42
Palmer Laura 5–42
Palyke Martin 36 OP–39
Palyke Maria 30 OP–39
Palyke Anna 4 OP–39
Palyke Maria 7 OP–39
Palyke Johanna 1 OP–39
Panizza Luizi OP–16
Panks David 25 labourer–34
Panshow Richard 22–28
Pantos Maria–32
Parcell Miss Ellen 23 I–32
Parish George–27
Pariss Frederick 19–27
Park John–9
Park Margaret–9
Park Mary–9
Park Thomas–9
Parken George 26 farmer–13
Parker G B adult–10
Parker Henry–11
Parker James 40 minister–13
Parker Michael 55 miner–16sy
Parker Jane 50–16sy
Parker Mary Ann 9–16sy
Parker Miss Emma 22–23
Parker William–23
Parker Robert 29–24
Parker Charles 35 labourer–26
Parker Ann 28–26
Parker (infant born 13.2.65)–26
Parker Lydia 5–26
Parker Mary 4–26
Parker Ann 2–26
Parker Robert 47–27
Parker Rev J –31
Parker Mrs–31
Parker Elizabeth E 7–31
Parker Fanny 6–31
Parker Herbert infant–31
Parker Mr–34
Parker Chris 34 mechanic I–36
Parker Lydia 22 I–36
Parker Alice infant I–36
Parker Gerald 22 I–41
Parker Rose 22 I–41
Parker Wm G 36 shipwright–43br
Parker Mrs 60–43br
Parkes Elizabeth 28 I–40
Parkinson Robert E 32 labourer–30
Parley Henrietta 22 servant I–42
Parnall Thomas 25 labourer–29
Parovicini Bendetto 39 OP–40
Parr Miss Elizabeth 29 I–24
Parr George 32–24

Parr William 36–32
Parr James 35 glazier I–35
Parr Margaret 35 I–35
Parr Bertha 7 I–35
Parr Frederick 3 I–35
Parr Walter 1 I–35
Parrott Thomas 60 blacksmith–37
Parry R 23 miner–10
Parry Elizabeth G 45 spinster–16
Parry Robert 29 labourer–20
Parry John 32 labourer–21
Parry Mons–22
Parry J R 28 labourer–23
Parry Miss Elizabeth 22 I–32
Parry J P –35
Parsons R –9
Parsons Mrs Mary 29–21
Parsons Jane 6–21
Parsons Henry 19 labourer–24
Parsons Edward 20–24
Parsons Ann 7–33
Parsons W H 22 labourer–33
Parsons I A 18–33
Parsons George 19–33
Parsons George–35
Parsons Elizabeth–35
Parsons George 10–35
Parsons Cecil 8–35
Parsons Adeline 1–35
Parsons Ephraim 17–36
Parsons John A 23 engineer–40
Parsons C M 19–40
Parsons George 24–40
Parsons George–41
Parsons Mrs–41
Pascoe Jonathan 34 miner–10
Pascoe Joshua 25 smith–10
Pascoe John 35 miner–11
Pascoe Nicholas 22 miner–11
Pascoe Richard 30 miner–13
Pascoe John 28 labourer–21
Pascoe Joseph 22–42
Pascoe Catherine 24–42
Pash Henry 27 traveller–42
Pasiani G 46 OP–40
Pasiani V 10 OP–40
Pasiani I V 8 OP–40
Pasiani Dom 11 OP–40
Pasiani Frans 9 OP–40
Patch Mrs servant–21
Pater John 21 farmer–13
Pater Matilda 22–13
Pates William labourer 45–20
Pates Eliza 42–20
Pates Susannah 20–20
Pates Elizabeth 17–20
Paterson Alexander–9
Paterson John–9
Paterson James 35 miner S–21
Paterson Carl 21 labourer OP–22
Paterson J C 26 labourer S–22
Paterson James–34

Paterson Mrs–34
Paterson Agnes 14–34
Paterson Marian 9–34
Paterson H B 18–36
Paton Miss Mary 26 S–21
Paton Walter 29 labourer S–21
Patrick Carl–11
Patrick Stewart 31 labourer–30
Patrick Mrs 29–30
Patterson W 50 architect S–10
Patterson Catherine N 25 S–10
Patterson David 22 joiner S–11
Patterson Thomas 25 miner–13
Patterson Elizabeth 27–13
Patterson Mary 2–13
Patterson Miss J –22
Patterson Miss Helen–23
Patterson Miss Matilda 21 S–23
Patterson James 19 labourer–25
Patterson Lancelot 23 lab.–25
Patterson William jr lab. I–26
Patterson J H –29
Patterson M S –31
Patterson R –32
Patterson Miss–32
Patterson Hugh 22–36
Patterson Robert 28–36
Pattinson I R 21 labourer–22
Pattinson William 30 labourer–24
Pattinson George 21–29
Pattinson John 48 miner–37
Pattison James 43–36
Pattison Mrs 40–36
Pattison Mrs 30–40
Pattison Ada 9–40
Pattison Hannah 10–40
Paul R 30 miner–10
Paul Edward–30
Paul Mrs Rosalie–30
Paul Annie M infant–30
Paulton Maria 52–42
Pause Richard 20 labourer–22
Paviso G –9
Paxton Adam 22 merchant S–11
Payne Robert–20
Payne Joseph 19–34
Payne Matthew R 47 S–36
Payne Henry 25–38
Paynter Miss–35
Paynter Ellen 23 servant–38
Payton James–41
Peace William 36 labourer–25
Peace Mary 33–25
Peacock Thomas 20 labourer–21
Peacock Robert 30 labourer I–24
Peake W F –22
Pearce Charles–9
Pearce Edward–9
Pearce William 43 labourer–11
Pearce William 26 miner–13
Pearce Miss Ellen 19–21
Pearce Josiah 16–21

Pearce William 20 labourer–22
Pearce Mrs Mary 36–23
Pearce Louisa 6–23
Pearce Clarissa 4–23
Pearce Thomas 70 I–32
Pears John 24 miner–27
Pearse Gardner 21 labourer–23
Pearson Mrs Margaret 25–16
Pearson Miss Susanna 20–23
Pearson Mrs Mary 49–24
Pearson William 19 labourer–24
Pearson Frederick 39–28
Pearson Frederick 12–28
Pearson David–43
Peart John 39 labourer–25
Peart Tamar 34–25
Peart Annie 6–25
Peart William 4–25
Peart Hannah 2–25
Peart Thomas 23–28
Peatt John 22 labourer–26
Peck Edward–9
Peck Hugh–9
Peck George–9
Peck E N –9
Pecos William 19 labourer–26
Pedretti Pietri 34 OP–43
Peebles John–9
Peel Eleanor spinster–11
Peel Hannah 22 spinster–16
Peel Alfred 24 compositor S–27
Peel Ann 24 S–27
Peel Thomas–41
Peers John G 22 labourer–23
Peers Robert–34
Peetra Gabrillo 21 OP–33
Pehas Henry 51 artisan I–37
Pehas Christine 41 I–37
Peill William 19 labourer I–24
Pelarchi Giovanni OP–38
Pelasio Giondomanico 19 lab.OP–13
Pellahie Jonathan 26 labourer–34
Pellahie E 25–34
Pelling John 25 clerk–13
Pellit Mr & Mrs J N N –30
Pellow Stephen 32 OP–33
Pemberton M –9
Pemberton Robert 23–21
Pemberton Harriet 39–39
Pemberton Melbourne 13–39
Pemberton Clara D 11–39
Pemberton Samuel 10–39
Pemberton Frederick C 7–39
Pemberton Henry C 6–39
Pemberton Percy G 4–39
Pemberton Thomas A 2–39
Pemberton Hope 1–39
Pemberty H 32 miner–10
Pemberty Eliza 30–10
Pemlatt Mrs Rush 34–34
Pemlatt Mary 4–34
Pemlatt John 35 labourer–34

Pender Michael 28 shepherd I–32
Pender Mary 26 I–32
Pender Patrick 2 I–32
Pender William 1 I–32
Pender Patrick 51 I–32
Pender Bridget 35 I–32
Pender William 19 S–40
Pendlebury James 26 labourer–26
Pendlebury Robert 27 labourer–22
Pendleton H L 18 I–10
Penfold Capt R –33sy
Penlington Thomas 42 clerk–38
Penman John 34 S–33
Penman Margaret 34 S–33
Penman William C 5 S–33
Penman Margaret E 3 S–33
Penman Elspeth 1 S–33
Penman Mary R 6 S–33
Pennell Henry 29–36
Penny Alfred 29–43au
Peoples Thomas 24 I–28
Pepper John G 45 labourer–23
Perch William adult–10
Percival William butcher–37
Perdue Diana 27 spinster I–20
Perinovi Mrs Caterina 39 OP–23
Perinovi Battina 9 OP–23
Perkin Miss Elizabeth 14–21
Perkin John–22
Perkin Ive 55–29
Perkins Edward 40–35
Perkins Mary 40–35
Perkins Sampson 10–35
Perkins Edward 5–35
Perkins Hannah 16–35
Perkins Thomas 14–35
Perks William 50–27
Perks William 59 labourer S–32
Perrey Charles 21–13
Perrey George 23–13
Perrier William 30–25
Perrot Horatio 25–11
Perrott D J –9
Perry F –9
Perry John–9
Perry John 29 coaler–10
Perry Bennett 24 miner–11
Perry Miss–23
Perry Samuel 30 labourer–26
Perry Elizabeth 25 spinster–26
Perry George 33 labourer–33
Perry George 19–34
Perryman Richard 17 labourer I–31
Peters H C –9
Peters J –9
Peters Thomas 21 miner–13
Peters Hilton 19–35
Petersen Jurgen 21 OP–29
Peterson James 29 surgeon–11
Peterson Andrew 25 surgeon–11
Peterson H J 21 labourer OP–27
Peterson I H 17 S–30

Peterson Christina 24 spinster–31
Peterson Ewald 5–31
Peterson Samuel 25–35
Peterson George 28 S–36
Petherbridge Thomas 23 lab.–11
Petrie Nusiel 24 glazier OP–16
Petrie Thomas 61 S–30
Petrie Mrs 63 S–30
Petrie Charles 22 S–30
Petrie Jane servant–34
Petterson P 22 OP–10
Petterson P 28 OP–10
Pettie Mrs Grace 46–21
Pettie James 14–21
Pettie Elizabeth 6–21
Pettie Isabella 4–21
Pettigrew J –9
Pettygrew A D –9
Pettygrew Miss–9
Pettygrew M E –9
Pezzioni Balestra 15 farmer OP–20
Phayer William 17 labourer I–21
Phelan James 22 labourer I–23
Phelan John 23 I–32
Phelan Dennis 32 I–36
Phelan Mary 18 I–36
Phelan Hannah 50 I–42
Pherson Mr–26
Philip Richard–35
Philips Mary 21–39
Phillip John 28 artisan–37
Phillip Elizabeth–42
Phillip Ann 11–42
Phillip Thomas 1–42
Phillips Frederick–9
Phillips William 41 miner–11
Phillips John W –16
Phillips Joseph 28 labourer–21
Phillips Griffith 27 labourer–22
Phillips James 36 labourer–22
Phillips George 29 labourer I–23
Phillips James 23 labourer–26
Phillips J Henry 21–labourer–26
Phillips Thomas 21 labourer–28
Phillips William 37–29
Phillips Miss Jane 34 S–36
Phillips John 21–36
Phillips Martha 27–40
Phillips Charles 27–43 1y
Phillips Frances 32–43
Pianta Joseph 30 OP–33
Piccoli Andrea 19 OP–40
Picken W H 19 former–10
Pickering Mrs 60–22
Pickering William 27 labourer–24
Pidmonte Bartotomo 28 lab.OP–21sy
Pidmonte Adeline 26 OP–21sy
Pidmonte Guiseppe 1 OP–21sy
Pieroni Enrico 41 OP–38
Pierossi Erico 31 labourer OP–20
Piers Robert 38 labourer–20
Piers Edward 16–20

Pifferini Batista 16 lab. OP–13
Piggott Louis J 45–43
Piggott Elizabeth 34–43
Piggott Emily 16–43
Piggott Edgar 12–43
Piggott Percy 11–43
Piggott Lily 8–43
Piggott Sydney 6–43
Piggott Stanley 3–43
Piggott Gerald 15–43
Pigott Patrick 26 labourer I–31
Pike John 24–36
Pilkington E 23 spinster–25
Pilling Sarah 31–20
Pilling Betsy 6–20
Pilling Sarah A 3–20
Pillow Henry 21 I–42
Pilten Mary H 28 I–41
Pinchen William 19 labourer–25
Pinckerton Charles 23 lab. I–32
Pinckerton Samuel 21 I–32
Pincus Marc 17 clerk OP–37
Pindue Samuel 26 carpenter–13
Pine Miss Catherine 18–36
Pipes George 28 carpenter–13
Pipes Mary 24–13
Pippard George 30 labourer I–27
Pisiana James 40 labourer OP–30
Pitman Maria 32 spinster–27
Pitman Albert 10–27
Pitt A adult–10
Pitt Robert 58–43
Pitty Thomas 59–32
Placzet Jacob 26–11
Plant Robert 24–41
Platmaner Louis 20 OP–10
Platt Richard 20 labourer I–22
Platt Jonathan 30–28
Playfair J H –9
Plevins C H –9
Plevins William G 30–10
Plumley Jessie 36 spinster S–27
Plumley Charles 3 S–27
Plumley Christopher infant S–27
Plunkett Capt–16
Pobjoy William 26 draper–16
Pocock E J –9
Poingdishe Edward J –29
Polaman Charles 30 OP–34
Pold Dominici 19 OP–35
Pole John 43 contractor–41
Polglase William Henry 22 lab.–21
Polglase Nanny 23–21
Polita Gianni 23 labourer OP–13
Polkingham Stephen 18 labourer–21
Polkington David 25 labourer–26
Pollard Thomas 40 warehouseman–13
Pollard Elizabeth 18–32
Pollard Esther 12–32
Pollard John 40 miner–32
Pollard Elizabeth 40–32
Pollard James 10–32

Pollard Thomas 7–32
Pollard Joseph 5–32
Pollard Mary A 4–32
Pollard Edward E 1–32
Pollard Christopher infant–32
Pollard John 18–32
Pollard Richard E 16–32
Pollard William C 15–32
Pollard Philip W 14–32
Pollard William 29–34
Pollock David–9
Pollock Hugh–9
Pollock Joseph James–9
Pollock J –9
Pollock John–9
Pollock William–9
Pollock James 30 trader–13
Pollock John 22 farmer I–38
Pollon John 39–13
Polmsar J –9
Polo Bernardo 29 OP–40
Pomeroy Meredith 50 matron–25
Pomeroy Richard 18–25
Pomeroy Margaret 16–25
Pomeroy Redmond 8–25
Pomeroy Mary 11–25
Pomjoy George–9
Pond Jonathan 38 labourer–24
Pond Mary 38–24
Pond Jonathan T 8–24
Pool John 10–34
Pool Ann 52–38
Poole Charles 32 labourer–22
Poole Maria 30 spinster–22
Poole Charlotte 27 spinster–22
Poole Henry E 37–33
Poole Campbell 40–41
Poole Sarah A 40–41
Poole James 37–42
Pope Mr E –27
Pope Mrs–27
Pope Joseph 22 labourer S–31
Pope Richard 35 labourer I–31
Pope Mayo 30 I–31
Pope Olivia 7 I–31
Pope Sarah J 6 I–31
Pope Matilda 4 I–31
Pope Richard 3 I–31
Pope Clare 1.1/2 I–31
Pope Joseph infant I–31
Porrer Pat 24 blacksmith I–37
Porteous John 22 labourer S–36
Porteous Emily 23–42
Porter H –9
Porter Robert–9
Porter William–9
Porter Thomas H 23 miner–13
Porter Charles 33 labourer–21
Porter Frances 26 labourer–21
Porter Jane 20 spinster I–22
Porter Thomas–23
Porter George 21 labourer I–32

Porter Edward 52-33
Porter Maria 46-33
Porter Alfred 17-33
Porter Agustin 16-33
Porter Edward 15-33
Porter Catherine 5-33
Porter John 26 labourer-34
Porvell E -22
Pott Joseph 36 miner-13
Potter Patrick 23 I-22
Potterson Moses 20 labourer-24
Pourfield Patrick 28-28
Pourfield Joseph 26-28
Poustie Donald 21 I-37
Poustie Matilda 20 I-37
Powel Richard 25 farmer I-16
Powell William E 20 watchmaker-16
Powell James 21 labourer I-21
Powell John 27 labourer-26
Powell William 24 labourer-27
Powell Miss E C 32-31
Powell Mary 12-31
Powell Thomas 50 labourer I-31
Powell Miss Margaret 26-32
Powell Mary J 21 spinster-37
Powell Frank W 14-42
Power Rev John-20
Power Robert-23
Power John 40 labourer-25
Power Jeffrey 20 labourer-27
Power Peter 22 labourer-27
Power Rev J P I-35
Power Pierce 24 I-36
Pozane James 34 I-34
Pozzi Graconi 36 labourer OP-37
Prag Julius 19 jeweller-42
Pratt Mrs Hannah 60-22
Pratt Harriet 20-22
Pratt Jonathan 21 labourer-27
Predeaux Richard E 30-labourer-24
Predeaux Mrs E 23-24
Prendegast Sel M 32 spinster-34
Prendergast Edward-28
Prendergast Ms Elizabeth 30 I-31
Prendergast John 50 I-35
Prendergast Ellen 50 I-35
Prendergast Mary 11 I-35
Prendergast Ellen 10 I-35
Prendergast Theresa 8 I-35
Prendergast Gertrude 7 I-35
Prendergast Geoffrey 5 I-35
Prendergast Joseph 17 I-35
Press Mrs 65-41
Pressland Thomas B 19 clerk-38au
Preston Mrs Margaret-11
Preston Mary-11
Preston David 26 labourer-26
Preston C W 28 labourer-34
Preston Mrs Alice 26-36
Preston Betsy 5-36
Preston Frederick 2-36
Preston Charles A infant-36

Pretty Richard 22 shoemaker I-31
Previs William 28-34
Price John-9
Price Enoch 25 teacher-13sy
Price George F 21 labourer-23
Price Mrs Sarah 42-23ad
Price Jonathan 24 labourer-24
Price Phillip C 22 I-32
Price Robert 33-41
Price Mary 30-42
Priestley Samuel 19 woolsorter-13
Priestley William 34 labourer-23
Priestley Catherine 33-23
Priestley William 9-23
Priestley Robert 7-23
Priestley Simon J 5-23
Priestley James 2-23
Prihoda John-9
Primple Samuel 20-36
Primrose Edward 12 labourer I-31
Prince John-11
Prince John 17 labourer-26
Pringle Joseph 24-10sy
Pringle Thomas labourer-22
Pringle Mrs Martha 30 I-37
Pringle Alexander W 8 I-37
Pringle Sarah 11 I-37
Prior Miss Anastatia 21 I-22
Prior Daniel 48 labourer I-22
Prior Alphia 32 I-22
Prior William 17 I-22
Prior Robert 14 I-22
Prior Thomas 10 I-22
Prior John 7 I-22
Prior Henry 4 I-22
Prior Gert 2 I-22
Prisk Thomas 27 miner-11
Pritchard Eliza 37-10
Pritchard infant-10
Pritchard Sarah 35 spinster-16
Pritchard John 19 farmer-20
Pritchard Miss Mary 22-24
Pritchard Miss Annie 19-24
Proberts Charles H 30-16
Proctor Joseph-9
Proctor Mary-9
Proctor Joseph 36 labourer-21
Proctor Henry 20 coachbuilder-31
Prosser I 22 miner-10
Proudfoot William-9
Proudfoot Robert 20-41
Proudfoot Sarah 20-41
Prout John P 24-32
Prout Elizabeth 20-32
Pruno John 31-35
Pryce Arthur P 26 labourer-31
Pryce Catherine 25-31
Pryor James 14 miner-13
Pryor Jemima 37-13
Pryor Mary 11-13
Pryor Harriet 9-13
Pryor Elizabeth 8-13

Pryor Joseph 5-13
Pryor Jemima 4-13
Pryor Jane 3-13
Pryor infant-13
Pryor John 23 labourer-20
Pryor Mrs Frances A-23
Puckle F A -27
Puckle Mrs-27
Puckle Selwyn 6-27
Puckle Louisa 4.1/2-27
Puckle Eleanor 2-27
Pugh Thomas-11
Pulbrook John P 30-13
Pullen William Charles 30-39
Pullen Sarah 30-39
Pullen Sarah A 8-39
Pullen William Henry 6-39
Pullen Amelia 4-39
Punch James 21 farmer I-16
Purars Angelo 11 OP-32
Purcell Thomas 20 labourer-13
Purres Mary 21 spinster S-31
Purser Robert-9
Purves William 11-24
Purves James-29
Purves Mrs-29
Purves Miss A 18-29
Purves Mary 17-29
Purves Fanny 11-29
Purvis Lawson 28 labourer-31
Putsch Samuel 22 labourer OP-29
Pynsent Burton-9
Pynsent Ogden-9
Pybus Thomas-9
Pyke John 36 joiner-10
Pyke H-31
Pyle William 25 I-32
Pyle Caroline 24 I-32
Pyle Robert 32 I-32

Q

Quaas Louis 38 labourer S-32
Quail Thomas 25 labourer-36
Quail Anna 30-36
Quail Harriet I-43
Quarell John-9
Quice Michael 24 labourer I-16
Quick Mrs Betsy 27-24
Quick Israel 7-24
Quigley Margaret 17 spinster I-20
Quigley Edward 58 S-32
Quigley Michael 17 I-32
Quigley Owen 29 I-38
Quin Henry 20 labourer-26
Quinar W 30 farmer-38
Quinlan Hannah 20 spinster-25
Quinlan Tim 21 I-28
Quinn Maurice 18 labourer I-26
Quinn Michael 21 I-33
Quinn Charles 24 farmer I-37
Quinns William 21 labourer-27
Quirk Martin 22 I-33

R

Rabbie Mr 36 labourer-27
Rabbie Jane A 11-27
Rabbie William 9-27
Rabbits N G -32
Race Joseph 27 labourer-27
Rachan Capt 53 labourer-26
Radcliffe John J 22 farmer I-38
Radd Guiseppi 32 OP-35
Rae Adam 23 labourer S-11
Rae Samuel 33 I-29
Raff George 49-26
Raff Harriet 42-26
Rafferty Hugh 26 I-28
Rafferty Ann 21 spinster I-28
Rafferty Mary 22 spinster I-28
Raffs Frederick 25 labourer I-20
Railey Isaac-30
Railey Rachel-30
Raine Mary Elizabeth-42
Rainer Mr jun.-11
Raines Geve I-28
Rainey Alfred J 9-41
Rainey Agnes P 8-41
Rainey Mrs Emiline 26-41
Rainey Henry 5-41
Rake William 32-34
Ralston David 25 farmer S-11
Ralston John 26 labourer S-31
Ralston Catherine 27 S-31
Ralston John 8 S-31
Ralta Pasqualo 28 labourer OP-30
Ramage Ann 30 spinster S-26
Ramsbottom James 33 farmer-16
Ramsbottom Elizabeth 30-26
Ramsbottom Jane 5-26
Ramsbottom Robert infant-26
Ramsden Thomas 23 joiner-13
Rance William-9
Randall Richard 24 labourer-30
Rankin William labourer-29
Rankin Mary-29
Rankin Angus-32
Rankine James S-33
Rantley John-9
Rappaile Pablicillo 27 OP-32
Raschen Dorothea 22 OP-40
Rash E 40 I-34
Rassi Giacomo 21 labourer OP-26
Ratagon Peter 18 I-34
Rathbone Frederick R 28 lab.-22
Rathbone A S -38
Rathbone Alfred-39
Rattery Margaret U 5 I-32
Rattery George F 3 I-32
Rattery Susannah A 1 I-32
Rattye Rockley 27-41
Rattye Sarah 24-41
Rattye Ann 9-41
Rattye Daniel L 2-41
Rattye N A infant-41

Rawcliffe Mary Ann 13-38
Rawley Johanna 20 spinster-25me
Ray William 26-34
Rayner George F 22-23
Rayner Joseph-38
Rayson William 28 farmer-27
Rea James 20 labourer I-22
Rea Robert 19 S-42
Read Cannell 35-13
Read Thomas 41-13
Read Ann 40-13
Read Harriet 15-13
Read William 46-16
Read Jane 46-16
Read E 10-16
Read William 5-16
Reade Mr Morris-9
Reade Mrs-9
Reader Capt Henry E -21
Reader Major William-21
Reading R G -31
Reading Mrs R-31
Ready Mrs June 32-32
Ready John 5-32
Reane Michael 23 labourer I-27
Reane Mary 23 I-27
Reane John infant I-27
Rearden Jeremiah 40 labourer-30
Reathaines Carpo 25 OP-40
Reckett Albert 39 labourer-34
Recketts Mrs Eliza 40 S-31
Recketts Jane 24 S-31
Recketts Henry K 1 S-31
Reddrop C 19 farmer-21
Reddrop Joshua 24-21
Reddrop Charles 19 labourer-23
Reddrop William 43 labourer-23
Reddrop Margaret 45-23
Reddrop Elizabeth 23-23
Reddrop Margaret 22-23
Reddrop Ann 20-23
Reddrop William 16-23
Reddrop James 14-23
Reddrop Richard 9-23
Reddrop Frances 7-23
Redfern Joseph 37 labourer-33
Redfern Mary Ann 39-33
Redfern Fanny 20-43
Redmond Mary 30 spinster I-27
Redmond Miss Catherine 28 I-27
Redmond Michael 38-34
Redmond Ann 32-34
Redmond Thomas 1-34
Redmond Andrew 23-36
Reed William-9
Reed Henry 33 miner-11
Reed Nicholas 25 miner-11
Reed Joseph 28-11
Reed William 35 miner-11
Reed John 21 farmer S-27
Reed Mrs E 36-29
Reed George 46-35

Reed Richard 20-35
Reed Mary 51-39
Reed Oliver adult I-40
Reed James 71 storekeeper-41
Reed Thomas 41-42
Reed William 14-42
Reed Thomas 10-42
Reed Robert 8-42
Reed Elizabeth 7-42
Reed John 5-42
Reed Sarah Jane 3-42
Reed William Dobson 60-42
Reegan John 40 farmer-20
Reekie Archibald 25 labourer-27
Rees J V -9
Rees Jenkins-9
Rees Jonathan 30 accountant-10
Rees Samuel 44 farmer-11
Rees Edward 12-11
Rees Sarah Ann 13-11
Rees John 29 miner-13
Rees Miss Martha 27 I-21
Rees George 20 labourer-23
Rees B 30-24
Rees Morgan 22 labourer-24
Rees Margaret S 7 I-27
Rees William 24 grocer-27
Reeves Thomas 25 carpenter-10sy
Regan James 22-35
Regangani Pietro-38
Reggetti Marco 16 farmer OP-20
Reggetti Guiseppe 15 OP-20
Reid H-9
Reid Henry 36 merchant-13
Reid George S-20
Reid Mr labourer I-21
Reid Mrs I-21
Reid W H 22 labourer I-27ad
Reid Charles 21 I-28
Reid Lucy 22 spinster I-28
Reid Moses 20 labourer I-31
Reid George P 34-33
Reid Eleanor 22-33
Reid Henry 20 S-34
Reid James 35 S-34
Reid William C 28 clerk I-40
Reig Ellen J 19 servant-38
Reig James 24-38
Reilley Peter 29 farmer I-16
Reilly Patrick 15 I-28
Reilly Anthony 30 I-32
Reilly Ann 25 I-32
Reilly James 7 I-32
Reilly Bridget 4 I-32
Reilly Pat 2 I-32
Reilly William 21 labourer I-32
Reilly Michael 24-33
Reilly David 25-36
Reily Ann 60 housekeeper-42
Reinhardt Andres 25 labourer-25
Rensan George-11
Renshaw Benjamin 33-36

Renshaw Mary Jane 32-36
Renshaw Annie E 4-36
Renshaw Walter 2.1/2-36
Renton Rev D 32 S-23
Renton James K labourer-25
Renwick George 26 mason-16
Renwick William 35-16
Renwick Catherine 30-16
Renwick Margaret Jane 3-16
Renwick Francis Henry 1-16
Renwick John 24 labourer-27
Ress James 33-43
Ressman Rembold 27 miller OP-37
Reston Joshua 53 engineer-43
Restrinket Martha I-21
Reusch C labourer OP-26ad
Reynold Mary A 43 I-39
Reynolds Patrick 22 labourer I-31
Reynolds Elizabeth 24 spinster-34
Reynolds Julia 29 barmaid-40
Rhodes Samuel B 35 artisan-38
Rhodes Isabella 26-38
Rhodes (female birth)-38
Rhodes Edith 7-38
Rhodes Ann 5-38
Rhodes Jael 60-42br
Rhrin Auguste labourer OP-35
Rhymer Tim 33-40
Rhys David 44 I-36
Riach I A -27
Riber Vincent 35 OP-36
Ricards E J -9
Ricards John-9
Rice Stephen 21 labourer-25
Rice Stephen 30 labourer S-26
Rice Stephen 40 dealer-27
Rice Mrs Ann 21-29
Rice Edward 23-29
Rice Stephen labourer-30
Rich Henry 22 labourer-20
Rich John 20 labourer-20
Rich George 33 I-34
Richard William 48 labourer-27
Richard Mrs 50-27
Richards James 31-10sy
Richards Eliza 30-10sy
Richards infant-10sy
Richards William 25 mason-11
Richards Richard 27 miner-13
Richards James F 28 painter-16
Richards Mrs-22
Richards Henry 29 labourer-23
Richards John 62 labourer-23
Richards Eliza 61-23
Richards Hannah 24-23
Richards Elizabeth 22-23
Richards Jane 21-23
Richards Frank 19-23
Richards John 22 labourer-25
Richards William J 17-32
Richards Thomas 20-33
Richards William labourer S-33

Richards John S-33
Richards Arthur 20 labourer-34
Richards Sampson 26-34
Richards Emily 21-34
Richards Emily 1-34
Richards James labourer-35
Richards John 26 I-35
Richards Philip 25-35
Richards Denham 21 corndealer-39
Richards Joshua 40-39
Richards Henry 18 farm lab.-42
Richards Thomas 21 clerk-43
Richardson Edward-9
Richardson W 30 miner-10
Richardson Mrs Frances-11
Richardson George-11
Richardson R -11
Richardson John 37 labourer-22
Richardson Hannah 35-22
Richardson Sarah 11-22
Richardson Emerson 8-22
Richardson Elizabeth 2-22
Richardson Joseph 50 labourer-24
Richardson John 30 labourer-30
Richardson Robert-32
Richardson Mrs Mary 33-35
Richardson Henry 19-36
Richardson Walter 20 S-36
Richardson Thomas W 17-42
Richberg Frederick 36 lab. OP-30
Richinson James 24-28
Richter Carl 38 labourer OP-26
Rickersteth John N 35-41
Rickersteth Mrs E 33-41
Ricketts Stephen 45 labourer-30
Riddle John 30 labourer-30
Riddle Mrs Agnes 26-32sy
Riddle Agnes E 6-32sy
Riddle Edwin 5-32sy
Riddle Maude 3-32sy
Riddle Edith infant-32sy
Riding Richard-26
Riding Ellen-26
Riding William 45 S-36
Ridler Sarah T 36 widow-37
Ridney William-20
Rierden Rev M 38 I-20
Rigan Maurice 30 labourer I-34
Rigby Peter-9
Rigbye Philip 19 labourer-23
Rigg Harriet S 18-10sy
Rigg P 18-10sy
Rigg Alfred 25-13sy
Riggetti Dominica 21 farmer OP-20
Riley Patt 28 labourer I-26
Riley Joseph 44 labourer-34
Riley Elizabeth 32-34
Riley Annie 5-34
Riley Ada 2-34
Riley Joseph 1-34
Riller Peter 28 labourer-27
Rimington George 27-37

Rimmer Randal 23 labourer-34
Rindall James 27 labourer S-35
Riorden Denis 29 labourer I-26
Riorden Honora 27-26
Ripper William 64-34
Ripper Mrs 38-35
Rippon Miss Mary S-43
Rishart E-22
Ritchie William 35 labourer I-31
Ritchie William 36 S-42
Ritchie John 33-34
Ritchins Joseph-22
Ritison James 21 labourer-26
Rivers Robert Hill 25 carpenter-41
Roache Tim 28 servant I-32
Roads William 25-43
Robb Robert 22 farmer S-38
Robbs Mary D 23-42
Robby Robert-10
Robby Mrs-10
Robe James 54 watchmaker-13
Robert Edward M 21 labourer-22
Roberts George-9
Roberts Thomas-9
Roberts John-9
Roberts William 45 miner-10
Roberts Peter 21 miner-13
Roberts James 21 miner-13
Roberts Thomas 27 miner-13
Roberts John-16
Roberts Henry 23 labourer-20
Roberts Robert 34 labourer-20
Roberts Robert 26 miner-20
Roberts David 21 miner-20
Roberts Thomas 18 farmer-20sy
Roberts William 24 labourer-20
Roberts Joseph 28 labourer-21
Roberts Thomas 19 labourer-21
Roberts Mrs Elizabeth 55-22
Roberts Jane 23 spinster-22
Roberts Mary 22 spinster-22
Roberts Mrs Ann 38-23
Roberts John 17-23
Roberts Mrs Georgina 30-24
Roberts Frederick C 21 lab.-26
Roberts John W 32 labourer-26
Roberts I S 26 labourer-27
Roberts M H 18 labourer-27
Roberts William F 31-28
Roberts Mary 30-28
Roberts William 4-28
Roberts Louisa infant-28
Roberts William 30-29
Roberts William 34 labourer-29
Roberts Mrs Mary 45-30
Roberts John Henry 7-30
Roberts T I S-32
Roberts Miss Margaret 22-33
Roberts William 30-34
Roberts Mrs Emma 52 S-35
Roberts Sydney 29 S-35
Roberts John-36

Roberts Mrs-36
Roberts John 34 trader-40
Roberts George E druggist-41
Roberts Mark 21 miner-42
Roberts William 36-43
Roberts Hannah 31-43
Roberts Alice 10-43
Roberts Florence 2-43
Roberts William 39-43
Robertson Ellen 22 milliner-11
Robertson infant-11
Robertson Ann 32 spinster I-20
Robertson Donald 26 I-21sy
Robertson Laurence 27 labourer-21
Robertson John 26 labourer S-22
Robertson Mrs A 68 widow-26
Robertson Miss Catherine 16-26
Robertson Duncan labourer I-26
Robertson William 40-26
Robertson Miss Catherine 52-29
Robertson Agnes 32 spinster-31
Robertson Mary 5-31
Robertson Kenneth 4-31
Robertson Daniel 29 labourer-31
Robertson Annie 25-31
Robertson Nathan 3-31
Robertson Willie infant-31
Robertson (male b. 12.2.1868)-31
Robertson James 28 labourer S-31
Robertson Maggie 26 S-31
Robertson J Jessie 7 S-31
Robertson J S infant S-31
Robertson David 43 labourer-35
Robertson Robert C S-35
Robertson Annie S-35
Robertson Helen S-35
Robertson James 20 S-36
Robertson Joshua 24 miner S-37
Robertson H A clergyman S-38
Robertson Mrs-38
Robertson G -39
Robertson James S-39
Robertson Mrs S-39
Robertson Christina S-39
Robertson Thomas S-39
Robertson M S-39
Robertson Donald 33 tailor S-40
Robertson George 25-40
Robertson Mrs R E-41
Robertson ? 10-41
Robertson ? 8-41
Robertson John 58-43
Robertson Mary 49-43
Robertson Annie 23-43
Robertson Isabella 21-43
Robertson Mary 17-43
Robertson Agnes 13-43
Robertson Catherine 10-43
Robins James 24 labourer S-24
Robinson Henry 42-10
Robinson Julia 28-10
Robinson William H Y 4-10

Robinson James 1.1/2-10
Robinson Adel F I 10mths-10
Robinson John 24 miner-11
Robinson Henry 20 labourer-13
Robinson John J 19 builder-13
Robinson Arthur 22-16
Robinson John 33 labourer-16
Robinson John 28 labourer-20
Robinson Sarah 25-20
Robinson Joshua 63-20
Robinson Isabella 63-20
Robinson Mrs-21
Robinson Jonathan 23 labourer-24
Robinson H C-26
Robinson Joshua 44 miner-27
Robinson Deborah 42-27
Robinson George 20 labourer-27
Robinson Mary 23 spinster-27
Robinson Mr adult labourer-27
Robinson Clara 19 spinster-28
Robinson Joseph labourer-28
Robinson Mrs-28
Robinson James E -29
Robinson Robert 22 I-30
Robinson Ellen 20 I-30
Robinson John 25 labourer-31
Robinson Robert 48 labourer-31
Robinson Martha 46-31
Robinson Joseph 21 labourer I-32
Robinson Henry 28 I-35
Robinson E G 17-36
Robinson William 40 S-36
Robinson Victoria 37 S-36
Robinson William 35-36
Robinson Anne 28-36
Robinson William 11-36
Robinson Samuel 7-36
Robinson Elizabeth 5-36
Robinson Sarah 2-36
Robinson Ellen infant-36
Robinson Barbara 30-37
Robinson Henry 45-37
Robinson Alice 45-37
Robinson Joshua 23-37
Robinson Mark 32 draper-38
Robinson Elizabeth 25-41
Robinson Eleanor 54-43
Robinson Margaret 29-43
Robinson Eleanor 25-43
Robinson Jeme 22-43
Robinson Alice 20-43
Robinson George 18-43
Robinson Sarah 16-43
Robson George 23 labourer-21
Robson Walter 20-21
Robson Jeffrey-28
Robson William 24 miner S-32
Robson Thomas 21 mechanic-35
Robson Matthew 33 miner-38
Robson Margaret 36-38
Robson (female birth)-38
Robson Sarah 7-38

Robson William 5-38
Robson Margaret 1-38
Roch Amelia 16 spinster OP-22
Roche Dr James-9
Roche Thomas 22 labourer I-31
Roche William Henry-41
Rodda W 25 miner-10
Rodda Benjamin 50 labourer-22
Rodda Tomasoma 47-22
Rodda Mary 26-22
Roddy Thomas M master mariner-41
Roden Robert B 42 labourer I-32
Roden Ann 14 I-32
Roden Robert T 11 I-32
Rodger Patrick 28 farmer I-32
Rodgers John 31 miner-13
Rodgers Henry 33 miner-13
Rodgers Alexander R 26 lab.-24
Rodgers James 36 labourer I-31
Rodgers Margaret 39 I-31
Rodgers Mary J 13 I-31
Rodgers James 11 I-31
Rodgers Robert 8 I-31
Rodgers John 6 I-31
Rodgers Samuel 3 I-31
Rodgers William 18 labourer I-31
Rodgers Hugh 26-36
Rodgers Edward J 25 I-42
Rodke Andrew 37 labourer I-31
Roger David 44 labourer-24
Roger Mary 38-24
Roger Mary 14-24
Roger Jane 12-24
Roger Hugh 9-24
Roger William 6-24
Roger Agnes 3-24
Roger Janet 25 S-32
Roger William 31 clerk-40
Roger Mary 21-40
Roger W R 2-40
Roger Edith 1-40
Rogers George 22 labourer-20
Rogers William M 25 labourer-23
Rogers James 20 labourer-27
Rogers John 24-28
Rogers John M 25 miner I-32
Rogers Eliza 23 I-32
Rogers John M infant I-32
Rogers Thomas 24-34
Rogers Jefine 24-34
Rogers I H 1-34
Rogers James 21 miner I-35
Roland John 26 I-42
Roland Mary 21 I-42
Rolfe Alfred 24-36
Rolland Ann 30 spinster-28
Rolland Adam-36
Rolland William-36
Rolland Richard 35-41
Rolston Elizabeth widow-37
Rominen William 20 labourer-30
Ronald George 31 miner-21

Ronald Miss-21
Ronald Catherine 57 I-28
Ronald Mrs-28
Ronald Fanny 8-28
Ronald Isabel 6-28
Ronald Margaret 4-28
Ronald Arthur 2-28
Ronald infant-28
Ronaldson James 40 labourer-35
Ronaldson Miss Margaret 34 S-35
Rooch T I 22 merchant I-10sy
Rookes Miss-9
Rooney Terence 23-41
Rooth E 30-10
Rootsey Isabella 60 spinster-41
Roscroft George 28-36
Rose Mr H -27
Rose Mrs (& infant)-27
Rose Benjamin 55 painter-39
Rosenbeelett M S 26 lab. OP-27
Rosenberg Theo 32 merchant OP-10
Rosenthal Louis 12.1/2 lab. OP-27
Rosenthal Sahra 10 OP-32
Roskringe Frank 27 labourer-27
Ross John-10
Ross John 32 merchant-10
Ross Alexander 26 mason S-11
Ross William 20 labourer I-16
Ross Jemima 20 spinster I-22
Ross George 19 labourer-23
Ross Donald 21 labourer-25
Ross James 38 miner S-27
Ross Sarah 37 S-27
Ross Charles 22-28
Ross William 25 farmer I-31
Ross John 24 I-31
Ross Hector 48-34
Ross Anne 27-34
Ross Margaret 60 spinster-34
Ross Alexander 31 labourer-34
Ross Reubin 21-34
Ross John 18-41
Rossa Pietro 23 OP-33
Rosseri Tommasso 23 lab. OP-26
Rossi Silvestro 18 OP-26
Rossillo Pietro 24 OP-35
Rotherham William-36
Rothwell E -9
Rottston William 40 I-43
Roughan Stephen 20 labourer-32
Roulston Samuel 23 labourer-32
Rourke Joseph 50 farm lab. I-31
Rourke John 24 I-36
Row Francis A-29
Rowan Miss Mary 35-23
Rowan Mrs Winifred 50-32
Rowan Martha 30-32
Rowe James 19 miner-13
Rowe Mrs Jane 33-21
Rowe William 31-21
Rowe James 38 labourer-21
Rowe Mrs 32-21

Rowe Julia 8-21
Rowe Martha 5-21
Rowe Nancy 1-21
Rowen James 20 I-35
Rowland J W 22 I-29
Rowland E R 19 I-29
Rowland William 56-33
Rowland Henry 37-36
Rowland Elizabeth 33-36
Rowland Charles 3-36
Rowland Annie 1-36
Rowland Arthur 18-40
Rowland Joseph 50-41
Rowlands Owen 21 quarryman-11
Rowlston Thomas 18-41
Rowney Mrs Ann 40 I-21
Rowney Margaret 18 I-21
Rowney John 16 I-21
Rowney Maria 13 I-21
Rowntree James 21 labourer I-31
Rows William H 24 labourer OP-26
Roycroft John 26 I-31
Ruane Margaret 14 spinster I-28
Rubeli Golshiel 23 labourer OP-26
Rubeli Frederick 17 OP-26
Ruddick Benjamin 21 I-28
Ruddock Miss Eliza 26-24
Ruffaline G OP-42
Rughan Mary I-31
Ruiel Francis 32 carpenter-43
Rule Thomas Henry 24-41
Rummington Miss-30ad
Rurd Alfred-11
Ruse Reuben 37-33
Ruse S H 29-33
Ruse female(born 26/3,died 8/4)-33
Rush Manby 22 spinster I-27
Russ Henry 45 labourer I-31
Russel James 62-29
Russell William 25 clerk-13
Russell George 44 labourer-20
Russell Miss Fanny 26-24
Russell Andrew-26
Russell Eliza J-26
Russell H -33
Russell William 31 farmer S-37
Russell Elizabeth 30-40
Russell Margaret 13-43
Rutherford Donald 25 gardener S-27
Rutherford Eliza 26 (& baby) S-27
Rutherford John 40-27
Rutherford Allen 17-27
Rutherford James 31 I-36
Ruthren Thomas 27 labourer S-20
Rutledge Albert M 18 I-35
Rya Hugh 28-29
Ryall John E -22
Ryan P 20 farmer I-10
Ryan Henry 22 miner-13
Ryan John 26 miner-13
Ryan Michael 40 farmer S-13
Ryan Bridget 20 spinster S-13

Ryan Mary 16 spinster S-13
Ryan Patrick 39 labourer I-13
Ryan Patrick 25 labourer I-20
Ryan John 21 I-20
Ryan John 16 labourer I-21
Ryan Margaret 18 spinster I-22
Ryan Jeremiah 16 labourer I-24
Ryan Miss Johanna 24 I-24
Ryan Jonathan 28 labourer I-24
Ryan Ann 20 spinster-25
Ryan James 30 labourer-25
Ryan John 40 labourer-25
Ryan Catherine 35-25
Ryan Mary Ann 10-25
Ryan Margaret 7-25
Ryan Johanna 2-25
Ryan Catherine infant-25
Ryan John 24 labourer-25
Ryan Thomas 15-25
Ryan Joshua 14-25
Ryan Pat 11-25
Ryan Michael 10-25
Ryan John 8-25
Ryan Michael 20 labourer I-26
Ryan Patrick 28 labourer I-26
Ryan Matthew 28 miner I-27
Ryan John 18 I-28
Ryan Bridget 16 I-28
Ryan Martin 21 labourer I-31
Ryan William 33 labourer I-31
Ryan James 33-32
Ryan Lawrence 19 I-32
Ryan Malachy 24 I-32
Ryan Michael 25 I-32
Ryan Richard 20 I-32
Ryan William 38 I-32
Ryan Dennis 28 I-33
Ryan James 22-34
Ryan Simon 58 I-34
Ryan Johanna 43 I-34
Ryan Patrick 10 I-34
Ryan James 8 I-34
Ryan Catherine infant I-34
Ryan Julia 37 housekeeper I-38
Ryan Thomas 31 farmer I-39
Ryan Michael 22 engraver I-39
Ryan Mary I-41
Ryan Thomas 22-41
Ryan Patrick 28-41
Ryan Patrick 22-41
Ryan Catherine 22-41
Ryan Patrick 28-41
Ryan Bridget 19-42
Ryan Patrick 27 I-42
Ryan Dennis 29 I-42
Ryder James Kent 27 labourer-25
Ryder Mary 24 spinster-25
Ryland Benjamin 49-35

S

Saber E -9
Saber Mr-9

Saber Mrs—9
Saber Miss—9
Sadleir John—9
Sadler Peter 21 farm servant—16
Sadler William 37—29
Sadler Mrs 36—29
Sadler Mrs H —34
Sailer Frederick 17 labourer—27
Sainsbury Elizabeth 41—33
Sainsbury Arthur James 10—33
Salfield William 28—34
Salit John adult OP—40
Salmann J miner OP—39
Saloman N —9
Saloway Miss Mary 19—36
Salt Thomas—9
Salt Miss Esther 37—24
Salter Charles adult—40
Salter Mrs adult—40
Salter Charles N 2—40
Salter Alex G 1—40
Salway William 14—32
Sampson William 57 labourer—21
Sampson Catherine 55—21
Sampson William 20—21
Sampson Richard Henry 18—21
Sampson Miss 10—22
Sampson A N —35
Sampson George Henry 21—42ot
Sand William B 21—28
Sanders William—27
Sanders Leonard 18 labourer S—33
Sanders John G 42 miner—37
Sanders Miss 45—37
Sanderson Nicholas 22 miner—11
Sanderson John 23 labourer—20
Sanderson Mrs Sarah 39—24
Sanderson Jonathan 43—24
Sanderson Margaret 19—24
Sanderson Sarah 16—24
Sanderson Ann 14—24
Sanderson Sarah 8—24
Sanderson Robert 21 I—36
Sandham Miss—13
Sandham John 27 labourer—22
Sandham John B 41 miner—37
Sandilands I B 24 labourer—27
Sanyon R E 26 I—28
Sanyon Agnes 21—28
Sanyon Rudolph—28
Sanyon infant—28
Sapper Mrs Sarah 30—36
Sapper William 10—36
Sapper Mary infant—36
Sarah William 25 labourer—13
Sardelle Pietro 24 labourer OP—26
Sargent Frederick 34—33
Sargint Mr—9
Sargint Mrs—9
Sartees John O —16
Satch Mr—27
Satcliffe John 24—24

Saults William 26 labourer—23
Saunder Arthur 22 shopkeeper—21
Saunders John 48 miner—13
Saunders Mr—30
Saunders Moses adult OP—40
Savell George C 24 labourer—25
Saviors Miss 27—21
Savigny Mrs 55—10
Savigny W H 28—10
Saville Henry 18 OP—32
Sawyer E 47 spinster—34
Sawyer Thomas L 20 labourer—34
Sawyer Sarah 17 spinster—34
Sawyer James 38 labourer I—34
Sawyer Eliza 32 I—32
Sawyer James 11 I—34
Sawyer John 5 I—34
Sawyer Harry 3 I—34
Sawyer Thomas 38 labourer I—34
Sawyer Alice 39 I—34
Sawyer Thomas 60 I—34
Sawyer Susan 60 I—34
Sawyer Alfred 28 I—34
Sawyer Ann 26 I—34
Sawyer John 26 I—34
Sayer Clara 21—42
Saywell Thomas—39
Saywell E A —39
Scadden James 27 miner—13
Scalletti G OP—42
Scally James 20—41
Scanlan Michael 44 labourer—25
Scanlen Winston 27—42
Scanlon Michael 28 labourer I—23
Scanlon Ganett 30 labourer I—24
Scanlon Ellen 28 I—24
Scanlon Mary infant I—24
Scanlon Honora 22 I—24
Scarr Christopher 54 grocer—37
Scarr Elizabeth 45—37
Scarlett James—11
Scartlebury Ephraim 41 tailor—20
Scaty Mary 25—28
Schaffer John workman OP—38
Schafner John 28 farmer OP—13
Schase Henrick 22 OP—35
Schascht John 43 OP—40
Schaun Michael 29 OP—43
Schifforte Joseph 32 lab. OP—35
Schifforte Johan 15 OP—35
Schinds August 22 labourer—22
Schlau Soloman 19 OP—26
Schmidt Fraz 26 miner OP—39
Schner Sunon 19 OP—40
Schoch Christian 30 OP—29
Schofield Benjamin 26—29
Schofield Frederick 17—33
Schofield John 26 fitter—42
Schreik Hein 30 merchant OP—16
Schroder Henrich 38 lab. OP—28
Schroder Elise 32 OP—28
Schroder Waliska 4 OP—28

Schroder Frederick 3 OP—28
Schroder Mary 40 spinster OP—28
Schules Miss Catherine 36 OP—29
Schulkraft Mrs F 42 OP—24
Schult John 22 farmer OP—16
Schultz Frederico OP—26
Schulz F 28 miner OP—39
Schwanan A 26 OP—10
Schwartz Miss Marione 24 OP—29
Schweder N W 24 artisan—38
Schweder Elizabeth 23—38
Schweder Elizabeth 1—38
Scorer Sarah 76 widow—24
Scotland James 40 labourer S—28
Scotland Jessie 36 S—28
Scott Mr—9
Scott Mrs—9
Scott Isaac 36 cabinetmaker—13
Scott Robert 20 farmer—16
Scott James 19—16
Scott Duncan 15 labourer S—21
Scott George 16 labourer I—22
Scott Glassford M 24 labourer—22
Scott John 24 labourer S—22
Scott Gideon—23
Scott Miss Mary 22 I—23
Scott Margaret 63 matron—25
Scott Alexander 20 labourer—65
Scott James 33 labourer—25
Scott Andrew—26
Scott Mungo 32 labourer S—26
Scott Mary 32 S—26
Scott Margaret 4 S—26
Scott Mary 3 S—26
Scott Wilhelmina infant S—26
Scott Robert 43—27
Scott Isabella 37—27
Scott William 10—27
Scott Elizabeth 8—27
Scott Alex 4—27
Scott Janet 1—27
Scott Walter 19—28
Scott John—29
Scott William 51 blacksmith S—31
Scott Walter 20 warehouseman S—32
Scott Robert S I—33
Scott William 34 labourer—34
Scott Ann 33—34
Scott Ann 11—34
Scott George 9—34
Scott Mary E 7—34
Scott Alice 4—34
Scott Elizabeth 1—34
Scott Margaret 13—34
Scott Hugh—35
Scott John S—37
Scott James 50 workman—38
Scott Helen 27—38
Scott Denison 47—41
Scott John 15—41
Scott Mary 24—42
Scott Walter 20—43

Scrivey Samuel George 33–33
Scrivey Mary A 35–33
Scriver George B 11–33
Scrivey Alice E 6–33
Scruder Jacob 26–36
Sculaci Bartholomew 27 lab.OP–33
Sculaci Dominimo 26 OP–33
Scullin Patrick 19 labourer I–30
Scully M 30 I–28
Scully Michael 65 labourer–31
Scully Bridget 60–31
Sealey George 24 labourer I–30
Searoyd Joe–34
Sears Arthur–40
Seaver Mrs Catherine 53 I–22
Seaver Mona M 32 I–22
Seaver John C D 8 I–22
Seaver Thomas H 7 I–22
Seaver Catherine I 5 I–22
Sedden Alexander 39 labourer–31
Seed Jonathan 40–41
Seeds W M –9
Sefton John H 27 labourer I–22
Segel Joseph 23 OP–43
Segard Frederick 50–28
Seitini Aboudia 21 OP–43
Selbrite Mrs Augusta 21–22
Selbrite child 1–22
Seligmann Johannes 26 OP–42
Selkirk Miss Isabella A 20 S–26
Sellar Richard 25 labourer–28
Sellers William 22 labourer–33
Sellwood Richard 25–43
Seniadine Andrew 33 lab. OP–26
Seniadine Paolo 37 labourer OP–26
Senior Benjamin 35 moulder–32
Senior Mary Ann 32–32
Senior Joseph 59–34
Senior Elizabeth 38–34
Senior Ellen 11–34
Senior Elizabeth 8–34
Senior John 5–34
Senior William 3–34
Senior Mary 1–34
Senior Jennett infant–34
Sensen Jens 18 OP–29
Serveder Joseph 18–37
Service John–23
Service Robert 21 labourer I–30
Service Samuel 19 labourer–30
Sett Jacques 32 OP–35
Sevy Markes adult–10
Sewell Thomas–21
Sewell John 22 labourer–27
Sewell Benjamin 31–29
Sexton Henry 23 labourer–30
Sexton Thomas 32–43
Sexton Daniel 27–43
Shackleton Mrs Anna 34–23
Shackleton Ann 36 spinster S–31
Shaler Thomas 19 labourer I–32
Shallcross Wright 30–41

Shanahan Michael 23–41
Shand George S–32ad
Shand George J S–32ad
Shand William 26 labourer–33ad
Shand Charles 18–33
Shand Mrs Mary 46–37ad
Shand Annie 14–37ad
Shand Margaret 11–37ad
Shand Mary Jane 9–37ad
Shand Andrew 18–37ad
Shanks Mary Ann 20–11
Shanks William John 34 farmer–11
Shanks Miss–34
Shannon Michael 23 labourer I–24
Shannon Michael 20 ploughman I–31
Shannon Thomas 40 farmer I–37
Shannon Sydney–41
Shannon Bessie–42
Shant Jane 26 spinster–20
Shapcott G E –22
Sharkie John 20 labourer I–21
Sharkie Mary Eliza 18 I–21
Sharland William C–31
Sharp D 32 steward S–10
Sharp Jonathan 23 labourer–25
Sharp Francis 35–30
Sharp Henry 35–35
Sharp John 21–35
Sharp Mary 20–35
Sharp E Edwin 1–35
Sharp David 22 clerk–42
Sharpe Benjamin 20 farmer I–31
Sharpe James 42 S–43
Sharpe Jessie 32 S–43
Sharples William H 30–43
Sharples William 18–43
Shaw William 25 labourer–13
Shaw W J 28 labourer–24
Shaw Alexander 35 labourer–26
Shaw Marion 24 spinster–26
Shaw J 33 spinster–27
Shaw Charles 42 labourer I–31
Shaw Mary J 42 I–31
Shaw John 33 clerk–35
Shaw John 27–35
Shaw Samuel S–36
Shaw George 26–41ho
Shawcross David 27 labourer–30
Shawcross Isaac 25 labourer–30
Shawcross William 30 labourer–31
Shawcross Isaac 32–42
Shcott Adam 20 farmer OP–16
Shea Margaret spinster–11
Shea George–11
Shea Ellen 20 spinster I–16
Sheahan Philip 23 labourer S–23
Sheahan Daniel 19 I–33
Sheahan Patrick 22 I–33
Sheahan Ann 20 I–43
Sheahan Daniel 27 I–43
Sheartson Joshua 22 labourer–24
Shedblick Otto 25 OP–42

Sheehy John 29 labourer I–23
Sheehy Miss Honora 22–23
Sheen James 18 servant–11
Shehan Patrick 18 labourer I–32
Sheldon Jabez 19 labourer–13
Shelvin John 36 labourer–22
Shenard Henry 40 labourer–24
Shenard Eliza A 40–24
Shenard Henry A infant–24
Sheover Archibald 25 I–13
Shepherd Thomas 50 miner–21
Shepherd Fanny 48–21
Shepherd Elizabeth 19–21
Shepherd Fanny 21–21
Shepherd Caroline 13–21
Shepherd Ann 9–21
Shepherd Henry 19 labourer–22
Shepherd George 26 I–32
Shepherd S H 19–34
Shepherd G –34
Shepherd Alexander 19 I–36
Shepherd Ann 59 teacher–39
Shepherd Joseph B 26–41
Shepherd Thomas 22–42
Sherham James 25 labourer I–24
Sherham Honora 23 I–24
Sherham Thomas infant I–24
Sherham Margaret infant I–24
Sherman W –28
Sheridan Thomas 30 engineer I–11
Sheridan James 22 labourer–24
Sheridan John 21 labourer I–27
Sherlock Francis 21 labourer–27
Sherton Robert 26 labourer I–32
Sherton Rebecca 19 labourer I–32
Sherwin John H 30 warehouseman–38
Shieblich Charles 44 OP–42
Shieblich Mrs Eliza 31 OP–42
Shieblich Emma 10 OP–42
Shield Patrick 23 labourer I–13
Shield Joseph 31 labourer–22
Shield Joshua 27 miner–34
Shields Jonathan 23 labourer–24
Shields Mrs Martha 56–34
Shields Martha 17–34
Shields Joshua 27–34
Shiels James 34 labourer–31
Shiers Joseph labourer–22sy
Shiers Mrs 26–22sy
Shiers Pauline 1–22sy
Shile Abraham 24 miner–13
Shile William 26 miner–13
Shile James 21 miner–13
Shillatti Stephanso 23 lab. OP–26
Shillatti Giovanni 18 OP–26
Shimick William 27–28
Shines Miss Johanna 19 I–21
Shoemate John 40 miner–16
Short Joseph 49 labourer–22
Short Jane 52–22
Shortis Patrick 20 labourer I–31
Shovelton Mrs Mary 55–22

Shovelton Peter 27 labourer–22
Shovelton Margaret 27–22
Shovelton Mary A 5–22
Shovelton Margaret 3–22
Shovelton Martha 1–22
Shovelton Jonathan W 30–22
Shrapnel Amelia B–38
Shrapnel Amy J 8–38
Shrapnel Joseph 7–38
Shrapnel Henry 5–38
Shrapnel Sydney 4–38
Shrapnel Alex 2–38
Shuckland William 14–27
Shumder Frederick 30 surgeon–11
Shunks Andrew 45 labourer I–32
Shuttleworth David workman–40
Siggins Jno 24 farmer I–31
Silcock Benjamin 14 I–31
Silcock Henry 23 artisan–38
Sim Mrs Robert 34–16
Sim William 9–16
Sim Thomas 7–16
Sim Mary Elizabeth 5–16
Sim Margaret 3–16
Sim William 23 joiner–16
Simcox Samuel 31 I–36
Simcox Betsy 34 I–36
Simcox Samuel 10 I–36
Simcox Richard 9 I–36
Simcox Benjamin 7 I–36
Simcox Emma M 4 I–36
Simeon Mrs–11
Simeon Miriam–11
Simeon Michael–11
Simeon Marcus–11
Simeon Miss–11
Simeon Miss–11
Simes Mrs Mary 49–32
Simes Mary A 18–32
Simes Louis Jane 16–32
Simmins Mrs Rebecca 24–21
Simmins Mary Ann 26–21
Simple A J C 26–24
Simpson Thomas 25 carpenter–10
Simpson W 19 I–10
Simpson George–11
Simpson William 37 labourer–11
Simpson Robert 21 miner–13
Simpson Thomas 27 joiner–13
Simpson Gavin 40 shopkeeper–21
Simpson Mary 35–21
Simpson Letitia 18–21
Simpson Elizabeth 16–21
Simpson William 8–21
Simpson Gavin 5–21
Simpson John 27 labourer–22
Simpson Joseph 44 labourer–25
Simpson George 42 labourer–25
Simpson Mary 40–25
Simpson Joseph 11–25
Simpson Mrs E M adult–27
Simpson Mrs Ann 70–32

Simpson James 36–32
Simpson Mary E –32
Simpson William 28 labourer S–32
Simpson Jessie 28 S–32
Simpson Annie 5 S–32
Simpson Helen 3 S–32
Simpson Isabella infant S–32
Simpson Thomas–34
Simpson Mary A –34
Simpson Emily 2–34
Simpson Mary A 1–34
Simpson John C 15–35
Simpson David R 19 S–35
Simpson Mrs Marian 45 S–35
Simpson Joanna 22 S–35
Sims Robert 29 baker–11
Sims John 24 miner–13
Sims Christopher 17–35
Sinclair Andrew 20 I–28
Sinclair Mrs Isabella 31 S–37
Sinclair Margaret F 9 S–37
Sinclair Helen B 7 S–37
Sinclair Agnes R 5 S–37
Sinclair Isabella W 3 S–37
Sinclair Charles 25–43
Sinclair Mary J 19–43
Sinclair Charles infant–43
Singer Edward 30 labourer–23
Singleton F C –23
Singleton Hugh labourer–23
Sinnott John 24 farmer I–20
Sinnott John J 24 I–40
Sirell Capt–10
Sivan Donald 40 farmer S–20
Skehan John 23 labourer I–24
Skehan H 24–42
Skehell Peter 19 labourer I–32
Skelly John 28 farmer–11
Skene William 51 sheep farmer–31
Skene Mrs 51–31
Skene Thomas 21–31
Skene William 17–31
Skene Mary 15–31
Skene David 12–31
Skewes William H 21–32
Skinner John–16sy
Skinner Mrs–16sy
Skinner William 28 labourer–33
Skinner Thomas–34
Skinner Thomas 35–42
Slack Garrett labourer I–23
Slade Lewis Wm 24 coachmaker–16
Slade Joseph 22–43
Sladen Charles–23
Sladen Mrs–23
Sladen Harvey–23
Sladden Edwin 30 servant–21
Slaren John 40 labourer I–20
Slark William 40–33
Slater John 22 miller–13
Slater John 37–28
Slater Abraham 24–35

Slattery B 21 farmer I–10
Slattery John 20 labourer I–21
Slattory William J 44 clerk I–32
Slattory Anne 26 I–32
Slattory John C 6 I–32
Slavin Michael 24 labourer I–26
Sleeson John–27
Sleeson Mrs–27
Sleigh Joshua 22 joiner–21
Sleigh George 30 labourer–26
Sleigh Mrs J T 33–26
Sliels John 21 labourer I–22
Slitt James 30–32
Sloan James 16 labourer S–23
Sloane James 31 labourer–30
Slrick William 32 labourer–23
Slubber Miss–36
Small Agnes 24–13
Small Thomas 3.1/2–13
Small David 25–41
Small William 40–41
Smart Mrs Clea 20 I–29
Smart William 10 I–29
Smellie Mrs E J 42–29
Smellie Miss J M 20–29
Smellie Elizabeth 18–29
Smethurst Mrs Martha 25–21
Smith John–9
Smith J H –9
Smith William–9
Smith W J –9
Smith F J 26 stationer–10sy
Smith James H 40–10
Smith Mary A 39–10
Smith Mary 31–10
Smith Mary E 9–10
Smith Daniel 3–10
Smith Miss–10
Smith S 17–10sy
Smith Sarah 31–10
Smith William 28 builder–10
Smith George 40–11
Smith Nicholas 13–11
Smith Thomas 9–11
Smith Sarah 40–11
Smith George 33 miner–13
Smith James 25 joiner–13
Smith Jessie 36 farmer–13
Smith Sarah 28–13
Smith Mary 7–13
Smith Sarah infant–13
Smith Thomas 20 farmer–13
Smith Patrick 26 labourer I–13
Smith James 26 labourer I–16
Smith Sarah 25 I–16
Smith Mrs Jane 55–16
Smith Emma 15–16
Smith Philip 21–16
Smith William 32 gas engineer–16
Smith William 28 baker–16
Smith Ann 25–16
Smith Elizabeth 3–16

Smith Mary 2-16
Smith Miss Sarah A 27-21
Smith Simon 20 labourer-21
Smith James 30 labourer S-22
Smith James 25 labourer-22
Smith Samuel 52-22
Smith Elizabeth 49-22
Smith Louisa 22-22
Smith Mary E 20-22
Smith Martha 24 spinster-22
Smith George 39 labourer-23
Smith W V -23
Smith Mrs-23
Smith William 32 labourer-23
Smith F N 40 labourer-24
Smith George 38-24
Smith H N 30 labourer-24
Smith Mrs P 39-24
Smith Miss 17-24
Smith William 27 labourer-24
Smith William S 34 labourer-24
Smith William 24 labourer-24
Smith Thomas 22 labourer-25
Smith William 32 labourer-25
Smith Edward 58 labourer-26
Smith Samuel John 14-26
Smith Robert 20 labourer I-26
Smith Thomas 25 labourer-26
Smith E C -27
Smith Elizabeth 40 spinster S-27
Smith Mr-27
Smith Charles 30-28
Smith Michael 58-28
Smith George-29
Smith Malcolm H 18 labourer-29
Smith James S-30
Smith Grace S-30
Smith Joseph 38-30
Smith Mrs Ellen 36-30
Smith N H -30
Smith Mrs-30
Smith Robert J 29 labourer-30
Smith William 28 labourer-30
Smith Mary 22 spinster-31
Smith Margaret 20 spinster-31
Smith Mary 26 spinster-31
Smith A M 21 spinster-32
Smith Mr-32
Smith Mrs-32
Smith Robert 33 labourer-32
Smith Wellington 18 labourer S-32
Smith John 24 S-33ad
Smith Robert 33-33
Smith Thomas 41-33
Smith Alfred 37-34
Smith Theresa 34-34
Smith Mr E G -34
Smith Margaret-34
Smith May A 25 spinster-34
Smith Charlotte 24 spinster-34
Smith Caroline 22 spinster-34
Smith W J 22-34

Smith Peter-35
Smith Thomas-35
Smith Mrs-35
Smith infant-35
Smith Albert 23 I-36
Smith Sophia 24 I-36
Smith Elizabeth 4 I-36
Smith J W -36
Smith Andrew farmer I-37
Smith Robert 28 farmer-37
Smith Catherine 28-37
Smith Thomas 10-37
Smith George 1-37
Smith John 20 farmer-38
Smith Thomas 48 S-38
Smith Bernard 26 I-39
Smith Henry 28 miner-40
Smith Caleb 30-40
Smith John M 48 printer-41
Smith Margaret 18-41
Smith Elizabeth 16-41
Smith Agnes 12-41
Smith Robert 18 clerk-41
Smith Thomas 51-41
Smith Caleb 18-41
Smith Henry 20-41
Smith William 26-41
Smith Charlotte 21-41
Smith Harry 2-41
Smith Annie 1-41
Smith George 40-42
Smith Mrs J -42
Smith Mary 3-42
Smith Thomas 24 farmer-42
Smithies Hugh 23-39
Smithies Ann 24-39
Smyth Mrs E -35
Smyth Frank L -35
Sneding Jno Henry 29-33
Snow D -9
Soddy Francis 66-36
Soleberg Mr OP-36
Solnes Bar 22-40
Soloman John 25 sailor-13
Sommers William 40 labourer-30
Sommers Susannah 40-30
Sommers Elizabeth 8-30
Sommers Mary E 6-30
Sommerset Rosa 28 spinster-33
Somerton Charles F 39-29
Somerton Susan-29
Somerville Ann 41 spinster-29
Sonnenberg Pino 41 OP-37
Sonnenberg Auguste 32 OP-37
Sorensen Harris 27 OP-29
Sounsen Joanna 22 spinster OP-29
Southera Walter adult labourer-27
Southera John adult labourer-27
Southern John 21-21
Soy Alexander 33 labourer-24
Soy Louis Ide 18 OP-27
Spaight Robert 29-24sy

Spaiter Mrs Ellen 46 OP-29
Spaiter Drotchen 3 OP-29
Spall Robert 27 guard-41
Spark Jonathan 33 miner-13
Sparks John-9
Spearman John 25 labourer-25
Spearman James 24 labourer I-31
Spears James 22 I-32
Spears William 17 I-32
Spears Edward 24 grocer-38
Speers Henry 25 grocer-13
Speers William 19 labourer-26
Speibrogle N F 23 labourer OP-27
Speller Susannah 44-43
Spen James 21-16
Spen Elizabeth 25-16
Spence John C 30-11
Spence David 22 S-43
Spencer Mrs 50-10
Spencer Miss 30-10
Spencer John W 19 S-13
Spencer Arthur C 17 S-13
Spencer Michael 21 smith-13
Spencer Henry 21 labourer-22
Spencer Mike 30 labourer-27
Spencer Elizabeth 55-34
Spencer R A 40 builder-38
Spencer Robert 27-38
Spencer Samuel 69-43
Spicer William 45-29
Spiers Felix adult-10
Spiers Thomas labourer-38
Spilshead John 28 farmer-41sy
Spooner Mrs Mary Ann 50-41ad
Spoor Thomas 37 mariner-13
Spraggon James 25 labourer I-26
Sprat Mark 39 I-36
Sprat Sabina 32 I-36
Sprat Maria 1.1/2 I-36
Spring Samuel 63 labourer-23
Spring Arthur 28 I-40
Spring Sandy 25 I-40
Squire I 30-10sy
Squires John H 22 grocer-39
Squires George-26
Stables David-41
Stack Patrick 26 I-33
Stack James 26 farmer I-40
Stackpool Mr-30
Stackpool Master A R 9-30
Staden M A W 24 labourer-20sy
Stafford W D 26 farmer S-35
Stafford Henry R 28-36
Stafford Sarah 24-36
Stainsby William 32-39
Standing John 22-34
Stands Carl 34 labourer OP-30
Stanhope Joseph 25 coachmaker-13
Stanley G H 33-10
Stanley Mrs 33-10
Stanley Alfred 20 clerk-13
Stanley Henry 17 clerk-36

Stanley Patrick 27 clerk–42
Stansfield Mary Ann 24–21
Stansfield Lewis 24 labourer I–21
Stansfield Henry 30–41ho
Stapleton Matthew 23–28
Stapleton Andrew 22 I–33
Stapleton Michael 21 I–36
Star William 26 farmer–10sy
Starmers Michael 17 I–31
Stathart James 18 labourer I–27
Staunton Thomas 40 miner–16
Staunton Thomas 11–16
Staunton John 19 I–35
Staveley H C –9
Staveley Mr S–32
Staveley Mr junior 6 S–32
Stead David–32
Stead Mrs–32
Stead Mary 34–38
Steads John 22–43
Stedman Robert 32–41
Stedman Elizabeth 32–41
Stedman Elizabeth 1–41
Steel Robert 35 labourer S–26
Steel Margaret 35 spinster S–26
Steel Philip J 15 I–32
Steel Michael 38–34
Steel Emma 30–34
Steel Louisa 7–34
Steel Eleanor 5–34
Steel Marian 4–34
Steel Emma 2–34
Steel William infant–34
Steel John R clergyman I–39
Steel Charles 15 I–39
Steel Mary 8 I–39
Steele James 26 labourer I–32
Steele T S –36
Steele William J 21 mechanic–36
Steen John 55–28
Steen Jane 48–28
Steen Jane 19–28
Steen Thomas 17–28
Steen John 14–28
Steen Irwin 11–28
Steen Hamilton 8–28
Steen Johnstone 5–28
Stefferson Hans P 22 lab. OP–30
Steir Jane 55 widow–25
Stenson Charles–25
Stenson Mrs–25
Stephen W R –9
Stephens John 36 farmer–13
Stephens Elizabeth 30–13
Stephens Mark 23 labourer I–21
Stephens John 25 labourer–22
Stephens Mrs 70–26
Stephens Miss 20–26
Stephens John 20–28
Stephens John 41–28ho
Stephens Charles 28 shoemaker–32
Stephens John 22 miner–32

Stephens John 20–32
Stephens Richard 22–32
Stephens Matilda 29–42
Stephenson Thomas 25 shoemaker–11
Stephenson H H –21
Stephenson Edward–21
Stephenson John 23 labourer–22
Stephenson John 27 I–32
Stephenson James 60–41
Stephenson Sarah 60–41
Steven John W–23
Steven Mrs–23
Stevens L W adult–10
Stevens Master–22
Stevens Alice 1–24
Stevens Henry 32–24
Stevens Jonathan 36 labourer–24
Stevens Elizabeth 32–24
Stevens Charles 3–24
Stevens Martha 16–24
Stevens John I–33
Stevens Miss L 30–35
Stevenson Robert 25 miner–11
Stevenson Fanny 38 spinster–25
Stevenson David 32 labourer–28
Stevenson Elizabeth 33–28
Stevenson Margaret 8–28
Stevenson John 6–28
Stevenson James infant–28
Stevenson Miss J 22–29
Stevenson J W 28–29
Stevenson Capt H –33
Stevenson James 27 labourer–34
Steward John M 26 carpenter I–11
Steward Bessy 20 I–11
Steward William 40–33
Stewart R I 20–10
Stewart F E –21
Stewart Robert–21
Stewart John 35 labourer–23
Stewart James 32 labourer–26
Stewart John 29–26
Stewart William 18 labourer S–27
Stewart John 36 S–29
Stewart George 35 S–29
Stewart William 57 S–29sy
Stewart William S 49 lab. I–30
Stewart Alexander 19 servant S–31
Stewart I H S–33
Stewart Mrs S–33
Stewart Matthew 37 lab. S–33sy
Stewart Mrs–34
Stewart Annie 4–34
Stewart Athol 2–34
Stewart Mr S–37
Stewart Mrs S–37
Stewart Thomas 22 I–37
Stewart Andrew 28 I–37
Stewart Sarah I–39
Stewart Robert 42 S–42
Stewart James 18 I–43
Stiles John 35–29

Stillings Edward–41
Stillong Miss E–31
Stitt James 20 farmer–16
Stitt Gibb 16–16
Stobbs Joseph adult miner–27
Stockenberg Jonas A 21 surgeon–11
Stockley William 21 clerk–13
Stoddart Isaac 33–37
Stoddart Mary Ann 28 spinster–37
Stoddart Elizabeth 40–43
Stoddert William A 25 farmer S–13
Stoker John 33 miner–13
Stokes Patrick 37 farmer I–16
Stokes John 31 farmer I–16
Stokes M J A 22 labourer–24
Stokes John 34 miner I–34
Stone Elizabeth spinster–11
Stone Ann 26–20
Stone Anna M 4–20
Stones John 20 farmer–13
Stoney Mrs Mary Ann 25–40
Stoney Alice 1–40
Storey Francis 26–41
Stornton William 22–26
Storr William 27 farmer–37
Stott Ann 60–34
Stott Ann 18–34
Stott Henry 35–34
Stott James 26 labourer–36
Stott George 50 storekeeper–42
Stovin Mr–9
Stovin Mrs–9
Stowton Arthur–43du
Strachan Miss Margaret 17 S–21
Strachan T A 39 S–36
Strackey Isabell–42
Strange John 35 labourer S–22
Strange Otts OP–39
Stratton John J–22
Street Samuel–22sy
Street Elizabeth–22sy
Street James 45 labourer–25
Street James 28 labourer–27
Street John 50–34
Street Mary 47–34
Street James 9–34
Street Lev.16–34
Street Elizabeth 20–34
Street Louis 37 I–34
Street Margaret 29 I–34
Strenson Mrs 28–20
Strenson Margaret 3–20
Stretton Mrs Louisa 26–34
Stretton Reginald H inf (died)–34
(died 28/8 of dysentery)
Stretton John 11–43
Strickland George–9
Stringer Henry 24 labourer–25
Stringer J H labourer–30
Strokarch Mr 47 OP–24
Strother Charles 38–11
Stroud Mr 20–21

Struchan John 26 labourer-13
Stuart William 27 labourer I-24
Stubbs C A 20-43
Stuckey Mrs Elizabeth-11
Stuckhouse Charles 23 butcher-13
Stucky J I -39
Studd Edward-38
Stulfield Charles H 38-16
Sturbridge Thomas 32-29
Sturdie Jane 18-43
Sturgeon Albert 31 labourer-27
Sturges Emma spinster-34
Suchalls Jonathan P 28 lab.-24
Sucher Carl 20 OP-43
Suck Henry 45-32
Suck Ellen 28-32
Suck Edward 10-32
Suck John 8-32
Suck Mary 3-32
Suck Henrich 1-32
Suffield William 20 clerk-21
Suffolk Charles 35 shoemaker-32
Suffolk Jane 31-32
Suffolk Louisa 5-32
Suffolk William 4-32
Suffolk George 2-32
Sugar Ann 25 spinster-26
Sugden Samuel 27 plasterer-16
Sugden William J 40 labourer I-35
Sugden Thomas 41 farmer-37
Sullivan James 25 labourer I-13
Sullivan John 21 labourer I-21sy
Sullivan Miss Mary Ann 15 I-21sy
Sullivan Daniel 33 labourer I-24
Sullivan Timothy 24 labourer I-24
Sullivan Pat labourer-25
Sullivan Miss Margaret 20 I-26
Sullivan Michael 23 labourer I-31
Sullivan John 19 S-32
Sullivan Mathias 24 I-32
Sullivan Peter 24 labourer-32
Sullivan Joanna 60-33
Sullivan Denis 35-33
Sullivan Jonathan 25 I-34
Sullivan John 12 I-35
Sullivan Samuel 20-41
Sullock Thomas 25-28
Summers William 27-16
Sumner Napolean 24 I-36
Sunderland Alexander 44 S-33
Sunderland Agnes 40 S-33
Sunderland James 20 S-33
Sunderland Isabella 18 S-33
Sunderland William 16 S-33
Sunderland Jane 12 S-33
Sunderland Agnes 10 S-33
Sunderland Alice 8 S-33
Sunderland Alex 6 S-33
Sunderland Margaret 4 S-33
Surgess Jonathan 19 labourer-25
Sussex Joshua 19 labourer-34
Sutcliff Mrs H 26-16

Sutcliff Alice 3.1/2-16
Suter Mahala 14-10
Sutherland H M -28
Sutherland H M 23 farmer S-39
Sutherland O C M 10-39
Sutherland Ann M 9-39
Sutherland G A W M 7-39
Sutherland Mr-16
Sutton John 20 labourer-27
Suukin (Le) Isaac 23-43
Swan George H-11
Swan William D 25 farmer I-37
Swann Miss 23-22
Sweeney Patrick 27 labourer I-30
Sweeney Miss Jane I-36
Sweet Henry 22 labourer-23
Swenton John 30 labourer-20
Swift Alfred 25 labourer-26
Swift Thomas 25 labourer-27
Swift Thomas 28 labourer-35
Swift George 27-36
Swift James 27 mason-37
Swift Mary 25-37
Swift Henry 6-37
Swift Arthur 2-37
Swindell Enoch 27 miner-31
Swindells James-41
Swindells Emma-41
Swindells Theodore 3-41
Swindlehurst Charles 23 lab.-31
Swires Henry 22 labourer-13
Swishbury Michael adult-27
Sydney George adult labourer-20
Sydney Mrs-20
Syers William 23 labourer-24
Sykes John 43-33
Sykes Benjamin 49 I-36
Sykes Miss Frances 20 S-36
Sykes Miss Jane 18 S-36
Symmers John-11
Symon Alexander 41 labourer-31
Symons Philip 55-29
Symons Jane 52-29
Symons James 19-29
Symons Charlotte 18-29
Syson Henry 35-29
Syson Charles 33-29

T

Tabiteau W A-9ca
Tadham Richard 60 miner-37
Taggart John 21 labourer S-22
Tahrig Oskar 20 OP-28
Tait William-28
Taite Jessie 20 spinster-30
Talbot Hon R G-35
Tallerman S -9
Tamsworth Frank 27 miner-37
Tanchero Hyman labourer-25
Tandle Michael D 17-32
Tangye George 38-41
Tanner James 19-37

Tapley Michael 26 labourer-27
Tapp James 23 labourer-25me
Tapscott Charles E 40 mechanic-41
Tarlton Joshua 24 farmer-21
Tarrant George 35-24
Tate James 30 farmer-11
Tate John 24 cabinetmaker-11
Tate George 20 miner-13
Tate Charles-30
Tattersall John-36
Tattersall Mary J-36
Tattersall Margaret 7-36
Taunton Sydney 22-34
Tawall William 30 labourer-24
Taylor Alfred-11
Taylor Elizabeth-11
Taylor Joshua 28 miner-11
Taylor James 43 clergyman-13
Taylor Christina 42-13
Taylor Mary 16-13
Taylor Isabella 11-13
Taylor Jane 8-13
Taylor Grace 6-13
Taylor William 3-13
Taylor Joseph 1-13
Taylor Josiah 24 farmer-13
Taylor Henry 20 slater-16
Taylor John 45 draper-16
Taylor Miss Ann 22-21
Taylor George 31 labourer-21
Taylor Jane 29-21
Taylor Bridget 5-21
Taylor infant-21
Taylor David 22 labourer-23
Taylor James 26 labourer-23
Taylor Duncan 31 labourer-26
Taylor John 26 labourer-26
Taylor Arthur 20 labourer-28
Taylor Esther 17 spinster-28
Taylor Warren 65-28
Taylor John 22-29
Taylor Thomas 33-29
Taylor Thomas 33-29
Taylor Thomas 30-29
Taylor Mrs Ann 54-30
Taylor Edward 13-30
Taylor George 15 S-32
Taylor James 65 cottoncorder-32
Taylor John 25 labourer-32
Taylor Robert 26 labourer S-32
Taylor William 26 bootcloser-32
Taylor Louisa 26-32
Taylor Marion 3-32
Taylor Charles 1-32
Taylor Ada infant-32
Taylor Frances 18 spinster-34
Taylor John 34-34
Taylor James 22 blacksmith-37
Taylor Thomas 31 brickmaker-37
Taylor Harriet 33-37
Taylor James W 8-37
Taylor Samuel 6-37

Taylor Charles 4-37
Taylor Robert 1-37
Taylor Sarah Jane 1-37
Taylor John 34 agri lab-38
Taylor Mary A 36-38
Taylor E 45 miner-39
Taylor Ellen 44-39
Taylor Alfred 11-39
Taylor Ernest L 7-39
Taylor Rebecca 21-39
Taylor C 29 chemist S-40
Taylor Henry 48-40
Taylor Mrs E 31 S-40
Taylor J A 18 S-40
Taylor William-41
Taylor Ellen-41
Taylor William J 7-41
Taylor Ellen 5-41
Taylor Arthur J 2.1/2-41
Taylor Mabel infant-41
Taylor James 18-41
Taylor Samuel 19-41
Tazer James 21 labourer-30
Teal John 64 miner-37
Teight George 30 workman-40
Telford Robert 32-27
Tempany Mrs-10
Temperley Henry 38 miner-13
Temperley I R 22-31
Temperley W A 20-31
Templeton William 23-25
Templeton Robert 20-28
Templeton Francis 50 platelayer-37
Templeton John 15-37
Templeton Agnes 13-37
Templeton Francis 10-37
Tennant James 9 S-21
Teolin Pat 23 labourer I-26
Ternaus Joseph 34 labourer-25
Terry Albert-23
Terry Miss-23
Tetley Edwin 29-29
Tetley William 21 landowner-42
Thackeray William labourer-23
Thin Miss Betsy 16 S-35
Thin Francis F 33 farmer S-35
Thistlethwaite D-9
Thomas John-9
Thomas R M -9
Thomas Jno 21-10sy
Thomas W 22 smith-10
Thomas Edward 27 sawyer-11
Thomas Richard 21-11
Thomas Richard 42 labourer-11
Thomas William 25 farmer-11
Thomas William 29 carpenter-11
Thomas Charles 25 miner-13
Thomas Richard 29 sailor-13
Thomas James 25 miner-13
Thomas Samuel 28 miner-13
Thomas David-13
Thomas Benjamin 28 miner-16

Thomas S 25-16
Thomas Mary Jane 1-16
Thomas George 25 labourer-20
Thomas Henry 37 labourer-22
Thomas Elias 23 labourer-23
Thomas Martin 22 labourer-23
Thomas William 30 labourer-23
Thomas Miss Ann 25-24
Thomas Miss Ann 20-24
Thomas Mrs Ann 37-24
Thomas Elizabeth 8-24
Thomas Cathering 5-24
Thomas Mary A 3-24
Thomas Ebbw 26 labourer-24
Thomas Henry 15 labourer I-24
Thomas Morgan 21 labourer-24
Thomas Ann 20-24
Thomas Morgan 45 labourer-24
Thomas Evan 21 labourer-25
Thomas Mrs R 52-25
Thomas Hugh 20 labourer-26
Thomas Daniel 25 labourer-27
Thomas John 24 labourer-27
Thomas Elizabeth 20-27
Thomas W R 27 labourer-27
Thomas Thomas 35-28
Thomas William 27-28
Thomas William 34-28
Thomas Honor 32-28
Thomas Mary E 16 spinster I-29
Thomas Thomas 22-29
Thomas David 28-29
Thomas John 22 labourer S-31
Thomas John 28-32
Thomas Richard 22-32
Thomas Thomas H 28-34
Thomas James 23-34
Thomas Thomas 27 labourer-35
Thomas Heale 25-35
Thomas Joseph 23-35
Thomas George 20-35
Thomas Daniel 17-36
Thomas William 30-36
Thomas Miss Ann 22-36
Thomas Ann 40 lodging keeper-38
Thomas Mary 15 nurse-38
Thomas George 16 coppersmith-38
Thomas Barbara spinster-38
Thomas Hugh 31 miner-38
Thomas Mord 18 I-38
Thomas Harriette 22 maid I-38
Thomas James 48 miner-39
Thomas E A 31-40
Thomas Bessie 11-40
Thomas Clare 8-40
Thomas Thomas C 6-40
Thomas William 4-40
Thomas Elizabeth 40-40
Thomas Alice 20-40
Thomas William 11-40
Thomas James 9-40
Thomas Elizabeth 7-40

Thomas Joseph 32 smith-40
Thomas James 52-41
Thomas Sarah 50-41
Thomas Thomas Taylor 20 miner-41
Thomas Kate 23 laundress-42
Thompson J J -9
Thompson I J 23 grocer I-10
Thompson W G 19-10
Thompson James 25 farmer-11
Thompson Matilda 11-11
Thompson William-11
Thompson Andrew 31 miner-13
Thompson George 24 farmer-13
Thompson John D-16
Thompson Mrs Annie-16
Thompson Mary-16
Thompson Joseph A-16
Thompson James 25 labourer I-21sy
Thompson John 32 seaman-21
Thompson Ann 31-21
Thompson Matthew 24 labourer-22
Thompson Miss 21-22
Thompson David 24 labourer S-23
Thompson James 25 labourer I-23
Thompson John 42 labourer-24
Thompson Sarah 39-24
Thompson Robert 14-24
Thompson Sarah R 11-24
Thompson Thomas 24 labourer-24
Thompson William 49 labourer-24
Thompson Alfred 26 labourer-25
Thompson Mrs 50-25
Thompson Jonathan 25-25
Thompson Mrs 25-25
Thompson infant-25
Thompson Frederick 22 lab.-25
Thompson David 25-28
Thompson William James 20 lab.I-30
Thompson Robert 22 labourer-31
Thompson William 23 I-32
Thompson G H 27-34
Thompson William 24 baker-35
Thompson Capt-36
Thompson Mrs-36
Thompson Mrs Elizabeth 46-36
Thompson Agnes 10-36
Thompson Norman-36
Thompson William 26 I-36
Thompson John 40-39
Thompson Mary J 36-39
Thompson Minnie 11-39
Thompson Harry P 10-39
Thompson Robert E 8-39
Thompson Alice 6-39
Thompson Winnie 4-39
Thompson Florence 1-39
Thompson Mary Ann 38-41
Thompson Thomas 7 (2nd class)-41
Thompson Margaret 32-42
Thompson William 26-42
Thompson Mrs 18-42
Thomson Mrs 47-20

Thomson Madeline 20-20
Thomson Margaret 15-20
Thomson Helen 10-20
Thomson Alexander 5-20
Thomson Alex P -21
Thomson Alex 29-21
Thomson Catherine 24-21
Thomson Alexander 28 lab. S-26
Thomson James 20 labourer-26
Thomson Alexander 29 lab. S-27
Thomson Ann 20 spinster S-27
Thomson Miss Elizabeth 19 S-27
Thomson David 25-28
Thomson James 45-29
Thomson Miss Elizabeth 30 S-30
Thomson Couray S-36
Thomson George-37
Thomson George 37 gardener S-38
Thorburn John 30-43
Thorburn E A 28-43
Thorburn Elizabeth 7-43
Thorburn J W 4-43
Thorley Ann 59-43
Thorne Robert-35
Thornley John 40-36
Thornley Ann 36-36
Thornley Thomas 11-36
Thornton A 20-10
Thornton John 18-10
Thornton George 22 mason-20
Thornton Robert 36 labourer-23
Thornton James 22 labourer-27
Thornton Miss 24-27
Thornton Joseph 44-42br
Thorp H -9
Thorp Alexander 31 labourer S-29
Thorpe Edgar 31 labourer-26
Thorton T D P 23-26
Threlfall Robert 29 labourer-23
Threlfall Mary 26-23
Threlfall Arthur 4-23
Threlfall Joseph 2-23
Throup William 37-33
Throup M 33-33
Throup Elizabeth 10-33
Throup Jane A 9-33
Throup James 7-33
Throup Sarah 5-33
Throup William infant-33
Thulbourne Lush-10
Thwaites John 45-43
Tiernan Francis 20 I-36
Tierney Bridget 17 spinster I-28
Tierney James 29 I-29
Tierney Ann 30 I-29
Tighe James 24 labourer I-21
Tilly Frank 42 labourer S-32
Tilly Mary A 17 S-32
Tilpot August 28 labourer OP-32
Timmons Robert 31 labourer-23
Timmons Mrs A J 29-23
Tindall Robert 21-41

Tinley Robert 34-24
Tinsley Jos S 43 labourer-27
Tipping John 22 labourer-34
Tipping William J 19-41
Titty Walter 34 labourer-22
Tobin Richard B 25 lighthouseman-16
Tobin William A 28 labourer I-23
Tobin Michael 51 labourer-25
Tobin Thomas 23 I-29
Tobke Ida 18 OP-35
Tocher E spinster S-37
Tocher Alex 61 watchmaker S-38ho
Tocher Jane 31-38
Todd Thomas J 38-13
Todd Elizabeth 40-13
Todd Mercer 15 labourer I-30
Todd W W 25 S-43
Toft Carl 22 labourer OP-26
Toll James 34-11
Toll Peter 30-11
Tolley Thomas 29-34
Tolley W C 39-34
Tomassini Mrs M 28 OP-20
Tomkins William Henry 24 lab.-35
Tomkinson John-16
Tomlin Alfred G 20-40
Tomlins Richard 47 labourer-30
Tomlinson Lettice 26 spinster-20
Toner Patrick 30 I-41
Tongue William 45 labourer-20
Tongue Eliza 46-20
Tonkin Emily-39
Tonkin William H 19-41
Toohey Timothy 50 labourer I-22
Toohey Alice 40 I-22
Toohey Tim 20 I-22
Toohey Hugh F 14 I-22
Toohey John 20 labourer I-27
Toohey Thomas-34
Toolsby Joseph 51 labourer I-31
Toop Hector 23 labourer S-24
Toquoli Giovanni 22 OP-40
Torfry John 27 labourer I-20
Torfry Mary 25 I-20
Torgill Francisco 9 OP-32
Tornell George 45 labourer-25
Torrance George 42 farmer S-37
Tottel William 26 labourer-25
Totton Hannah 50 spinster-25
Tough Isabella 55 knitter S-37
Toung Edward 35 labourer-11
Toung Jane 36-11
Toung Samuel 8-11
Toupey Patrick 21 I-35
Tovsey M D 50-26
Towers James 27 labourer S-21
Towle Benjamin-9
Towle Edward-9
Townley W A 24 labourer I-33
Townsend R H adult-10
Townsend John R 20 labourer-22
Townsend G 68-28

Townsend Helen-42sy
Townsend John 32-42
Townsend Anna 31-32
Townsend Anna 3-42
Townsend Jessie 2-42
Townsend John 1-42
Toy H labourer-25
Toy Mrs-25
Toy Oliver labourer-25
Tozer James 21 labourer-20
Tozer Mrs 60-37
Tracy William 22 farmer I-13
Tracey Patrick 25 I-28
Tracey Mary 15 I-43
Traenkel Carl 18 labourer OP-30
Traherne Arthur-21
Traherne Llewellyn P-21
Travers Anthony 30 labourer S-21
Travers Rosanna 25 S-21
Travers Ann 7 S-21
Travers Mr 28-24
Travers M 33-27
Travers Mrs 25-27
Travers Roderick 38 squatter-42
Travers Mrs 20-42
Travers infant-42
Treacey Peter 26 labourer-21
Treacey Mrs-31
Treacey Eva-31
Tregallis Alisha 25 miner-11
Tregallis Samuel 24 farmer-11
Tregallis Josiah 19-11
Tregarty Catherine infant I-36
Tregeder John 28 S-35
Tregeder Mary 22 S-35
Tregise Mrs Margaret 48-28
Tregise Hugh 18-28
Tregise Grace 14-28
Tregise Thomas 20-28
Tregise Elizabeth 24-28
Tregoine Michael 27 labourer-35
Tregoine Mary 27-35
Tregoine Mary 7-35
Tregoriss Miss Jane 62-32
Trembath William J 17 miner-31
Trembeaith Sarah A 18-42
Tremelling Henry 30-35
Tremelling Jane 23-35
Tremlett Ada-9
Tremlett Frederick-9
Tremlett Mr-9
Tremlett Mrs-9
Tremlett infant-9
Tremlin James 26 I-36
Tremlin Esther 29 I-36
Trenhalt Martin T 20 lab. OP-30
Trenselling Mrs Myriel 58-34
Treparne William 33 labourer-30
Tresidor Edward 22 miner-11
Trevana Henry 22 miner-13
Trevarton George 28 miner-16
Trevarton Harriet 24-16

Trevarton Charles 1-16
Trevise John 22 miner-21
Trevithnick John 75 farmer-41
Trevithnick Thomas 40-41
Trevithnick Henry J 25-41
Trevithnick Jane 28-41
Trevonon John 31 labourer-23
Trevorrah Richard 38 miner-13
Trevorrah Miss Jane 16-32
Treweeke William labourer-26
Trewheela Joseph H 28 miner-37
Trewheela Minnie 19-37
Trewhella Chris 33-34
Trewins E spinster-11
Trezider Thomas 22 miner-13
Trezider Thomas 33 miner-13
Trezider Mr 27 I-35
Trezider Mrs 23 I-35
Trillo William-11
Trim Mrs Alice 35 I-40
Trim Mrs M P I-41
Trimbath Samuel-21
Trinfield Joseph 28 bricklayer-11
Trinfield William 24-11
Trisiddan W 42-10
Tristrail Martha 23-21
Tristrail Martha 9-21
Tristread Martha 1-21
Trollope Anthony-37
Trollope Mrs-37
Tromencie John 33 labourer-26
Tronney Michael 25 farmer I-37
Trooney Thomas 25 labourer I-27
Troulan Robert 18 labourer-24
Trouton Charles-9
Trouton Moses 35-34
Troup John U engineer S-16
Trumbolt William 22 labourer-22
Truscott Charles-35
Truscott Mary-35
Tubridy Patrick 22 I-33
Tuck A -27
Tuckett Mrs-9
Tuer Jonathan 27 S-24
Tuer Ruth 29 S-24
Tuer Joshua infant S-24
Tuffnell Robert 25 labourer-38
Tuffnell Mary Ann 26-38
Tuffnell Harry 4-38
Tuffnell Emily infant-38
Tuhey Patrick 19 I-28
Tulin Michael 22 labourer I-32
Tullock Mrs Elizabeth 40 S-41
Tullock Helen 24 spinster S-41
Tulloh W H -30
Tullwan E O 23 I-40
Tully William C 30 labourer-21
Tully Catherine 25-21
Tully William 25-21
Tully Mark 21-21
Tully Robert 18-21
Tully Mrs Beatrix 57 I-22

Tully Jane 16 I-22
Tully Beatrix 12 I-22
Tully Henry 35 I-22
Tully Elizabeth 38 I-22
Tully David 9 I-22
Tully Mary 7 I-22
Tully Elizabeth 5 I-22
Tully Jane 3 I-22
Tully Beatrix 1 I-22
Tully Mrs Jane 38-23
Tully Lucy 2-23
Tully Pat 24 labourer I-24
Tully Mrs Jane 44-33
Tully Lucy 8-33
Tulva Giovanni 37 labourer OP-26
Tunnicliffe Miss Mary 34-21
Tuohy Michael 25 labourer-27
Tuomay Miss A 22 I-29
Tuomey Cornelius 34 blksmith I-32
Tuomey Mary 30 I-32
Tuomey Mary 7 I-32
Tuomay Catherine 5 I-32
Tuomey Julia 3 I-32
Tuomey Ellen 1 (died 17/8) I-32
Tupper Emily 31
Tupper Emma-31
Turgensen C H miner OP-39
Turkington Samuel 24-41
Turnbull Robert 23 lab. S-211a
Turnbull John F 35 labourer-23
Turnbull Gideon P 27-24
Turner H J -9
Turner William 24 enginetender-13
Turner Mary 21-13
Turner Grace 39 spinster-16
Turner Jessie 27 spinster S-16
Turner Sarah 29 spinster S-22
Turner John 18 labourer-23
Turner Thomas 50 labourer-23
Turner William 22 labourer-23
Turner George F 21 labourer I-24
Turner Mrs 18-24
Turner Charles 24-28
Turner William 50 I-33
Turner Eliza 49 I-33
Turner James 28-34
Turner W -36
Turner Mrs-36
Turner William 42 clerk-38
Turner James 19-42ot
Turner Mary 23-42ot
Turner Arthur 23-43
Turney John 23 labourer S-33
Turtan Miss Mary J 18-23
Turtle Samuel 25-36
Tusby John 21-28
Tuscini Miss Julia 35-36
Tuscini Carolina 13-36
Tusin William W 26 lab. I-32
Tuvohy Miss Ann 18 I-22
Tuvohy Catherine 21 spinster-22
Tweddle Richard 20 labourer-22

Tweedie James-9
Tweedle Mr-27
Tweedle Mrs-27
Tweedle John 3-27
Twiss George 21 labourer-25
Twyncross Thomas 20-13
Tyas John W -31
Tyers John 44-42ad
Tyler Benjamin 30 labourer I-32
Tyler John 35-36
Tyne Samuel 33 miner-13
Tynew Joseph 27 labourer-25
Tyrer William 21-36
Tyrer Hannah 24-36
Tyrer Margaret infant-36
Tyril Barbara 54 widow-25
Tyrrell Adam L-28
Tyson Miss Mary 20-23
Tyson Mary 38 spinster-28
Tyson Jonathan 24 labourer S-31

U

Udy Thomas 29-29
Uglow Robert 25-39
Uglow Elizabeth 27-39
Uglow William 22-39
Ulray Ann 20 spinster-41
Ulrica Hannah 12 S-43
Underwood Capt.-9
Unwin James-41
Uphill Charles 17-16
Uphill Miss A 19-31
Uprichard James 19-41
Upton Charles J 44 labourer-31
Urindram Robert 47-41sy
Urindram Hiriam 17-41sy
Urquhart John 53 farmservant S-40
Urquhart Isabel 50 S-40
Urquhart Jessie 7 S-40
Urquhart David 9 S-40
Urquhart John 18 farmservant S-40
Urquhart James 12-40
Urquhart William-42
Urthole Adolph OP-42
Usher R -32
Utley James 19 spinner-37

V

Vale Emma 32-40
Valentine Elizabeth 44 I-13
Vallance Miss M L 25 OP-41
Van Arnstel E P 38-24
Vance W P I-39
Vance Eliza 20 I-42
Vaughan Annie 20 servant-39
Vannick Hon Walker-35
Vardy Mrs Mary J 21-33
Vardy John E 2-33
Vardy John E 27-33
Varty John 41 miner-13

Varty Isaac 39 joiner-21
Varty Isaac 40 labourer-25
Varty Elizabeth 39-25
Varty Robert 11-25
Varty Joseph 8-25
Varty Isaac 3-25
Varty John infant-25
Vasicton James F 30 labourer I-22
Vasicton Mrs 28 I-22
Vaughan Ralph-11
Vaunton James 20 draper-16
Veal John 15-28
Vedova Bernard Wella 25 OP-43
Vedova Benedicioni 37 OP-43
Venn George 32 farmer-33
Venn Catherine 22-33
Venn Mary 26 spinster-33
Vennick Hon.A-30sy
Venus Robert 22-43
Verga Thomas-11
Verga Christopher-11
Verga Thomas 30-29
Verity William 35-34
Vernon Harry 32 baker-11
Vero Charles E 33 labourer I-22
Vettler Johann 57 workman OP-38
Vettler Anna 60 OP-38
Vettler Catherine 20 OP-38
Vettler Joseph 17 OP-38
Vial S 23 miner-10
Vial Samuel 33 miner-13
Vial William 19 miner-13
Vicar Abraham 26 labourer-22
Viccars Alice 22-43sy
Vickery Samuel K 21 labourer I-20
Vincent James 31 labourer-20
Vincent Henrietta 36-26
Vincent Thomas 11-26
Vincent Margaret 6-26
Vincent Matthew 4-26
Vipound Mrs Mary Ann 28-23
Vipound John 7-23
Vipound Margaret Ann 5-23
Vipound William 3-23
Vipound Ellen 1-23
Vippon Joseph 29 labourer S-24
Vippon Mary 22 S-24
Vippon Alexander 5 S-24
Vippon Nicholas 3 S-24
Vivian William 36 miner-11
Vivian John 23-11
Vivian Joseph 30-11
Vivian William 24 miner-11
Voegal Chis 16 OP-40sy
Vohey Honor 21 spinster I-27
Vohey Catherine 20 spinster I-27
Von Bayen I C 43 OP-10
Voyce Joseph 27 blacksmith-40ly
Voyce Mrs 20-40ly
Voyce William 1-40ly
Vyvyan C -9
Vyvyan E -9

W

Waddell William 25 mechanic-27
Waddie Thomas 29 labourer-24
Waddington Robert 27 labourer OP-22
Waddington Amelia 27-22
Waddington Jane 1-22
Wade John 31 labourer-24
Wade Charlotte 31-24
Wade Arthur 2-24
Wade Samuel 38 labourer-31
Wade Patrick 22-41
Wades Jenzean A 35 labourer OP-22
Wades Margretta 28 OP-22
Waig George G 23 S-28
Waigh Sarah Ellen 30 I-42ot
Waise Ernst E H 26 merchant OP-37
Wait Charles-9
Waite Henry 28 labourer-23
Waite Jonathan 41 labourer-24ad
Waite Jonathan T 10-24ad
Waite Emma 11-24ad
Walcott E L 32-10
Walcott Mrs 36-10
Walcott Mary E 11-10
Walcott Henry L 9-10
Walcott Dorothea 8-10
Walcott Katherine 6-10
Walcott Charles 3-10
Walcott Elizabeth 2-10
Walcott Robert 5-10
Waldron Thomas 20 I-40
Walford S -9
Walford F A-39
Walford Arthur-40
Walkden Basil-9
Walkden Cecil-9
Walkden Clarence-9
Walkden Francis-9
Walkden Frederick-9
Walkden George-9
Walkden John-9
Walkden Emily-9
Walkden Mr Richard-9
Walkden Mrs-9
Walkden Miss-9
Walke W H 21-10
Walke W H 21-10
Walker Miss-16
Walker W G -16
Walker Mrs-16
Walker James 32 butcher-21
Walker Mrs H 28-21
Walker Joshua B 1-21
Walker Miss Mary Ann 23 S-21
Walker Mrs Susanna 33-21
Walker Thomas 4-21
Walker John B 17 labourer-22
Walker Joseph 35 labourer-22
Walker Matthew 36 labourer-22
Walker Henry 40 labourer-24
Walker Jessie 26-24

Walker Rebecca 20 spinster I-30
Walker William B 22 labourer I-30
Walker Sarah A 20 spinster I-30
Walker Elizabeth 14 I-30
Walker William Percy 24 S-33
Walker G 24-34
Walker Colin 28-34
Walker James 20-34
Walker Archibald 18-34
Walker Miss M 29-34
Walker Christopher 1-34
Walker Miss S 39-34
Walker Edward 22 clerk (d.5/4)-35
Walker Elizabeth 20 spinster-37
Walker Charles 20 farmer I-38
Walker Henry 22 miner I-39
Walker William 40 farmer-42
Walkes William 23-28
Walkes George 23-28
Wall Jane spinster-11
Wall Albert B 24-16
Wall Michael 21 labourer I-28
Wall Samuel 61-29
Wall Martin 26 car driver I-31
Wall Daniel 50 painter-38
Wall Rachael 35-38
Wall Robert 11-38
Wall Edmund 9-38
Wallace James 30 clerk I-10
Wallace William Ritchie 40 S-16
Wallace Thomas 18-16
Wallace Harry Edmund 16-16
Wallace Mary 20 spinster-25
Wallace Robert 23 labourer-26
Wallace Miss Frances-32
Wallace Hugh H S-37
Wallace James 27 platelayer-37
Wallace Helen 25-37
Wallace Mary 4-37
Wallace Janet 2-37
Wallace Catherine 1-37
Wallerd Mr-9
Wallerd Mrs-9
Wallerd (6 children)-9
Wallen Miss-9
Wallis John 30 miner-21
Wallis Alice 30-21
Wallis Sarah A 9-21
Wallis Thomas 7-21
Wallis John 6-21
Wallis Frances 5-21
Wallis Alice 1.1/2-21
Wallis Richard 1-21
Wallis James 22-41
Walls Mrs Elizabeth-11
Walls Thomas 26 labourer S-27
Walls William 26-33
Walmsley Mary 35 spinster-22
Walsh Jeremiah 25 farmer-16sy
Walsh William 22 labourer I-20
Walsh James 25 labourer I-22
Walsh Michael 18 labourer I-22

Walsh Patrick 38 labourer I-22
Walsh Mary 32 I-22
Walsh William 11 I-22
Walsh Eliza 9 I-22
Walsh Mary 6 I-22
Walsh Patrick 1 I-22
Walsh Maurice 20 labourer I-24
Walsh James 24 labourer-25
Walsh Miss E 22-26
Walsh Henry-26
Walsh John 17 labourer-27
Walsh Miss-27
Walsh John 21 I-28
Walsh Agnes 56 spinster I-29
Walsh John 19 I-29
Walsh Daniel 24 labourer-31
Walsh John 25 I-32
Walsh Robert 20 labourer I-32
Walsh W -34
Walsh Elizabeth-34
Walsh Anne 20 spinster-37
Walsh Thomas J 20 carpenter-38
Walsh Patrick 22 I-39
Walsh John 23-43
Walter Kellener 22 OP-29
Walter Thomas 23 mechanic-36
Walters Lewis 29 joiner-11
Walters Marie 20 spinster I-30
Walters Mrs Ellen 41-35
Walters John 10-35
Walters George 15-35
Walters Thomas 27-35
Walters James Y 19-35
Walters John 40 mason-38
Walton William jun 30 surveyor-11
Walton John 46 miner-13
Walton Aaron 24 OP-28
Wappel Aug 18 labourer I-24
Warall Walter 29 labourer-35
Ward Benjamin 20-13
Ward Thomas 26 pointsman-13
Ward James 30 I-16
Ward Jane 24 spinster-22
Ward Thomas 30 labourer-22
Ward Harrison 23 labourer-22
Ward William 22 labourer-22
Ward Michael 21 labourer I-23
Ward Elizabeth 24-26
Ward Henry 18 labourer I-27
Ward Samuel 24-28
Ward John 24 I-32
Ward Richard 32-33
Ward James 25-33
Ward Col E W-34
Ward Mrs-34
Ward E 8-34
Ward F 10-34
Ward H 6-34
Ward Master J W 4-34
Ward Mark R I (died 29/9)-34
(died of scarlatina)
Ward Matthew 46-36

Ward Bernard I-37
Ward Thomas B 47 merchant-38
Ward Jane 46-38
Ward Jane E 11-38
Ward Kate G 8-38
Ward Mary L 6-38
Ward Thomas E 14-38
Ward Frederick 19-41
Ward Owen 21-41
Ware John 34 labourer-21
Ware Mary 28-21
Ware Samuel 4-21
Ware Betsy 3-21
Warfield Thomas 30-41
Warfield Catherine 35-41
Warfield John 13-41
Warfield Thomas 8-41
Warfield Mary 6-41
Warfield William 4-41
Warfield George 2-41
Warfield Harry 1-41
Waring Susannah 18 spinster-34
Warnock Robert 35-41
Warnock Elizabeth 42-41
Warnock Thomas L 3-41
Warner Mrs 45 I-24
Warner Miss 21 I-24
Warner Thomas 35-36
Warner Jane 40-36
Warner Annie 11-36
Warner Thomas 9-36
Warner Frank 7-36
Warner John 1-36
Warnock Samuel 33 labourer I-23
Warnock Mary E 22 I-23
Warnock Elizabeth M 4 I-23
Warnock Maria 2 I-23
Warnock James 1-23
Warren Martin 30 miner-16
Warren George 27 labourer-28
Warren Arthur 28 farmer I-32
Warren Elizabeth 27-34
Warren Agnes 8-34
Warren Holmes 6-34
Warren Veda 4-34
Warren Isabella 2-34
Warren Archelaus 31-37
Warren Mary Jane 24-37
Warren John 19-40ot
Wase Edward B 18 labourer-31
Wasner John 28 labourer-25
Wastin Clark 19 labourer S-35
Watchouse G M-34
Watchouse Mrs L-34
Watchouse Fanny-34
Watchouse Lizzie-34
Waterhouse Mrs Ellen 45-22
Waterhouse Alfred 10-22
Waterhouse Emma 8-22
Waterhouse Joseph 55 labourer-22
Waterhouse Mrs-22
Waterman Isaac-21

Waters David 33 farmer-11
Waters Ellen-11
Waters Mr 28-16
Waters William 35-16
Waters Rosina 30-16
Waters Herbert E 6-16
Waters Alfred J 3-16
Waters William W 24 labourer I-31
Waters Joseph 24 miner-41ad
Waters George 21-41
Waterson Miss Catherine 35 I-20
Waterson Thomas 18-32
Waterworth George 63-38
Watkins Mrs Mary-11
Watkins infant-11
Watkins David E 46 labourer I-27
Watkins Bridget 30 I-27
Watkins Thomas 2 (died) I-27
(died from whooping cough)
Watkins William infant I-27
Watkins Gilbert 19 labourer-28
Watkins D 42-36
Watkins Margaret R 56 S-36
Watkins Algern 36 butcher-38
Watkins William E 29 squatter-41
Watkins Deborah 24-41
Watson Miss-9
Watson A 42 S-10
Watson N -11
Watson John 30 miner-13
Watson Sarah 25-13
Watson Robert 10-13
Watson John 8-13
Watson James 3-13
Watson Robert 24 miner-13
Watson E -22
Watson John A 30 labourer-22
Watson Joseph 30 labourer-22
Watson A R 32 labourer S-23
Watson Thomas 22 S-23
Watson David 63 labourer S-24
Watson Miss Eliza 24-24
Watson Alice 28 matron-25
Watson Thomas 9-25
Watson Emma 7-25
Watson Matilda 5-25
Watson Robert 4-25
Watson Abraham 1-25
Watson Alfred 28 labourer-26
Watson Mr-27
Watson Mrs-27
Watson William 35-28
Watson Alex 29-28
Watson George-29
Watson Edward-29
Watson Mrs H 58 widow S-30
Watson George 21 draper S-30
Watson James-32
Watson Kezia 20 servant-34
Watson Miss B V-35
Watson Robert 22 I-43
Watt Mrs Janet 30 S-29

Watt Sarah A 11 S-29
Watt Catherine 5 S-29
Watt John 30 labourer-35
Watt Mrs 26-35
Watt Barbara 2-35
Watt Jennie 1-35
Watts James 38-13
Watts Pamela 32-13
Watts Henry 4-13
Watts Henry G 25 labourer-24
Watts William 37 labourer-26
Watts Ellen 30-26
Watts Lucy 10-26
Watts William 8-26
Watts Alfred 6-26
Watts Anney 3-26
Watts Ellen infant-26
Watts William 16-36
Watts Mary 54-36
Waugh William 31 draper-21
Waugh Mrs R 29-21
Waugh Ann 8-26
Waugh Hugh 28 labourer-28
Waugh Hugh 30 I-29
Waugh John 25 I-39
Wauliss William 30 labourer I-35
Wayte George H-21
Wearne John 26 labourer-26
Weatherbum Henry 22 engineer-38
Weatley Henry 20-13
Webb Samuel 40 builder-13
Webb Henry-22
Webb William 40-41
Webb Mary A 40-41
Webber F G -9
Webber H -9
Webber Johanna 34-42
Webber Elizabeth 9-42
Webber Robert Henry 5-42
Webber Lucy 3-42
Webber Thomas 40-42
Webber Caroline 31-42
Webber Annie 7-42
Weber Emil R OP-43
Weber Anna OP-43
Weber Arthur 10 OP-43
Webster William 20 labourer-23
Webster James 38 labourer-25
Webster James S-29
Webster John 22-29
Webster Francis B 45-30
Webster Robert 53 labourer-38
Webster Robert 41-42
Webster Alice 41-42
Webster Joshua 11-42
Webster John 7-42
Webster Mary Jane 5-42
Webster Sarah 3-42
Webster Elizabeth 20-42
Webster Alice 17-42
Weely William 44-33
Weightman Charles 21 workman S-38

Weir Jarvais 19 labourer I-24
Weir John 16 labourer-30
Weir N 20 labourer-32
Welch Richard 27 grocer-11
Welch James A 20 labourer-31
Welchman Edward-35
Weldon Miss Jane 22-36
Wellington Pat 39 I-32
Wellington Ellen 39 I-32
Wellington Thomas 11 I-32
Wellington William 8 I-32
Wellington John 4 I-32
Wellington Patrick infant I-32
Wells Thomas 23 grocer-13
Wells William 17 labourer-34
Wells William 50 shipowner-41
Wells Mary 41-41
Wells Ellen 18-41
Wells Susan infant-41
Welsh Michael 28 labourer-21
Welsh John 20 labourer-26
Welsh Fergus 28 labourer-27
Welsh Mrs Kate 28-40
Welsh Lillie 4-40
Welsh Bella 2-40
Welsh Mrs Jane 43 nurse-41
Welsh Elizabeth 31-43
Welsh Frederick 3-43
Welsh Florence infant-43
Wenkley E B -27
Wepplemann H 21 bookkeeper OP-33
Wesley Thomas 18-41
West Mary Ann 25 spinster-27
Westby Ashley-34
Weston Thomas 30-33
Wettig Julius 38 miller OP-10
Wettig Andreas 28 butcher OP-10
Wettig Mathias 23 baker OP-10
Wharton R -9
Wharton Elizabeth 32-10
Wheelan Kate 19 K-42
Wheeler Charles 19 labourer-22
Wheeler Henry 30-28
Wheeler Arthur 50 labourer-33
Wheeler Edwin 22-35
Wheeler James 23-35
Whelan John labourer I-21
Whelan Eliza-21
Whelan John 24 labourer I-31
Whelan Bridget 18 I-31
Whelan Margaret 1 I-31
Whelan Kate 18 servant I-31
Whisker William labourer I-37
Whitaker Mrs Hannah 29-23
Whitaker Walter 2-23
Whitaker Maria-23
White Mr-9
White Mrs-9
White William 30 engineer-16
White Sarah Ann 29-16
White William 23 labourer I-21
White Samuel 21 labourer-23

White George 33 labourer-24
White Benjamin 23 labourer-25
White Elizabeth 24-25
White Charles J infant-25
White Pat 27 labourer-26
White William 31 labourer-26
White Mary Ann 30-26
White Mary Jane 8-26
White William 16 labourer-26
White Frederick 31 printer-27
White Mr A B-27
White Mrs-27
White Marjery 32 spinster-27
White Richard 22 merchant-27
White Ann spinster-28
White Charles 60-28
White Mary 50-28
White Charles 16-28
White James 14-28
White Frances 13-28
White Elizabeth 11-28
White Frederick 9-28
White Lydia 9-28
White H W -28
White George 48 labourer-33
White Joseph 20 (died 12/3)-33
White George 29-34
White W M -34
White George 34 miner-41
White John-41
White John-41
Whitehair William 22 mason-11
Whitehead Mrs Eleanor 25-21
Whitehead John 4-21
Whitehead William 44 labourer-23
Whitehead Charles 50 labourer-30
Whitelaw J 29 tailor S-10
Whitelaw W 26 painter S-10
Whiteley John 32 farmer-42
Whiteley W F 35-42
Whitelock Mrs Louise 23-23
Whitelock Isabella 1-23
Whiteman Robert 35 stonemason S-16
Whiteman Janette 32 S-16
Whiteman Margaret 8 S-16
Whiteman Charles 6 S-16
Whiteman Alice 2 S-16
Whiteman Robert 1 S-16
Whiteman William T 27-27
Whiteman William 40-27
Whiteman Emma 33-27
Whiteside William 32 farmer-35
Whiteside Ann 25-35
Whiteside Samuel 8-35
Whiteside William 2-35
Whiteside James 1-35
Whitfield Edward 37 miner-11
Whitiford Mr labourer-28sy
Whiting Elizabeth S-36
Whitlaws Henry 43 farmer-10
Whitley Thomas 25-36
Whitmore John-40

Whitmore John P-40
Whitta Valentine A-37
Whittaker R 50-27
Whittaker James H 21 labourer-30
Whittaker Reuben 20-34
Whittaker Thomas 30-34
Whittaker Edward 21 spinner-37
Whittaker Mrs 21-37
Whittall George M 22 lab. I-32
Whittan Moses 21 labourer I-24
Whittard George 18 (d. at sea)-40
(died on 2.4.1873)
Whittington Rd Henry 22-31
Whittle Eliza adult I-20
Whittle William 24 labourer I-23
Whittle Ann J 27 I-20
Whittle Catherine 3 I-20
Whittle Mary J I-20
Whitworth Miss Fanny-32sy
Whitworth Henry 30 S-36
Whitworth Ann 31 S-36
Whitworth Samuel 23 S-36
Whitworth Hannah 25 S-36
Whitworth Emma infant S-36
Whyte Lawrence 23 I-36
Wickliffe James 17 labourer I-26
Wiechman F adult trader OP-40
Wienka Carl 25 labourer-22
Wier Miss Matilda 19 I-24
Wightman Mrs Anna M 39 I-23
Wightman Anna B 22 I-23
Wightman Elizabeth 17 I-23
Wightman Jane 15 I-23
Wightman David J 11 I-23
Wightman Martha J 8 I-23
Wilcockson Thomas 40-13
Wilcox Thomas 20 draper-11
Wilcox W E 26 labourer I-24
Wilcox Alfred 24 I-24
Wilcox Joseph 27 draper-38
Wilcox Mrs Ann 36-41
Wilcox Rupert 8-41
Wilcox Ada 4-41
Wilcrynoke E S 24-26
Wild James 22 I-32sy
Wild Luke 21-34
Wild Thomas 27-36
Wild Elizabeth 25-36
Wilding Joseph 38-37
Wilding Ann 31-37
Wilding Margaret 7-37
Wilding Robert 6-37
Wilding Joseph 4-37
Wilkins John 36 I-41
Wilkins Mrs Mary J 20 I-41
Wilkinson Joseph 26 tea dealer-10
Wilkinson Henry H 25 grocer-11
Wilkinson William Henry 30clerk-21
Wilkinson George 54 labourer-24
Wilkinson Mrs Mary 56-24
Wilkinson David R 24 labourer-29
Wilkinson Joshua 45-36

Wilkinson John 21 farmer-40
Wilkinson Richard 20 farmer-40
Wilkinson Edmond 26-42
Willamson Miss C M 30-24
Willamson Walter 17 labourer-24
Willett Charles 21 labourer-23
Willey Samuel 35 labourer-23
Willey Frances 39-23
Willey Mrs Mary A 30-35
William Thomas 24 labourer-21
Williams E P -9
Williams George 28-10
Williams Joseph 35-10
Williams I W H 26-10
Williams Jane 26-10
Williams infant-10
Williams P 34 miner-10
Williams W 30-10
Williams Christopher 30 miner-11
Williams John 42 miner-11
Williams John 23 quarryman-11
Williams John 32 labourer-11
Williams John 32 miner-11
Williams Richard 28 farmer-11
Williams John 25-11
Williams Humphrey 21 sailor-13
Williams Thomas 34 miner-13
Williams George 39 farmer-16
Williams Edward 31-16
Williams William 34 I-16
Williams Mary 27 I-16
Williams John 2.1/2 I-16
Williams William N 29 clerk-16
Williams Dan 22 labourer-20
Williams Jane adult-20
Williams Mr labourer-20
Williams John 8-20
Williams Jane 26 spinster-20
Williams John 37 labourer-20
Williams Rev M 28 I-20
Williams Thomas 24 miner-20
Williams William 32 labourer-20
Williams Jane 29-20
Williams Margaret 8-20
Williams Miss Catherine 15 I-21
Williams Mrs Margaret 26-21
Williams David 4-21
Williams Mrs Margaret 21-21
Williams Mary infant-21
Williams Pryce 19 labourer-21
Williams Miss Margaret-22
Williams John 24 labourer-23
Williams Sarah 21-23
Williams Sarah A 2-23
Williams N 35 labourer OP-23
Williams Thomas 21 labourer-23
Williams Eliza 20-23
Williams infant-23
Williams David 25 labourer-24
Williams Jonathan 22-24
Williams Ellen 18 labourer-24
Williams Hugh 20 labourer-24

Williams W G 23 labourer-24
Williams William 22 labourer-25
Williams Charles 20 labourer-26
Williams Miss M 11-26
Williams Selina 24-26
Williams Simon P labourer-26
Williams Frederick 19-28
Williams Edward 17-28
Williams Humphrey 22-28
Williams James-28
Williams David 31-29
Williams Margaret 25-29
Williams Mrs Julia 30-30
Williams John 4-30
Williams O 25 labourer-30
Williams G P-33
Williams D 22-34
Williams Miss Elizabeth M 25-34
Williams William 60 S-34
Williams Thomas 50 S-34
Williams Edward 25-35
Williams John G 18 labourer S-35
Williams Stephen T 18-35
Williams ? miner-35
Williams Stephen-36
Williams Esther-36
Williams Ellen 10-36
Williams John 9-36
Williams Emily 7-26
Williams Matilda 6-36
Williams Bessie 2-36
Williams Hugh 28 farmer-37
Williams James Henry 25-37
Williams Richard 26 miner-37
Williams David 60 farmer-38
Williams Mary Ann 35-38
Williams Nilervin 23-38
Williams Ivor 19-38
Williams Richard 44-38
Williams Mary 30-38
Williams Mary 25-39
Williams Arthur 21-41
Williams Owen S 31-41
Williams Owen S 31-41
Williams Henry 26-41
Williams Emma 20-41
Williamson Richard 27 labourer-16
Williamson Robert T 20 lab. I-21
Williamson Samuel 21 clerk-21
Williamson John 24 labourer-27
Williamson George 36-34
Williamson Elizabeth 22-34
Williamson William 7-34
Williamson George 5-34
Williamson Theresa 2-34
Williamson William 21 eng. S-35
Williamson David 21 I-40
Willing Robert P 32-16
Willis Edward-30
Willis Maxwell D 20-30
Willis Herbert S 17-30
Willis Mrs-34

Willoughby John H 20 labourer—21
Wills John 25—10
Wills John 36 farmer—13
Wills Joseph 30—13
Wills Robert 49 farmer—13
Wills Mary 30—13
Willson R G 38 labourer—34
Willson Annie 31—34
Willson W E 8—34
Willson R G 5—34
Willson Ann G 3—34
Willson Ann G 25 spinster—34
Wilme Charles 18 farmer I—40ad
Wilshin D —9
Wilson J —9
Wilson J W 22—10
Wilson O 21 OP—10
Wilson P 21 OP—10
Wilson Andrew 26 farmer I—11
Wilson Joshua—11
Wilson Andrew 27 farmer—13
Wilson Charles H 25 engineer—13
Wilson Daniel 31 miner—13
Wilson Eliza 26—13
Wilson Miss Mary 22 S—21
Wilson Miss Charlotte 20 I—22ad
Wilson Jamina C 20—23
Wilson Alfred 56 labourer—24
Wilson Edward 26—24
Wilson James 20 labourer—24
Wilson Miss Jessie 32 S—24
Wilson William 23 labourer I—24
Wilson Isabella 22 I—24
Wilson George labourer—25
Wilson Samuel 16—26
Wilson Alexander 14—26
Wilson Catherine 30 spinster S—27
Wilson William 23 labourer—27
Wilson Rev G H 40 I—28
Wilson Ecipheuma 40 I—28
Wilson Thomasina 16 I—28
Wilson Thomas 10 I—28
Wilson George 7 I—28
Wilson Mary 5 I—28
Wilson William 3 I—28
Wilson Louis infant I—28
Wilson Charles 28—29
Wilson Erasmus 30 labour—32
Wilson George 50—32
Wilson William 32 S—32ad
Wilson James 16—33
Wilson John 14 S—33
Wilson Matthew 11 S—33
Wilson Mrs—33
Wilson Mary 15—33
Wilson Anne 11—33
Wilson Alfred John 8—33
Wilson J G —35
Wilson William H —36
Wilson Caroline 27 spinster—37
Wilson John F farmer I—37
Wilson Florence 14—38

Wilson Matthew 50 I—38
Wilson James clergyman I—39
Wilson Margaret I—39
Wilson George 19—40
Wilson William 60—40
Wilson F W 28 (2nd class)—41
Wilson Thomas 20—41
Wilson Frederick W 28 baker—41br
Wilson J Rankin—41
Wilson Alexander S—42
Wilson Mrs 23 S—42
Wilson Alexander J infant S—42
Wilson Eliza—42
Wilson Sophia 31 servant I—42
Wilson Miss S—43sy
Wilson Thomas 31—43
Wilton Henry 29 labourer—31
Wiltshire Charles R 21 printer—27
Winchester Thomas 27—29
Winchester Emily 30—29
Windel Calsin 60 labourer OP—32
Windel Maria 60 OP—32
Windham James E—29
Windibank Harry 21—35
Windsor Arthur L—23
Windsor Mrs—23
Windsor Thomas J 28—36
Wingad David 19—40
Wingate Walter 45 labourer—25
Wingate Mary 49—25
Wingate Margaret 14—25
Wingate John 10—25
Wingate Andrew 8—25
Wingate Major Thomas—33
Wing Ralph 60—35
Wing Elizabeth 53—35
Wing Ralph M 18—35
Winn James Lucy 19 labourer—33
Winnan Miss Catherine 21—23
Winter James 50—30
Wisch Carl 36 OP—10
Wise Henry 36—37
Wiseman Arthur 20 engineer—33
Wiseman James 24 gamedealer—11
Wiseman Thomas 27—11
Wiseman Mrs Agnes 62—35
Wiseman Isaac 25 labourer—35
Wish B F 22 OP—10
Wishart William 22 labourer—26
Wishart Alexander 19 S—36
Withers Anne 70—31
Withers Henry 26 engineer—34
Wittowski Isidor 35 OP—29
Wittowski Mrs L 20 OP—20
Wixted James 18 blacksmith I—32
Wolf John 30 labourer OP—23
Wolf Marianne 28 OP—23
Wolf John 5 OP—23
Wolf Sophia 9 OP—23
Wolf Mrs R 32 OP—23
Wolf Miss 6 OP—23
Wolf Miss Phoebe 36 OP—23

Wolf Solomon 21 OP—23
Wolf Alfred 15 labourer I—26
Wolf Henry 35—29
Wolf Mrs 34—29
Wolf Sarah 11—29
Wolf Elizabeth 8—29
Wolfe A 17—10
Wolfe Solomon 19 labourer—26
Wolfender Joseph 22 labourer—13
Wolff August 28 miner—37
Wolff Auguste 22—37
Wolff Clara 1—37
Wollard M H 23 farmer—10sy
Wolley H—9
Wollf Rose 30 spinster—37
Wolstencroft Joseph 5—40
Wolstencroft William 32 trader—40
Wolstencroft Margaret 2—40
Wood James 20—10
Wood William 33 miner—13
Wood Mrs Mary 29—21
Wood Edward 5—21
Wood Charles 11—23
Wood William—23
Wood Samuel 27 labourer—24
Wood Catherine 25—24
Wood Anna 3—24
Wood John infant—24
Wood Mary 21 spinster S—27
Wood May 27 spinster S—27
Wood Mr 29 labourer—28ad
Wood Mrs 29—28ad
Wood William Riley 36—29
Wood William 35 I—33
Wood John 21—34
Wood Sarah—34
Wood Joseph 50—36
Wood Mary 45—36
Wood James I—37
Wood John spinner—37
Wood Thomas 34—37
Wood Harriet 26—37
Wood R Bertie—39
Wood Charles 25 cottonspinner—41
Wood Hammond 54—42
Wood Mary Ann 25—42
Wood Bennet G 4—42
Wood Ethel Helena infant—42
Woodhouse Joseph 25 millwright—10
Woodman Miss Mary 25—22
Woodmansey Henry 16—33
Woodmass Miss Ann 29—23
Woodmore Miss servant—40
Woodmore Henry 32(died 12/5)—40
Woodraber E —32
Woodraber Agnes 3—32
Woodraber William F 2—32
Woods Charles 40 labourer I—20
Woods Mrs W H 30—21
Woods Fanny 6—21
Woods Elizabeth servant—33
Woodside Alex 30—28

Woodward Edward–9
Woodward Jemima 28–13
Woodward Isabella 5–13
Woodward Amy 1–13
Woolcock Miss 30–23
Woolfe Elizabeth 30–29
Wooldridge Alice 14 S–36
Woolley Peter 31 farmer–43
Workman James 21–41
Worrall Charles–9
Worthington William 33–43
Wotherspoon John 19–34
Wotherston Archibald–11
Wraughan Thomas–9
Wray William 28–35
Wren John 31 butcher S–10
Wren Bennett 27 miner–13
Wren Martin 24–28
Wren Jane 24–28
Wren Joseph 31 painter–42
Wren Samuel 22–42
Wrew John 46 labourer–27
Wrew Maria 50–27
Wrew John 17–27
Wrew Thomas 16–27
Wrew Henry 11–27
Wright Richard 12–13
Wright William 34 clerk–13
Wright Mary 30–13
Wright Miss–16
Wright William R 35 farmer–16
Wright Mr I–20
Wright John 24 labourer–20
Wright Samuel 22 joiner–20
Wright Charles 56 labourer–22
Wright Ralph 24 labourer–22
Wright George–23
Wright Mrs–23
Wright George 26 labourer–24
Wright Mrs Mary 49–26
Wright Anne 30 spinster–27
Wright John 40 labourer–27
Wright Harriet 38–27
Wright Isaac W 3–27
Wright Walter J 1.1/2–27
Wright Jeffrey infant–27
Wright Thomas 38 labourer–27
Wright Mary 35–27

Wright John 10–27
Wright Thomas 8–27
Wright Duncan J 29 labourer–33
Wright George 30 labourer–34
Wright Sarah 30–34
Wright Emily 4–34
Wright Joseph 15–34
Wright Frederick 13–34
Wright Richard 28–34
Wright Olivia 30–34
Wright Olivia 5–34
Wright Emily 3–34
Wright Richard 1–34
Wright Maria 22–34
Wright Nathaniel–36
Wright H 34–38
Wright Richard 35–40
Wright John 25–41
Wrigley Mary spinster–20
Wrigley Miss–20
Wrigley John 49 grocer–21
Wrigley Hannah 47–21
Wrigley Jane Elizabeth 18–21
Wrigley Martha 14–21
Wrigley Mary 11–21
Wrigley Tom 7–21
Wrigley Stephen 31 labourer S–31
Wurn Ned 22 OP–40
(married Dorothea Fischer)
Wyatt Benjamin 31–28
Wyllie Mrs 58 S–43
Wyllie Jessie 23 S–43
Wynne Miss Jane 24–36
Wynne James 25 clicker–40
Wynne Jane 22–40

Y

Yates Thomas–9ca
Yates Andrew 24 labourer–13
Yates Henry 17 merchant–16
Yates Ann 23 servant–31
Yates Joseph 33–42
Yeatman Charles 32–13sy
Yeo James 23–28
Yeoman Richard Ellis–41
Yeoman Kitty–41
Young James 22 labourer S–11
Young James 28 butcher–11

Young Isabella 26–11
Young George 6–11
Young Thomas 4–11
Young James infant–11
Young Alexander 21 labourer S–13
Young Peter 25 mason–13
Young Thomas 30 labourer S–22
Young Catherine 26 S–22
Young Catherine 4 S–22
Young Jane 2 S–22
Young George 1 S–22
Young George 38 labourer–24
Young Jonathan 22 labourer–24
Young Fanny 21 spinster I–26
Young William Henry 23–28
Young Charlotte 13–29
Young John 30–31
Young Jno 22 farm lab I–31
Young John 50 labourer–33
Young Joshua draper–34
Young Philip S 23–34
Young Mrs–34
Young Thomas 49 labourer–35
Young Mary 49–35
Young Radores 11–35
Young Mary A 9–35
Young Elizabeth 18–35
Young Thomas G 45–36
Young Charles 35 colporter S–39
Young Jane 26 S–39
Young Mary A 3–39
Young Margaret 13 S–39
Young Jane 1 S–39
Young James 24 mechanic S–40
Young Margaret 26–40
Young William 22 mechanic S–40
Young Oliver 39–41
Young Jes–42
Youngman T C –29
Younghusband Mrs 41–24
Younghusband Miss 20–24
Younghusband Miss 18–24
Younghusband John 39 S–35

Z

Zabel Henry 28 labourer S–35
Zala Ramigro 20 OP–33
Zender Simon 30 labourer OP–24

Author's Postscript

The preparation of this book has been a double labour of love, firstly because I have had the privilege since 1968 of being involved with the ship and secondly because it has led me to research my own family tree. Like so many people I have considered through my early and middle years that there were more pressing demands on my time than indulging in genealogical studies. Writing 'Is *Yours* an SS Great Britain Family?' has changed all that.

As an Australian long resident in Britain, I have always been aware that my Scottish ancestors travelled to Melbourne in the 1850s and 1860s while my English forbears went out in the 1870s and 1880s. When the *Great Britain* was brought home to Bristol in 1970 my mother told me she believed her mother's family had travelled to Australia in the ship. She had no further information.

I recalled her chance remark when working on this book and was plunged immediately into a series of instructive research exercises in Edinburgh, Melbourne and Sydney. From these enquiries I am now all but certain that mine *is* an 'SS Great Britain Family'.

It appears that great-grandparents on my mother's side (he aged 25 and she 26) together with an infant daughter sailed to Melbourne in the ship in 1865. I am not naming them at this stage because, as this book goes to press, I am still awaiting the formal documentary proof from the authorities in Sydney. But I have little doubt that one set of great-grandparents sailed in the Brunel ship and discovering this information has been both a fascinating and a salutary experience for me. I trust that the foregoing information provides a similar excitement for many readers of this book.

Adrian Ball